EXPLAINING INEQUALITIES IN
SCHOOL ACHIEVEMENT

D0947768

Dedicated to the memory of Roy Nash

Explaining Inequalities in School Achievement

A Realist Analysis

ROY NASH
formerly Massey University, New Zealand

Edited by
HUGH LAUDER
University of Bath, UK

LONDON AND NEW YORK

First published 2010 by Ashgate Publishing

2 Park Square, Milton Park, Abingdon, Oxfordshire OX14 4RN
52 Vanderbilt Avenue, New York, NY 10017

Routledge is an imprint of the Taylor & Francis Group, an informa business

First issued in paperback 2020

British Library Cataloguing in Publication Data
Nash, Roy, 1943-
    Explaining inequalities in school achievement : a realist
    analysis.
    1. Academic achievement. 2. Educational equalization.
    3. Educational sociology.
    I. Title II. Lauder, Hugh.
    306.4'3-dc22

Library of Congress Cataloging-in-Publication Data
Nash, Roy, 1943-
    Explaining inequalities in school achievement : a realist analysis / by Roy Nash ; edited by Hugh Lauder.
        p. cm.
    Includes bibliographical references and index.
    ISBN 978-0-7546-7904-2 (hardback)
    1. Educational equalization. 2. Academic achievement. 3. Educational sociology. I. Lauder, Hugh. II. Title.
    LC213.N365 2010
    302.43--dc22

                                                            2009046910

ISBN 978-0-7546-7904-2 (hbk)
ISBN 978-0-367-60278-9 (pbk)

Contents

PART 1: THEORETICAL FOUNDATIONS

PART 2: EARLY CLASS DIFFERENTIALS IN COGNITION

PART 3: CLASSED IDENTITIES IN FORMATION

PART 4: SECONDARY EFFECTS AND STATISTICAL MODELLING

List of Figures

List of Tables

Acknowledgements

I would like to gratefully acknowledge the collegial contribution made to this work by Professor Hugh Lauder. Without his determination to help find a publisher and to write the introductory chapter, this work would not now be available to readers.

There are many who should be acknowledged for their contribution to this work and Professor Dick Harker would be the first to come to mind as one of Roy's closest colleagues and research partner for many years.

During Roy's last few months I recognised more clearly the part played by his colleagues through the lively discussions held in the staffroom at the College of Education, Massey University. I know how much they supported, challenged and stimulated his thinking.

This book represents the development of ideas to the point where the questions they raise have become clear. Answers and solutions are important, and there are strong indications within the chapters as to where they may best be sought. Here acknowledgements are due to all those who, at times to their dismay, fuelled Roy's determination to find realist explanations for policies that were not working in order to produce policies that would work.

Finally, acknowledgements are due to Roy's family: his family of origin who struggled through poverty to succeed through education and who have been highly successful, and Roy's children who inspired him and gave him every good reason to remain grounded in his realist philosophy.

Versions of some of the chapters in this book were published in the following journals: *British Journal of Sociology of Education* (http://www.informaworld. com), *Journal of Curriculum Studies* (http://www.informaworld.com), *British Educational Research Journal* (http://www.informaworld.com), *Educational Philosophy and Theory, Interchange, Journal for the Theory of Social Behaviour, New Zealand Journal of Educational Studies, Sociological Review* and *Teaching and Teacher Education*. Thanks are due to the editors of these journals.

Mary Nash

Roy Nash
A Biographical Note

Roy Nash was born in Birmingham, UK, on 24 November 1943 and died in New Zealand, on 24 October 2006. This publication is testimony to his contribution to ongoing debates about why students succeed at school. In New Zealand, where he lived and published from the late 1970s, his identification of class and the family as the key determining factors in a child's scholastic success set him apart from other thinkers and made him a controversial figure. His subtle thinking on educational issues could not easily be expressed in a sound bite and was often misunderstood or misrepresented. Author of eight books and 65 academic articles, he was one of the most published writers on education in New Zealand.

Nash was born to working-class parents, the eldest of ten surviving children, and grew up in a three-bedroom council house. His mother knew the value of education and, having bought a copy of the *Encyclopaedia Britannica*, kept it in its wrapper until the last hire-purchase payment was achieved. Living on the poverty line, she would not risk missing payments and being unable to return it. His father was an electrician and Nash left school with no qualifications and began work as a grocer's delivery boy. He became an apprentice jeweller and earned a passage to the Soviet Union on an organised trip behind the Iron Curtain. The experience of Soviet factories and witnessing life in the isolated USSR would influence Nash when he returned to the United Kingdom. Shortly afterwards he was admitted to the newly established Sussex University on its successful Early Leavers' Scheme, and, left the jeweller's trade to read psychology from 1964 to 1967. He would talk of how he was introduced to deficit theory (to which he took an instinctive dislike) and the idea that working-class people could not defer gratification, and he started on his intellectual career in the course of which he never lost sight of the significance of structural causes of inequality.

After graduating in Educational Psychology, Nash qualified as a secondary school teacher and then sought to apply his ideas in the classroom, teaching in Birmingham from 1968 to 1969. He went up to Edinburgh to do his PhD under Professor Liam Hudson. In 1973 it was published as his first book, *Classrooms Observed*, which was eventually translated into several languages. He taught Sociology of Education at the University of Bangor and became fluent in Welsh. Nash believed in fairness and social justice and his bid to represent Clwyd as a Labour candidate in 1974 was based on socialist ideals, the rights of the worker and protection of the poor and oppressed.

Figure 0.1 Roy Nash (top left) with siblings, 1954

In 1978 Nash emigrated to New Zealand with his family. He settled in Palmerston North where he had accepted a lectureship at Massey University. Numerous books followed including *Schools Can't Make Jobs*, *Succeeding Generations* and two volumes analysing how class and the family influence the scholastic attainment of New Zealand pupils. His 1990 book, *Intelligence and Realism*, made a challenging addition to the body of work critiquing IQ theory.

The six-year Progress at School project followed a sample of students through secondary school and shed considerable light on the reasons why some children succeed at school while others do not. The statistical analysis of questionnaire responses confirmed Nash's contention that a family's social capital is one of the crucial determining factors in a child's success at school, challenging the received wisdom in New Zealand that structural problems inherent in the school system determine the success or failure of certain groups – in particular disadvantaging certain groups on the basis of their ethnicity.

An uncompromising critic and controversial intellectual, Nash carried on a number of lively academic conversations both within New Zealand and internationally. In the last piece he wrote, commissioned by Professor Marie Duru-Bellat, he reflected on the problem of sociology of education, describing it as 'once at the centre of our sub-discipline, and all but definitive in any account of its theories and methods' and which has become little more than one speciality among many. He observed that:

sociological research into state policy, the School, the teaching profession, the examination system, parental choice, and so on, are typically carried out with no more than a rhetorical acknowledgement of their contribution to inequality of educational opportunity. Even the central problem is usually fragmented in such a way that race, gender, and class are isolated as social facts suitable for investigation by concepts and methods distinct to the case.

Although all this can be supported by reasonable argument, the cumulative effect is to inhibit the production of an integrated theory of inequality of educational opportunity that seems so clearly needed. Such a theory will, according to good evidence, require that we move forward resolved to develop a more satisfactory relationship with psychological theory in as much as it is concerned with the development of durable schemes of thought and language. There is every reason to suppose that the directions indicated by Bernstein and Hasan point a way compatible with the robust intellectual frameworks supported by Bourdieu and Boudon.[1]

A few weeks before he died, Nash held a seminar for his colleagues, arguing that the:

construction of an adequate explanatory model of the processes involved in the generation of social disparities in education is much more difficult than many advocates of educational reform suppose. There is always some thought to be applied when deliberating on the evidence for a case. The judicial metaphor is entirely appropriate, of course, for reaching a conclusion beyond reasonable doubt is exactly what we must do.

The entire relationship between educational advocacy, educational policy, and educational research requires discussion that is both lengthy and complex and the explanation of difference in educational attainment among children from working and middle-class backgrounds is, in fact, a matter far from settled. It is important to have good theories, if only because the development of successful policies intended to improve educational performance is likely to depend to some extent on their being grounded in reality.[2]

Nash's creativity was not limited to the academic sphere. He tried his hand at hobbies from bee keeping, building and flying model airplanes, and patchwork quilting to photography, carpentry and jigsaw making. He devoured literature, filling his home with books, and was a font of historical knowledge. The one

---

1   Nash, R. (2006). 'The sociology of education and its ambivalent relationship with IQ'. A short article written for Marie Duru Belat.

2   Nash, R. 'Fancy that: Discrepant research evidence on how Maori children think about their teachers'. Paper presented in September 2006 to Massey University College of Education seminar.

interest that never dwindled was his love for cooking. As the family cook he dished up a variety of local and international fare, earning fame at home for his paella and pizzas.

His conviction for his intellectual principles and his commitment to a fairer society and better education drove him to the top of his discipline. In October 2006 he was awarded the Mackenzie Prize, New Zealand's highest award for educational research. His work remains as an invaluable contribution to practical efforts to improve the ways children and young people are taught as well as to the body of academic work on educational attainment.

Mary Nash

Introduction
Educational Policy and Social Inequalities in School Achievement

This book provides a systematic account of the sources of inequality in school achievement. It appears at a time when the issues concerning educational inequality are once again prominent and with good reason: where 30 years ago it seemed that incomes in modern industrial societies were narrowing, now we are seeing polarisation of the kind that has not been witnessed since Victorian times. Not surprisingly, we are also witnessing the shattering of another fundamental assumption of modern societies: that upward social mobility would steadily increase. Instead, we are now witnessing the closing of opportunities. The paradox is that these fundamental changes have emerged at a time when the expansion of the educational system might predict the opposite effect. The idea that education can create the conditions by which the polarisation of income can be reduced and that it can provide the equality of opportunity leading to upward social mobility is now being challenged. This book cuts to the heart of the sources of educational inequality and, by combining theory with quantitative and qualitative analyses, provides an account that will be of interest to policymakers at such a pressing time.

What was the basis of the belief that education could reduce inequality and promote greater upward social mobility? Here we need to examine the consensus theorists who were writing in the post–Second World War period. At root, they thought that the introduction of various forms of new technology, most apparent now in electronic communication technologies, would lead to a steady increase in the demand for educated workers. In turn, this demand would 'pull up' those from the working class into middle-class occupations, reducing poverty. The future, they thought, would be one of an expanding middle class made possible through education. Moreover, consistent with this account, Goldin and Katz (2008), in a recent well-publicised book, have argued that the polarisation of incomes has occurred because the demand for skilled workers has outstripped the supply. The policy drive in many countries towards mass higher education has been predicated on these assumptions.

Yet the consensus account is flawed in many ways: it does not explain why the already privileged continue to prosper in education and indeed have done throughout the period of rapid expansion of the middle class in the post-war era, and it does not explain the structural point that, in Britain and America, the middle class is not expanding and indeed may be declining. The challenge is to comprehend why we are witnessing the increased differentiation of education systems according to social class at a time when more students are staying longer in education. Moreover, while average levels of achievement seem to be rising, there is also increased social class polarisation in the credentials gained in Anglo-Saxon countries such as the United States, the United Kingdom and New Zealand.

The vision of raising educational standards for all seems to be something of a chimera. Just when it appears progress is being made, it becomes clear that success is at best qualified. It is not for want of trying. Governments in many developed and developing countries that have seen education as the solution to the problems of economic competitiveness and social justice have increased the resources flowing into the sector and have taken a close interest in its regulation and control. The most extreme example of the latter is perhaps England, although, since the No Child Left Behind policy in the United States, it too is following the same route.

Central to the efforts in both these countries is what has been called the State Theory of Learning (STL). It is so called because, in setting a framework of accountability based on the repeated testing of students, the state has made some fundamental assumptions about the motivations of teachers to teach well and students to learn, as well as how schools can best be improved. The STL sees the testing of students as the basis for making judgements about school performance and student progress. Schools are judged against benchmark test levels in which a significant proportion of their students are expected to reach a certain level. For students, the testing is meant to be a way of providing feedback on progress and for setting targets for improvement. This system is backed up by a rigorous system of inspection, by which schools are judged and evaluated, in large part by how well their students do.

Underlying this framework are assumptions about the motivations of both teachers and students. For teachers, success in tests is both a spur and an incentive as it is for students in that both have clear targets they are supposed to reach. However, as has been shown, this is rather too simple an account of how to motivate success in education. There have been many criticisms of the STL but here it is worth mentioning those that relate to Roy Nash's research, for in terms of motivation the impact on students appears to vary with social class. Booher-Jennings (2008), Reay and Wiliam (1999), Brown (2008 and Hempel-Jorgensen (2008) have all shown that the pressure imposed by this system of high-stakes testing generates anxiety, discipline problems among the less successful and attitudes of disdain among the most successful. That factors such as this have been identified is not surprising because, in the UK, the performance of those identified as being disadvantaged declines as they progress through their school careers.

It is at this point, when there has been a major, some would say draconian, effort to eradicate the persistent inequalities of social class with limited success, that it is important to return to the fundamental questions: what causes social class inequalities in achievement at school and what can be done about it? It is here that Roy Nash's path-breaking work assumes significance. With his longtime colleague Richard Harker, Nash developed an account of the way that social class structures family resources, which in turn he regarded as crucial to understanding social class differences in educational achievement. Inevitably, this means looking at education not as a simple vehicle for educational progress, as so many policymakers do, but to consider it as a site of conflict in which success is measured in the credentials gained, for they provide the passport to the labour market and possibly upward mobility into the middle class.

In order to construct a theory that seeks to explain the causes of persistent inequalities, Nash engages with the history of recent sociology of education and philosophy of the social sciences to develop a particular realist account of social class inequalities. His work is not eclectic; rather its strength is derived from developing what promises to be a coherent theory. But, in doing so, he provides a masterclass in how theory construction should be undertaken. By charting a course through the key theoretical positions in the sociology of education, he engages with all the major contemporary thinkers from realists such as Bhaskar and Bunge through Bourdieu and Bernstein to Vygotsky. And, on the way, he challenges some of the key positions currently held within the discipline. He does not consider the inequalities that we observe to be primarily or fundamentally determined by education but rather by classed family resources. This does not mean that schools are neutral institutions in the creation of inequality; rather we need to understand what happens within them by reference to the wider processes relating to the family. But Nash is also aware that there is some upward mobility, hence not all working families, for example, can be seen to adopt the same practices and processes relevant to education. Additionally, it becomes apparent that much of the so-called 'school effect' is as much related to the selection of students attending any particular school, as it might be to the school's policies, practices and curriculum.

While Nash provides a particularly strong case for believing that much of the inequality in education stems from the very early years of childhood, he is also concerned with the possibility of what Bourdieu called a universal pedagogy: with the power to bring children with all entry-level skills to the same standard of achievement within a manageable period of time. To this end, he is concerned to argue against one of Bourdieu's positions regarding the school curriculum: that in a sense it is an intellectual arbitrary that reflects the impositions of a dominant class. Rather, like Michael Young's (2008) more recent work, Nash argues strongly that there are forms of powerful knowledge, rather than the knowledge of the powerful, that schools can communicate. In a sense, this can be seen as paradoxical: on the one hand he considers schools as classed institutions and, on the other, that the curriculum, which has been singled out, by Bourdieu, as being one element of the manifestation of class, nevertheless has the potential, through the reasoning processes underlying the social and natural sciences, to emancipate. One of the great intellectual frustrations is that Nash was never able to engage in a debate through which this paradox might have been resolved.

It will be clear that in order to construct a theory that is in dialogue with data, Nash not only developed a realist methodology but also was able to integrate both what he called 'narratives and numbers' – the qualitative and the quantitative – and to show how by embracing both they could still conform to the tenets of a realist methodology.

In respect of theory development and an engagement with the empirical world through a realist methodology, Nash demonstrates the systematic nature of his thinking and the ambition of his project. While this book can be seen as a three-way conversation between academics (philosophers and sociologists of education), policymakers and the reader, it is a particular kind of conversation in which he is never frightened to challenge what he considers orthodoxy or to demonstrate to policymakers that 'quick fixes' will not do. Some of his views may be considered either unduly optimistic or pessimistic and, while he spent a life engaged with issues of social justice, he has troubled those on the Left as much as those on the Right.

For those on the Left, his view that inequalities originate in the cultural practices of the home may offend because it suggests that, if these cultural practices could be changed, then the persistent inequalities of education could be tackled. It may seem like a deficit theory in which working-class families whose children fail at school are to blame. The charge that he is involved in such an account exercised him and he is careful to defend his theory against such a view. And, in case readers consider that he can easily be pigeonholed in this way, his view of Meyer's (1997) much publicised research in the United States should prove a corrective. Although it may seem that Nash was advocating a 'cultural' solution to inequality in terms of the practices and processes of the family at the expense of the material questions of income and wealth he was critical of Meyer, who argued that raising the income of the poor would not address inequality. The key here is that, for working-class families, cultural resources are but one element of inequality; income is another. It is surely in the interplay between these two factors and that of school culture that the sources of inequality must be found.

While those on the Left might be troubled by his theory, so would those on the Right who take the view that educational inequality is simply to do with IQ and genetic inheritance. Nash's account is embedded in an understanding of the social. For him there is no simple *deus ex machina*, like genetic inheritance, that visits a simple, plausible explanation for inequalities upon us.

It will be clear that there is much for the reader to engage with in Nash's position. Like many who have sought to understand how inequalities may be addressed, there are points of tension, if not contradiction, that he has to negotiate. While he takes the view that family practices and processes create what he calls the cognitive habitus that sets the trajectory for learning and achievement, it is not clear from his theory what responsibilities schools have for inequality. Indeed, this is made more difficult by his attack on Bourdieu's notion of the cultural arbitrary. He may well be right in insisting that there is powerful knowledge that the school can communicate, but if that knowledge also provides greater opportunities for those who have had the appropriate family environment to succeed, then this presents a problem.

However, these points of tension will be found in any systematic theory and especially in an area as difficult as education. What prescriptions does his theory offer for policymakers? We could begin with the obvious point that, if family cultural processes generate a cognitive habitus that makes success in education difficult, then is early childhood education not the solution?

While there is much evidence to recommend such a view, it needs to be considered with some caution. Esping-Andersen (2006) has shown that early childhood education is one component for addressing inequality but there are others to do with the labour market and with the way work is constructed and rewarded. In other words, a single policy in one field, education, is not enough to address inequality. Much has been made recently of the importance of joined-up policy, and the example of the Nordic countries where education has made a difference in reducing inequality of opportunity reinforces the need for it. But Nash has more words of caution for policymakers.

In the final chapter of this book he points out that, while it is attractive to think 'if policymakers understand the causes of social disparities in achievement they will be better able to eliminate them', he cautions that 'Things are, however, a little more complicated'. The complications are not only about the difficulties in implementing policies derived from the best theories of educational inequality available but about the limitations to the knowledge claims that can be made by the discipline. However, considering the political issues that surround socio-economic and ethnic differences in school attainments, it is vital that policymakers know as much as possible about the mechanisms responsible for such disparities. They must look beyond the politically correct conclusions and get to grips with the best theories and data available. As he notes:

> Policymakers might find this discussion of some value in helping to clarify the theoretical and methodological limitations sociology of education necessarily faces in its attempt to construct realist explanations of the origins of social disparities in educational achievement. These limitations cannot be overcome, but they can be accepted without great loss, and may even provide a context in which the relationship between the concerns of policymakers and those of sociologists can be placed on a more secure basis. (p.259 below)

In the past 30 years there have been few sociologists of education who have engaged with the issues of inequality in such a systematic and rigorous way. Nash was an academic who enjoyed debate and there will be readers who will want to dispute his claims. However, researchers, students and policymakers who come to this book will leave it understanding the scope of the challenge that confronts anyone aspiring to reduce educational inequalities.

Hugh Lauder

References

Booher-Jennings, J. (2008). Learning to label: Socialisation, gender and the hidden curriculum of high stakes testing, *British Journal of Sociology of Education*, 29(2): 149–60.

Brown, C. (2008). *The Making of Ideal Pupils: Explaining the Construction of Key Aspects of Primary School Learner Identities* (The HARPS Project: Education Department, University of Bath).

Esping-Andersen, G. (2006). Social inheritance and equal opportunities policies. In H. Lauder, P. Brown, J. Dillabough and A.H. Halsey (eds), *Education, Globalization and Social Change* (Oxford: Oxford University Press): 398–408.

Goldin, C. and Katz, L. (2008). *The Race between Education and Technology* (Cambridge, Mass.: Harvard University Press).

Hempel-Jorgensen, A. (2008). *The Construction of the 'Ideal Pupil' and Pupils' Perceptions of 'Misbehaviour' and Discipline: Contrasting Experiences an a Low and a High Socio-economic Primary School* (The HARPS Project: Institute of Education London University).

Meyer, S. (1997). *What Money Can't Buy: Family Income and Children's Life Chances* (Cambridge, Mass.: Harvard University Press).

Reay, D. and Wiliam, D. (1999). 'I'll be a nothing': Structure, agency and the construction of identity through assessment, *British Educational Research Journal*, 25 (3): 343-354.

Overview
Approaches to Inequalities
in School Achievement

Inequalities in educational opportunity – referred to here as inequality/difference – have been a persistent feature of all school systems for generations. This introduction argues that a realist framework for the sociological explanation of group differences in educational attainment can be constructed, and the chapters that follow should go some way to build on that structure. Conventional explanations in the sociology of education essentially reduce to two: non-quantitative 'list' theories, usually incorporating one or more 'standard' theories; and quantitative 'list' theories, where items are treated as measured variables and subjected to statistical analysis. It will be useful to review these allied approaches. Most list theories are recognisable as more or less coherent amalgams of Flude's (1974) classical meta-account of theories of social difference in education. Flude distinguished four theories with distinct causal mechanisms: (i) 'deficit' theories, in which certain deficiencies in IQ, linguistic forms and family resources are the effective variables; (ii) labelling theories, which maintain that teachers' expectations influence the self-conceptions of students and so affect their learning; (iii) school resource theories, which regard the schools' definitive practices in the domains of curriculum, pedagogy and evaluation as being fundamentally classed and thus accessible only to those already disposed to respond to its arbitrary forms; and (iv) structural theories, in which the economic, political and cultural structures constrain educational access for dominated social classes and cultural groups. These accounts are not necessarily exclusive or incompatible, and the last provides an explanation at a different level to the others, but the structures of the theoretical, methodological and political fields in which they are generated effectively discourage attempts at their integration.

Non-quantified List Theories

One of the most elaborate non-quantified list theories to be found in the sociological literature – which deserves to be reproduced in an unexpurgated form – must be that given by Marshall, Swift and Roberts (1997: 138):

> It has been argued ... that class disparities in educational achievement are the result of one (or some combination) of the following: labelling, by middle-

class teachers, of working-class children as 'under-achievers' in the classroom; prejudice … in tracking working-class children into less ambitious and less adequately resources streams, schools, or colleges; the culturally loaded organizational ethos of schools, which includes a (sometimes 'hidden') curriculum and examinations that favour children from middle-class homes, or having middle-class verbal and other skills; residential segregation or zoning, which – together with catchment-area policies practiced by schools – serves to isolate working-class children from their middle-class peers, invariably in financially disadvantaged establishments; and, perhaps most obviously, the continued provision of private education for those whose parents are able to pay. This list, of course, is far from exhaustive.

Marshall, Swift and Roberts do not discuss the multiple hypotheses of the theories informing this list; still less do they hint that some, at least, of these hypotheses may be less than adequate, and there is no attempt to provide any supporting evidence. The declared purpose of the list is to show that the hypothesis of an 'unequal distribution of meritorious attributes' can be given alternatives enough in a sociological account to be persuasive: a matter of 'never mind the quality, feel the length'. It thus positions the sociology of education in open competition with psychology to explain the between-class variance in school attainment and presumably for that reason excludes the contribution of cognitive ability as a source of class differences in attainment. Although the passage suggests a certain academic distance – the 'take it or leave it' tone is unmistakable – the context suggests more than a guarded endorsement for this position. It is as if the very structure of this text, as its intricate clauses and subclauses build up, were sufficient to give it the authority of unchallenged truth. But this list should, indeed, be accompanied with a visible shrug of the shoulders.

A brief critique will bring out the central problems. Labelling is actually a weak theory that lacks substantial evidence as a significant source of inequality/ difference; streaming, 'fair' or otherwise seems to have little or no effect on attainment; the effects of the classed nature of schooling on attainment are difficult to observe; and the effects of class-segregated schools are much less apparent than is popularly supposed (Lynch, 2000; Pallas and Entwisle, 1994). The idea that schools arbitrarily 'favour' middle-class verbal skills is taken for granted, and the possibility that this preference has a necessary educational function, which is a defensible reading of Bernstein (1996), receives no mention. The treatment of theories in this kind of list – sophisticated and unsophisticated, testable and non-testable, all lumped together – is particularly objectionable. To include as contributing mechanisms with apparent equivalent status, on the one hand, such complex mechanisms that might be generated by classed forms of schooling associated with 'verbal skills' and, on the other, the processes generated in response to school zoning, is in essence to endorse the characteristic nominalist error of the most atheoretical forms of quantitative modelling. It would require a complex chain of argument to sustain the view that these processes or their effects might be regarded as additive in a particular empirical model. One must also ask on what basis this list has been ordered: how is it known, for example, that it is 'perhaps most obviously' the case that private schools are a major cause of inequality/difference? This very phrase, 'perhaps most obviously', indicates the rhetorical position being taken. Has any satisfactory, longitudinal research shown the educational attainments of middle-class students (when adequately matched – a difficult state of affairs to achieve) who attend private schools to be higher than those who attend state schools? A quantitative model of social disparities in education including every variable on this list, to suppose that such a model could actually be constructed, would be unlikely to account for much more than 20 per cent of the attainment variance observed between social classes (Hanushek, 1997).

Quantitative List Theories

The discussion of list theories has exposed several problematic features that can actually be found reproduced in many statistical models. Among the most important of these are the specification of the social processes that need to be included in an explanation, and the theoretical principles to be used in the construction of indicator variables for that purpose. A clear illustration of the muddles that can occur when theoretical guidance is not available is provided by Riordan (1997) in an introductory US textbook on 'mainstream' quantitative approaches to the sociology of education. The text presents two apparently incompatible statements:

> Assume that the vast majority of variability in educational outcomes is due to the factors at home, school, and peer group. The goal is to unpack the relative influence of each of these factors and to understand the nature of these interrelationships. (36)

> Research clearly shows that three factors consistently influence academic success in education: (1) academic resources (human capital), (2) financial resources (physical capital), and (3) social resources (social capital). (69)

This is worth some comment. Riordan first informs his readers that the three important factors are home, school and peer group, and then that they are cultural, financial and social capital. How has this apparent contradiction, of which the author seems completely unaware, occurred? What confusion of thought can be responsible for it? Two major reasons should be noted: first, Riordan has no term other than 'variable' or 'factor' to refer to causal properties of the social and physical environment that make a difference to educational attainment; and, second, the theory he subscribes to is unable to recognise ontological distinctions in its objects of study because it regards all properties (and all objects within the terms of the model) as 'concepts' subject to operations of measurement. In this empiricist epistemology, physical entities, social connections and social organisations have an identical status. In this approach, there is apparently nothing inherently absurd in a statistical model that allocates, for example, x per cent of the variance to the home and y per cent to cultural capital. This is not acceptable and is incoherent within an adequately formulated realist theoretical framework. But does Riordan think there are three variables or six? It is quite likely that there are actually intended to be nine, for the specified social organisations (home, school and peer group) are identified as distinct sites where the three independent resources (financial, cultural and social capital) are located. The interpretation of quantitative modelling is not nearly as straightforward as it looks.

The resistance of many sociologists of education to quantitative methods is, to a large extent, based on a well-founded dissatisfaction with two related dogmas of statistical methods. These concern the construction of indicators and the interpretation of statistical associations between them. The problems of constructing indicators are not purely technical, and certainly not ones that can be resolved by routine checks for 'validity' and 'reliability', and the interpretation of correlations is not purely a statistical problem requiring ever more advanced techniques of multilevel modelling and the like (Byrne, 1998). On the contrary, patterns of correlation are almost meaningless unless interpreted with a wealth of information that can come only from outside the model, and that is not usually available from statistical databases alone. A model that included, for example, indicators of school administrative autonomy, co-educational or single-sex status, school size, social class composition and teachers' focus on academic attainment would quite likely find that these 'variables' were virtually interchangeable, because in the system studied single-sex schools tend to be large, to enjoy semi-independent status, to be selective, and to provide a rigorous academic curriculum. But it is quite possible that all of these indicators point to the same processes and ones that are, furthermore, not described by any of the indicators used. The confusions that can result from this are bad enough even were this set of indicators to be included in the same model, but they are likely to be compounded four- or fivefold when it is necessary to compare different models that have included only one or another of these variables. It is commonplace, of course, to encounter one study that reports higher attainments in single-sex schools and another that reports higher attainments in schools with a strong academic programme, when the real mechanism in both cases is likely to be a selective intake. The implications of all this, and some proposals for reform, are discussed more fully in Part 4.

From List Theory to Explanatory Framework

We need to move from a list theory to an explanatory framework (Gasper, 1990; Wartofsky, 1979). A family resource framework is one such within which various hypotheses can be formed and tested. Such a framework might include, for example, the following propositions:

- The economic system generates social classes differentiated by their possession of economic, political and cultural power; this structure gives class-located families endowed with different levels of financial, cultural and social capital.
- As a consequence of the classed distribution of cultural capital (in a specifically literate form), it may be hypothesised that classed families differ in their socialisation practices in such a way that schemes of cognition and speech are linked to class origin.
- The structure of modern economies imposes constraints on: (a) the curriculum, which is required to provide students with the knowledge, which has both necessary and arbitrary elements, required to function competently in a complex economic, political and cultural system; (b) evaluation, by which system must supply qualifications in some approximation to the demand for them; and (c) pedagogy, which must attempt in its forms to resolve tensions that arise from contradictions in these twin demands.
- In consequence of these constraints the contexts of schooling are such that: (a) rates of educational progress, identified by comparing relative level of attainment at one point with those at a later point, are associated with class origin; and (b) rates of transition to selective courses and post-school destinations to tertiary education and employment are associated with class origin even when prior attainment is controlled.

These major propositions about the economic basis of social stratification, the transmission of specialised modes of cognition, and the nature of schooling in an educational system that must provide real knowledge, particularly in its techniques of textual and mathematical analysis, in a competitive examination system, are intended as a framework of social facts and hypotheses within which explanations open to empirical test can be constructed.

There are, it is suggested, three distinct processes, in an approximate temporal sequence, that contribute to the generation of inequality/difference. These are: (i) the development of cognitive schemes in early childhood; (ii) rates of learning at school as indicated by changes in relative levels of attainment; and (iii) transition to post-school destinations. The framework contains, in effect, the resources for the construction of models in which the causes of class differences in cognitive ability on entry to school, relative progress at school, and secondary effects can all be studied and provided with an explanatory narrative that includes reference to the structural properties of social organisations, the dispositions to act possessed by those involved, and the practices through which the effects are created. This framework is not a theory. It is offered as an heuristic structure for the development of a theory with explanatory capacity. Each of the processes mentioned is likely to make different demands on theoretical knowledge. The study of cognitive development in early childhood, for example, will certainly require some engagement with psychology. It is not supposed, moreover, that these processes are discrete, that they necessarily involve different structures, dispositions and practices, nor that they are without temporal overlap.

The development of cognitive skills, for example, continues throughout childhood, and indeed throughout life, but there is adequate scientific reason to accept that language-based modes of conceptual thought, established by the age of five or six years, confer a durable personal capacity with long-lasting consequences for school learning (Plomin, 1994). The relative progress of students at school is, by definition, a bounded temporal process. The processes driving such progress, although made in relation to the school, do not necessarily occur at the site of the school and need not even be associated with school properties. The degree to which rates of relative progress are structured by their school context is a hypothesis open to test. There is some evidence, for example, that self-concepts, aspirations and willingness to accept the disciplinary regime of school are dispositions of students associated with progress at school, but the extent of the relationship between these and social class needs to be shown (Nash and Harker, 1998). Classic secondary effects, those revealed by statistics that show a discrepancy associated with class origin in the destinations of students with equal attainments, also have an arbitrary temporal boundary (Boudon, 1973). Whether the processes that generate differences in relative progress and in destination choices are actually different is a contested matter in the sociology of education. It also goes without saying that these differences in the selection of in-school courses and post-school destinations can be influenced by properties of the home, community (peer group) and school. Each of these processes, in so far as they are distinct, can be explained, as already outlined, by an explanatory narrative that recognises three levels: (i) properties of social organisations, (ii) dispositions to act and (iii) activities that can be subsumed under recognised social practices.

Although this division might not withstand critical scrutiny it may be justified for methodological purposes. First, it allows the effects of early childhood development, which serious workers cannot ignore, to be taken into account (when Bernstein (1990: 158) remarks that 'the basis of symbolic control is laid down before reading is possible', he refers to codes that facilitate later access to classed modes of thought), but as this whole area is tainted with toxic waste from the IQ industry it is dangerous to traverse it without the protection of an effective conceptual apparatus. Second, the importance of self-identity, all those dispositions quantitative researchers attempt to pin down as 'aspirations', 'self-concepts' and so on, and which postmodernists theorise as 'the adoption of subject positions' – a social process, of course – are crucial to students' relative academic progress, particularly in the middle years of secondary school, and these practices must be given their own space. Third, explicit recognition of so-called secondary effects, the tendency of working-class students to choose lower destinations than middle-class students even when their qualifications are similar, may also be justified. Boudon (1973) assumes for the purposes of quantitative modelling that this effect is the result of classed decision-making contexts in which it is rational for a working-class student to adopt that path most likely to generate a rise in relative economic status at the lowest cost: in short it is 'rational' for working-class girl with A levels that would get her into medical school to take a pharmacy course rather than attempt a medical degree, but less rational for a middle-class girl for whom pharmacy would represent no advancement. There is almost certainly something in this theory and it, too, needs its space. The three phases of this analysis, which form a structure for this collection, need to be described in a little more detail.

Phase One: Cognitive Formation

Is it possible to distinguish the effects on school learning of cognitive structures, however conceptualised in psychological theory, that have been acquired to variable levels as a result of socialisation in literate family environments? If there are any more or less durable mental formations – to use a term with much the same reference from a different theoretical lexicon – developed in early childhood, in social contexts organised to respond to different symbolic forms, then those individual properties, which should be recognised as reflections of a property shared by a social group, may properly be included in sociological accounts of class differences in learning. This realist theory argues that the possibility of more or less durable cognitive structures exercised in processes of thought necessary to the acquisition of school knowledge should be investigated. There is a direct reference to the level of generative mechanism and to performances held on theoretical grounds to be those so produced. It should be possible to refer, in this sense, to the nature of the cognitive habitus.

There is no need, for the purposes of the argument advanced here, to suggest that cognitive structures developed in early childhood provide specific information processing capacities that cannot be acquired at a later point of maturation, although in the case of natural language acquisition the evidence for such a critical period is fairly robust, but it is to assert that the hypothesis of social variation in school learning resulting from differences in cognitive structures formed in this period is neither illegitimate nor incoherent. Whether this domain of human capacity is best analysed in the theoretical framework of, for example, Piaget (1969) or Vygotsky (1994), is perhaps less important to sociologists than the general scheme which needs recognise only that durable cognitive structures are acquired in the early years of life. It is arguable that sociology may leave the elaboration of cognitive structures, their identification by suitable test performances, and the functional relationship between their possession and school learning, to cognitive and educational psychologists. The investigation of the contexts of their acquisition, however, is a matter in which sociologists of education should have a distinctive contribution to make. If effective cognitive structures, or mental formations, are acquired differentially, with respect both to rate of development and relative level of effective capacity, in social environments marked by the material and symbolic resources of social class, then it can be expected that this will make some contribution to the generation of inequality/difference. It is reasonable, moreover, to suppose that performance on an appropriate set of tests might reveal the state of cognitive functioning developed as a capacity of the individual.

Phase Two: Learning at School

The period of schooling is characterised by differential rates of progress in learning. When performance on standardised tests is compared at different times it can be established that some children, usually most, have maintained their relative position, that some have shown a degree of relative progress, and that some have declined. Such relative shifts in standardised position are associated with processes of classed, gendered and ethicised identity formation. This focus on educational attainment does not imply that the cognitive habitus, the level of the generative mechanism, is not constantly developing, for the processes of intellectual development are continuous, but it is to suggest that, for these purposes, attainment in specific domains can be distinguished from the tools of thought, verbal concepts, specialised mathematical concepts and so on, that are incorporated into the cognitive habitus as effective mechanisms of thought. A model that treats the level of the cognitive habitus at five or seven as given at that point, and attempts to examine attainment in school as relative to that, can be defended. There is good evidence that aspirations, self-concepts and mode of adaptation to school are associated with relative academic progress (McCall, Beach and Lau, 2000). These non-cognitive psychological dispositions, although they may be analysed within the framework of that discipline, are related to social origin in complex ways. The significance of the concept of the educated person, in the school's discourse, to the trajectory of young people may be crucial to their success. The secondary school imposes a structural grid that shapes the patterns of identity (Ortner, 2003; Bernstein, 1971). The school becomes a stage, but by no means necessarily the largest, on which these processes are played out. The fact that a process takes place at school does not mean that it is a consequence of institutional practices at that site (even if an 'institutional effect' by definition), and the capacity of schools to accommodate and manage forms of resistance warrants careful discussion.

Phase Three: Secondary Effects

Boudon's (1973) analyses have made most sociologists of education familiar with the concepts of primary and secondary effects. It is possible to observe at any given stage of schooling a disparity in the attainments of students with different class origins and these may be definition as primary effects of class relations. The term refers to effect, not cause, and it is necessary only to accept that such observed differences are a consequence of variation in class experience, of whatever kind and at whatever site, that affect school attainment. It is almost invariably possible, however, to detect class differences when attainments at a later stage are compared with those obtained at an earlier stage. This is exactly the procedure already shown to be employed in the identification of relative shifts in attainment levels. The term 'secondary effect', however, can be restricted to those instances when more or less distinct points of transfer from one course of study or stage of education are involved. Boudon has demonstrated, for example, that the destinations of middle-class students are typically higher than those of working-class students even when their formal attainments are comparable. In as much that the presence of a secondary effect is by definition not caused by variation in attainment, there is some reason to suppose that it might be due to a different set of processes. Whatever the influence of class socialisation might be on the development of the cognitive and non-cognitive dispositions that affect educational attainment, for example, it cannot account for secondary effects. This argument enables Boudon to present a sociological theory powerful enough to displace those narratives of psychology, with their emphasis on working-class deficiencies, that for so long dominated the explanation of educational inequality. Boudon further argues that secondary effects can most adequately explained, not by differences in class-cultural values, but as a necessary outcome of the rational actions of agents with similar preferences but operating in competitive markets with different effective resources and relative opportunity costs. These distinct phases in the generation of inequality/difference, which are quite possibly due to different processes, need to be distinguished and included within a realist explanatory framework.

Structure–Disposition–Practice: The Terms of a Social Explanation

According to realist philosophy, the task of science is to discover the essential structures of natural things and specify the mechanisms by which effects observable at the level of appearances are generated (Bunge, 1998). Of course, the procedures for demonstrating the existence of social properties, and showing that particular observed events are effects of those properties, are peculiarly difficult. The effort, however, may be worthwhile. To be able to describe the mechanism by which some event, process or state of affairs has come to be is to provide a causal explanation of those things. In social science, the most complete explanations are those that include a reference to the structural properties of society, the dispositions of individuals and the practices of social groups. The emphasis on the multi-level character of sociological *explanations* can bring a new perspective to debates between agency and structure. There is nothing novel, in this sense, about the explanatory scheme outlined. On the contrary, structure–disposition–practice models are actually the common provision of empirical investigations in sociology and anthropology.

It may give the wrong impression to suggest that this explanatory scheme should be associated uniquely with my name. I derived it in an attempt to present a headline introduction to Bourdieu for first-level students: 'Social positions give rise to socialised dispositions which enable people to adopt social practices adjusted to those positions,' and so on. The ideas were first published in New Zealand (Nash, 2000a; 2000b), and developed for an international audience in the hope of attracting critical notice (Nash, 2002; 2003). But it turns out that López and Scott (2000) have developed a similar position. In any event, these authors – and López sees critical realism as the successor to postmodernism – recognise 'relational structure' as a system of social relations and 'institutional structure' as a system of customary social practices. Having defined these two necessary concepts of structure, they declare:

> ... patterns of institutions and relations result from the actions of individuals who are endowed with the capacities or competencies that enable them to produce them by acting in organized ways. The capacities are behavioural dispositions and so social structure has to be seen as embodied structure. (193)

I submit that this is a tripartite structure–practice–disposition scheme. López and Scott are interested in 'structure', a term so ambiguous that I prefer to use it only for relational structures and their emergent properties, but 'structure' can be employed to refer to any organised collection of elements and, if these concepts can be separated in substantive discussion, then all will be well. There is no obvious point in possessing such concepts if they are not to form the basis of explanation in social science. That is what the structure–disposition–practice scheme attempts to do. The familiar thesis that the structures of working-class life generate dispositions of opposition to the dominant classes, with the consequence that practices of resistance are adopted and manifested in schools, has, it will be noted, precisely this explanatory structure.

Structure

Social organisations have their existence as real entities by virtue of the relations and interactions between the people who constitute them. The social relations and interactions that bring them into existence, and as a result confer certain emergent system properties, necessarily structure all organisations. Social organisations, let us say families, factories and schools, all possess: (i) a definitive set of internal social relations (parent–child, employer–employee, teacher–pupil); (ii) a definitive set of practices (nurturance, production, education); and (iii) a set of resources, which includes material objects (homes, factories, schools) and cognitive and non-cognitive dispositions, necessary to the successful adoption of practices (love, productive skills, specialist knowledge). All these conceptually distinct properties are structured, in as much that they are composed of elements related together in some ordered way, and so may all be recognised as 'social structures' of one sort or another. This wide reference of the term 'social structure' is responsible, in fact, for considerable ambiguity in sociological theory (Porpora, 1989). The connection between relationships (forming a structure of positions), individual dispositions (forming internally related structures of knowledge) and practices (structured by function, hierarchy and distribution) is intrinsic to the emergence of social systems. A social organisation, therefore, may be recognised as the kind it is by having regard to the nature of the social relations that constitute it, the practices appropriate to that relationship, and the dispositions of the agents necessary for the maintenance of those relations and practices. A realist ontology of the social is crucial to the identification of properties treated as objects of measurement and included in statistical models.

Disposition

To acknowledge the dispositional properties of people necessarily brings the discipline of sociology into conversation with psychology, for the methods of observation, both clinical and cultural, become essential in this scheme to sociological explanation. Dispositions, frames of mind, 'mentalities', all the cognitive and non-cognitive habits of mind and body that sociologists and psychologists recognise in their studies of social behaviour, are properties of individuals. The demonstration of psychological dispositions must be approached through the various methods of clinical psychology, not excluding the psychoanalytic tradition, in addition to those of anthropology and interactionist sociology. This open acknowledgement of the relevance of personal characteristics to sociology represents, in this respect, a break with structuralist theory, and a rejection of Durkheim's form of realism in which 'collective representations' are supposed to influence social members without any form of psychological mediation (Schmaus, 1994; Durkheim and Mauss, 1963). The recognition of disposition in this sense contrasts with the parallel universe strategy adopted by Riordan (1997: 1), who proposes to avoid 'the temptation to psychologise about success and failure at school ... not because psychology is useless to furthering our understanding, but rather because it is overused'. This position makes little sense, and Riordan, who includes dispositional variables such as teachers' expectations and students' self-concepts in his models, is unable to maintain it, but the fact that it is held at all in this field is significant. The problem of inequality/difference, of course, is not one that sociologists can expect to be left solely to them, and the intelligent response of sociology is not to compete for the variance with psychology (which, in practice, means to settle for what is left), but to engage in a principled co-operation with that discipline with the aim of generating complex structure–practice–disposition explanations.

Practice

To adopt a position, to follow a custom, to take up a form of institutionalised conduct, all mean much the same thing. Practices and customs – Radcliffe-Brown's (1958) institutions – are necessary to an account of the performances, modes of conduct and activities associated with particular social positions or roles. The nineteenth century has bequeathed sociology, as Turner (1994: 6) has stated, 'a problem about practices, a problem about their status as objects, their causal properties, and their "collective" character'. This approach gives rise to some fundamental questions, of which perhaps the most important is: Do practices, customs, or institutions have a function? It is worth the effort to work this through, even though the argument will be much abbreviated, as there are confusions at the highest level in this area. The existence of a social practice – bedtime stories will afford a relatively trivial but non-contentious example – always has some consequences for those who adopt it. Reading children stories at bedtime provides a routine point of contact between parent and child – it is actually a good way to get children to sleep – and it might instil in some children habits of reading. At the same time, as a strongly classed practice, bedtime stories might well have certain consequences for the classes that provide them, such as contributing to the reproduction of their relative position, that need not be known to any of the individuals who adopt it, let alone provide a reason for them to do so (Heath, 1982). Practice is a concept that must be understood in relation to structure and disposition and in the context of a complex explanatory narrative.

This outline of a realist explanatory scheme recognises the emergent properties of social organisations (understood as constituted by social relations) and allows them a causal effect on human conduct. This causal effect must be described with reference to the dispositions possessed by individuals that give them the capacity to enter into social relations and adopt the practices they require and are associated with. The capacities of people are causal. Only human practice gives causal properties to social organisations. It is human practice that has brought into being the function states, such as demographic structures, that affect what can be done. Individuals related in such ways that they constitute a social system are so authorised by the positions they hold to adopt certain practices and must possess the personal capacities to do so. As to the effects of practices, if bedtime stories contribute to the development of literacy, then so they do, and to say that this is an effect of a practice should not be misleading in that sense. But the force of this explanatory scheme is to make explicit the connections between the properties of social organisations as systems, the nature of dispositions to act held by social members, and the nature and function of the practices they adopt. The task undertaken in this collection is to examine in context how the development of such explanations should proceed with regard to concrete evidence for the processes at each phase of educational differentiation.

The Organisation of the Text

The collection is divided into four sections each comprising three chapters: theoretical foundations; early class differentials in cognition; classed identities in formation; and secondary effects and statistical modelling. Part 1 includes: Realism in the sociology of education: 'explaining' social differences in attainment (1999); Numbers and narratives: further reflections in the sociology of education

(2002); and Social explanation and socialisation: on Bourdieu and the structure–disposition–practice scheme (2003). These chapters are all concerned with realism as a philosophical basis for the explanation of group disparities in educational achievement. The earliest chapter uses empirical data from the New Zealand Progress at School project in order to examine explanatory schemes developed by Jencks et al. (1972), Boudon (1973), and Bourdieu and Passeron (1977). The positions of quantitative modelling, in different forms, and non-quantitative studies in a realist sociology of education are explored in an examination of the causes of social differences in educational attainment. The second chapter makes the case for a realist framework integrating quantitative and qualitative methods: it argues for 'numbers and narratives' as the basis for a combined approach to research in the sociology of education. Many of the problems that arise with quantitative work are shown to have their origin in an inadequate theory of measurement and to be sustained by an unsound concept of 'statistical explanation'. The chapter provides an outline of the structure–disposition–practice scheme in this context. The final chapter in this section interrogates the competence of socialisation in sociological explanations of social events and processes and provides a more detailed account of the Bourdieusian-inspired structure–disposition–practice scheme.

Part 2 includes: Class, 'ability' and attainment: a problem for the sociology of education (2001); Cognitive habitus and collective intelligence: concepts for the explanation of inequality of educational opportunity (2005); and Bernstein and the explanation of social disparities in education: a realist critique of the sociolinguistic thesis (2006). The first chapter in this second part considers the ambivalent relationship between the sociology of education and IQ and 'ability' testing. Some accounts of inequality/difference incorporate 'measures' of intelligence; others restrict their explanations to the 'sociological' rather than the 'psychological' variance, and still others entirely reject psychometric theory and subject it to vigorous critique. But there are certain contradictions in this area. Studies that show environmental (rather than genetic) effects on 'ability' test scores are welcomed even as 'ability' is treated as a 'social construct'. Standardised tests produced within the psychometric paradigm are employed in certain research applications even as their theoretical rationale is dismissed. The chapter argues that this situation is unsatisfactory and that a realist account of cognitive socialisation based on the research of Vygotsky (1994) and Bernstein (1990) would represent an advance in our capacity to explain social differences in educational attainment.

The second chapter is also concerned with intelligence and introduces the concept of cognitive habitus in the context of a discussion of Brown and Lauder's (2000) Deweyian notion of 'collective intelligence'. Sociologists of education attempting to explain social inequalities in educational attainment have suggested that, despite the thoroughgoing criticism of the classical IQ concept, teachers continue to maintain practices that ensure their taken-for-granted ideas about the social distribution of 'ability' are realised in patterns of school attainment. The chapter accepts that this pragmatic idea may have a contribution to make in the struggle to replace the established individual reference of classical IQ theory but argues that there may be something no less important to be gained for radical interests in education from the realist concept of cognitive habitus. The case is made for this thesis by means of an investigation necessarily concerned with the conceptual clarification of certain essential terms, with reference to the guiding thought of Dewey and Bourdieu. The focus is on the concepts necessary for the construction of a coherent theory of the explanation of social disparities in education that attempts to incorporate reference to the effects of cognitive socialisation on inequality of educational opportunity.

The final chapter takes up references to Bernstein, often made in these chapters, in a considered examination of the once widely accepted sociolinguistic thesis. It poses the question whether an explanation of the origins of social disparities in educational achievement can be assisted by a critical examination of Bernstein's sociolinguistic thesis. The status of the sociolinguistic theory has been uncertain for at least 30 years. Davies (1976) presented an account of Bernstein's emerging ideas that barely mentioned the sociolinguistic thesis at just the same time that Stubbs (1976), in a parallel text, subjected it to a dismissive critique. Atkinson's (1985: 10) influential introduction to Bernstein declined to discuss the sociolinguistic theory so as not to 'recapitulate major misunderstandings' and this view seems to have been widely shared. This famous thesis has all but disappeared from view. Yet Bernstein never conceded that his most vociferous critics had weakened the theory in any respect (Bernstein, 1990) and for decades the sociolinguistic explanation of differential achievement has been left in a discursive limbo. The chapter argues that accounts have yet to be settled with this central and once highly influential aspect of Bernstein's theoretical and empirical work.

Part 3 includes: Can the arbitrary and the necessary be reconciled? Scientific realism and the school curriculum (2004); Social capital, class identity and progress at school: case studies (1999); and Pedagogy and the care for knowledge: reproduction, symbolic violence and realism (2003). The curriculum chapter was written several years before it was published and reflects on an influential interpretation of Bourdieu's theory of knowledge and its contribution to class disparities in access to education. The curriculum has been placed at the centre of a narrative of how social and cultural reproduction is effected through the symbolic power of the school. An influential body of critique maintains that the forms of the curriculum are characterised by a class arbitrary that effectively confines access to knowledge to those students who possess the code required for its acquisition. The insights of this critique are invaluable. A realist ontology demands, however, that the necessary elements of education, including respect for reality, knowledge and truth, should be an integral part of the school curriculum. It is concluded that the possibility of reconciling the arbitrary with the necessary should be grasped.

The second chapter presents the contrasted lives of two Year 11 girls, one of middle- and the other of working-class origin through a close interrogation of conversations with them. These case studies examine, with particular reference to social capital, how classed identities are adopted and maintained. Our longitudinal New Zealand Progress at School research suggests that progress at school is associated with high aspirations, positive academic self-concepts and a willingness to accept the regime of the school. These complex dispositions are interrelated and have their origins in social identities with a class origin: they are, it is argued, derived in a fundamental sense from familial and age-peer social capital. The second chapter in this section also draws on individual case study material from the Progress at School project and confronts one of the most difficult problems facing the integration of sociological and psychological approaches. Although the apparatus of self-administered questionnaires will generate – especially if the questions have been selected to generate the patterns desired – analyses that suggest, for example, that aspiration, academic self-concept and perception of schooling are significantly associated with relative progress at school, but this ought to be the beginning rather than the end of the matter for sociology. It is suggested, in fact, that these characteristics of the successful student are elements of the stratified self, unified by an overarching concept of education. Interview material with senior secondary school students is used to show how the desire to be educated within a specific concept of education is essential to their success. It is argued, with close reference to Bourdieu, that the concepts of education and the educated person need to be founded on the educational necessary as real knowledge.

The third chapter in this group extends these themes to an examination of pedagogy and the care for knowledge. The importance of care for learners is properly recognised as fundamental to teaching: it is argued here that teaching equally requires a care for *knowledge*. Within a realist theory, to care for knowledge, moreover, must involve taking into account its relationship to the real world. The implications of this ontological consideration are worked out with particular reference to Bourdieu's theory that social reproduction is effected in educational contexts where arbitrary knowledge is experienced, particularly by working-class students, as symbolic violence. The 'universal pedagogy' advocated by Bourdieu may need, in fact, to be based on a scientific realism in which the definitive knowledge of the school, taking up a theme raised in the curriculum paper, is regarded not as *arbitrary* but as *necessary*. The case for a realist approach, reflecting the different classed, gendered and cultural origins of students, is made in the context of a secondary school science lesson observed in the course of the longitudinal Progress at School project.

The final part includes: Controlling for 'ability': a conceptual and empirical study of primary and secondary effects (2006); Explanation and quantification in educational research: the arguments of critical and scientific realism (2005); and The explanation of social disparities in achievement: what has the sociology of education to offer policymakers? (2006). These chapters, with the exception of the last, have appeared in various academic journals as detailed in the acknowledgements. The first chapter considers Boudon's concepts of primary and secondary effects. Although this distinction, and its associated rational action models of inequality of educational opportunity, has been somewhat more influential in the field of social stratification and mobility than in the sociology of education, there is good reason to reconsider the theoretical and practical implications of this approach. The investigation brings conceptual analysis and empirical research to bear on Boudon's arguments in a manner that may be somewhat unorthodox. The theoretical arguments are developed in the context of a detailed empirical investigation of three transitions, age ten to O level, O level to A level, and A level to degree, using the extensive 1970 British Cohort Study. It is concluded that primary and secondary effects should be recognised as methodological rather than theoretical concepts, that the techniques used to identify them are independent of rational action theory, and that, contrary to an influential position, the evidence suggests that primary effects are more important, at least with respect to the cohort studied, than secondary effects in the generation of social disparities in access to education.

The following chapter argues that scientific realism, including critical realism in the opinion of several authorities, can provide a philosophical basis for the interpretation of certain forms of statistical modelling much superior to the orthodox neo-positivist discourse favoured by traditional experts in this field. The argument is illustrated by substantive analyses of the relationship between poverty and educational attainment (reading) using the PISA 2000 UK data-set (OEDC, 2000). It is concluded that an approach to the construction of explanatory narratives based on scientific realism is more likely to effect a principled integration of the theory and practice of qualitative and quantitative research.

The final chapter in the collection uses a later PISA 2003 UK data-set on the literacy attainments of 15-year-olds which, as is invariably the case, also reveals significant disparities associated with parental occupation, number of books in the home, and 'cultural' possessions (OECD, 2003). This data-set is used to examine some theoretical and methodological constraints on the construction of explanations of the causes of social disparities in education. It is argued that a clear distinction should be made between the analysis of population variance, to which the properties of social class will contribute, and the analysis of social disparities as such. Policymakers may need to accept that there might be no 'best model' available in order to estimate the sources of variance in educational achievement attributable to the resources and practices of social class. The whole question of what causes group disparities in education is much harder to answer in a more or less complete and satisfactory manner than most workers in the field of education often suppose.

Some Implications for Practice

If social differences in educational attainment are the result of three distinct phases, each with separate, but no doubt overlapping, generative mechanisms, then the implications of this for policies intended to reduce their cumulative effect as multi-level causes of recognised educational inequalities need to be considered. There is every reason to provide whatever resources can be offered to support parents in the critical period of early childhood development. The importance of formal and informal pre-school education is widely accepted and can be justified on grounds quite independent of this theory, but if it is well founded then those grounds are that much more solid. There is also, of course, a strong argument for any social or economic policy designed to improve the collective and individual living standards of working-class people, for there is good evidence that the well-being of parents is crucial to their capacities to home environments where children may develop and flourish in every area of competence (Brown and Lauder, 2000).

The processes of relative progress at school have been given less attention than might be expected by the standard models of quantitative educational research. The only way to obtain the quantitative data necessary requires extensive longitudinal studies that are rarely available, and perhaps for this reason the relative magnitude of this process is not sufficiently widely acknowledged. This is an area, moreover, where principled collaboration between quantitative and qualitative approaches has the potential to make an important contribution. The conventional assumption of ethnographic research that students from different social groups have an identical capacity to succeed at school is, in that sense, essentially concerned with the conditions of relative progress and decline. The school is a setting within which young people learn to be who they are and take on identities structured by the classed distribution of income, cultural and social capital. It is a setting, however, that may have relatively little power to interrupt these processes. Where schools are able, nevertheless, to raise aspirations, sustain positive academic self-concepts, and provide a moral order able to accommodate modes of adaptation to school that do not inherently prevent learning within the necessary forms of the institution.

The secondary effect, the tendency of similarly qualified students from high- and low-social backgrounds to select high and low destinations, is likely to be a product both of classed preferences and of differential opportunity costs. To the extent that preferences are responsible it would seem that effective policies should concentrate on modifying aspirations and the ideas on which they are based. Such policies will not be different in character from those designed to interrupt the processes of relative educational progress for in this thesis the phases here regarded as distinct are merged and the processes that generate one are those that generate the other. In as much as the secondary effect is a product of differential opportunity costs, however, the policies should concentrate on support mechanisms, and financial incentives in particular, that might be expected to counterbalance the individual cost–benefit calculations made by working-class students.

In conclusion, 'list' theories, including those that incorporate general theories of 'reproduction' that fail to recognise the distinct processes of differentiation (which have a temporal aspect and which to some extent involve different processes), inhibit the construction of complex multi-level explanations of inequality/ difference necessary to the introduction of effective intervention policies. The case made has been complex, but this 'conclusion' is, of course, but the last word in an introduction to a dozen chapters that take the argument deeper and further.

References

Atkinson, P. (1985). *Language, Structure and Reproduction: An Introduction to the Sociology of Basil Bernstein* (London: Methuen).

Bernstein, B. (1971). *Class, Codes and Control, Vol. I: Theoretical Studies towards a Sociology of Language and Socialization* (London: Routledge & Kegan Paul).

Bernstein, B. (1990). *Class, Codes and Control, Vol. IV: The Structure of Pedagogic Discourse* (London: Routledge).

Bernstein, B. (1996). *Pedagogy, Symbolic Control and Identity: Theory, Research, Critique* (London: Taylor & Francis).

Boudon, R. (1973). *Education, Opportunity and Social Inequality* (New York: Wiley).

Bourdieu, P. and Passeron, J.-C. (1977). *Reproduction in Education, Society and Culture*, trans. R. Nice. (London: Sage).

Brown, P. and Lauder, H. (2000). Education, child poverty and the politics of education. In S.J. Ball (ed.), Sociology *of Education: Major Themes, Vol. IV: Policies and Practices* (London: Routledge/Falmer): 1753–79.

Bunge, M. (1998*). Social Science under Debate: A Philosophical Perspective* (Toronto: University of Toronto Press).

Byrne, D. (1998). *Complexity Theory and the Social Sciences: An Introduction* (London: Routledge).

Davies, B. (1976). *Social Control and Education* (London: Methuen).

Durkheim, E. and Mauss, M. (1963 [1903]). *Primitive Classification*, trans. with intro. R. Needham. (London: Cohen & West)..

Flude, M. (1974). Sociological accounts of differential ability. In M. Flude and J. Aheir (eds), *Educability, Schools and Ideology* (London: Croom Helm): 15–22.

Gasper, P. (1990) Explanation and scientific realism. In D. Knowles (ed.), *Explanation and Its Limits* (Cambridge: Cambridge University Press): 182–206.

Hanushek, E.A. (1997). Assessing the effect of school resources on student performance: An update, *Educational Evaluation and Policy Analysis*, 19(2): 141–64.

Heath, S.B. (1982). What no bedtime story means: Narrative skills at home and school, *Language in Society*, 11: 49–76.

Jencks, C., Smith, M., Acland, H., Bane, M.J., Cohen, D., Gintis, H., Heyns, B. and Michelson, S. (1972). *Inequality: A Reassessment of the Effect of Family and Schooling in America* (Harmondsworth: Penguin).

López, J. and Scott, J. (2000). *Social Structure* (Buckingham: Open University Press).

Lynch, K. (2000). Research and theory on equality and education. In M.T. Hallinan (ed.), *Handbook of the Sociology of Education* (New York: Kluwer Academic/ Plenum): 85–105.

Marshall, G., Swift, A. and Roberts, S. (1997). *Against the Odds: Social Class and Social Justice in Industrial Societies* (Oxford: Clarendon Press).

McCall, R.B., Beach, S.R. and Lau, S. (2000). The nature and correlates of underachievement among elementary schoolchildren in Hong Kong, *Child Development*, 71(3): 785–801.

Nash, R. (2000a). Educational inequality: The special case of Pacific students, *Social Policy Journal of New Zealand*, 15: 69–86.

Nash, R. (2000b). On violence: A realist(ic) commentary for workers in schools, *Social Work Review*, 12(3): 20–25.

Nash, R. (2002). A realist framework for the sociology of education: Thinking with Bourdieu, *Educational Philosophy and Theory*, 34(3): 273–88.

Nash, R. (2003). Social explanation and socialization: On Bourdieu and the structure, disposition, practice scheme, *Sociological Review*, 51(1): 43–62.

Nash, R. and Harker, R.K. (1998). *Making Progress: Adding Value in Secondary Education* (Palmerston North: ERDC Press).

OECD (2000). *Manual for the PISA 2000 Database* (Paris: Organisation for Economic Co-operation and Development).

OECD (2003). *Programme for International Student Assessment*, data-set (Paris: Organisation for Economic Co-operation and Development).

Ortner, S.B. (2003). *New Jersey Dreaming: Capital, Culture and the Class of '58* (Durham, NJ: Duke University Press).

Pallas, A.M. and Entwisle, D.R. (1994). Ability-group effects: Instructional, social, or institutional? *Sociology of Education*, 67: 27–46.

Piaget, J. (1969 [1947]). *The Psychology of Intelligence* (New York: Humanities Press).

Plomin, R. (1994). *Genetics and Experience: The Interplay between Nature and Nurture* (Newbury Park: Sage).

Porpora, D.V. (1989). Four concepts of social structure, *Journal for the Theory of Social Behaviour*, 19(2): 195–211.

Radcliffe-Brown, A.R. (1958). *Method in Social Anthropology: Selected Essays*, ed. M.N. Srinivas (Chicago: University of Chicago Press).

Riordan, C. (1997). *Equality and Achievement: An Introduction to the Sociology of Education* (New York: Longman).

Schmaus, W. (1994) *Durkheim's Philosophy of Science and the Sociology of Knowledge: Creating an Intellectual Niche* (Chicago: Chicago University Press).

Stubbs, M. (1976). *Language, Schools and Classrooms* (London: Methuen).

Turner, S. (1994). *The Social Theory of Practices: Tradition, Tacit Knowledge and Presuppositions* (London: Polity Press).

Vygotsky, L. (1994). *The Vygotsky Reader*, ed. R. Van der Veer and J. Valsiner (Oxford: Blackwell).

Wartofsky, M.W. (1979). *Models: Representations and the Scientific Understanding* (Dordrecht, The Netherlands: Reidel).

PART 1
Theoretical Foundations

Chapter 1

Realism in the Sociology of Education: 'Explaining' Social Differences in Attainment

Introduction

Realist approaches to sociology have been stimulated by recent works, of which the rigorous investigations by Bunge (1979) and Archer (1995) have been particularly influential, in the philosophy of science and social theory. The sociology of education, by no means the least important area for the practice of sociology, may stand to benefit from these attempts to reposition the nature of sociological enquiry and explanation. This chapter will seek to explore some implications of realism for the sociology of education in the context of a presentation of empirical findings from a New Zealand research programme. Two large-scale projects carried out in the last ten years, Access and Opportunity in Education (Nash, 1993a) and Progress at School (Nash and Harker, 1998), have attempted to develop an integrated approach to the investigation of socially differentiated access to education constructed around a 'family resource framework' informed by realist theses, and data from the second of these will be presented in some detail. Although basically constructed with reference to Bourdieu's (1977) analyses of social and educational reproduction, and strongly influenced by his methodology, several characteristics of Bourdieu's theory, particularly its functionalism and relativist epistemology, are rejected, and it would consequently be misleading to position our research programme as 'Bourdieusian'. In fact, the immediate problem for research with statistical data is to analyse it in the most appropriate and informative manner, but that is an issue requiring more discussion than is sometimes offered, and the influence of Bourdieu's work in this respect is not uniquely problematic. Bourdieu's theory of educational inequality is related only indirectly to methods of statistical enquiry and, while engaged with correspondence analysis, it is not dependent on any specific technique and lends its support to no particular form, but as much cannot be said for all theoretical approaches. On the contrary, in the structural models of 'causal sociology', based on correlational methods and employed with considerable effect by Jencks et al. (1972), the analytical technique has a dominant position in the construction of theoretical accounts, and in Boudon's (1981) theory of socially differentiated access to education flow models in the form of tables have a similarly important role. The techniques of statistical analysis and the forms of explanation associated with them, in fact, require to be examined in the context of an enquiry directed to the nature of the relationship that exists between them. Inspired, therefore, by a search for realism in sociological accounts of educational inequality, the following discussion will examine the approaches of Jencks, Boudon and Bourdieu to statistical data with specific reference to an empirical study concerned, above all, to discover the answer to a real problem: What are the main causes of social differences in educational attainment?

The Progress at School Project

The data discussed in this chapter are from the Progress at School project, which followed the educational careers of 5,384 students who entered 37 New Zealand secondary schools in 1991: this is virtually a 10-per-cent sample of the annual cohort. In New Zealand students enter secondary school in the third form (Year 8) when they are usually 13 or 14 years of age, and may leave at age 16, but most complete sixth form (Year 11) and a considerable minority remain to seventh form. The research was designed as a school effects study (Smith and Tomlinson, 1989), but few differences in students' attainment that could be attributed to any property of the school attended were observed, and the data are examined here with other interests in mind. Student attainment was assessed at five points: at third-form entry by New Zealand standardised tests of reading and 'scholastic ability' (IQ); at the completion of fourth form by specially designed tests of English, mathematics and science; at fifth form by results in the nationally assessed School Certificate examination; at sixth form by results in the nationally monitored Sixth Form Certificate award; and at seventh form by the nationally assessed University Bursary examination.

Correlational Models: Jencks

In many respects the Progress at School data set is comparable to those used by Jencks et al. in their influential study *Inequality*. Jencks's team set out to report the extent of educational and income inequality in American society and investigate its causes: their investigation remains a classic example of orthodox quantitative methodology in the sociology of education and provides an appropriate starting point. The object of correlational analysis, of which path analysis is an advanced form, is to estimate the relative degree of influence of the several variables included in the analysis by discovering the amount of variance 'explained' by each. When Jencks et al. (1972: 139) state, in a proposition entirely representative of this form of argument, that 'about a third of the discrepancy between economically advantaged and disadvantaged students is explained by differences in their test scores', a statement of causality is made that is based on nothing more than a 'descriptive presentation' of certain relationships that exist in the data. When information is collected on students' test scores and their parents' occupations it is invariably observed, if the sample is representative and of adequate size, that students from richer homes are more likely to have higher scores than those from poorer homes. The degree of association between the two variables can be expressed by a correlation coefficient. If, for example, the correlation between social class and test score is about 0.35 (a value typical of the association between IQ-type tests and scales of socio-economic status), then it is consequently established that about 12 per cent of the variance in each set of scores is shared with the other set and, by a long-standing convention, it is said that 12 per cent of the variance has been *explained*. In this instance, as children's IQ is obviously not a cause of their parents' class position, it must be that 12 per cent of the variance in the intelligence of children is due to their social origin. As a result of analysing data from several US studies available at the time of their investigation Jencks et al. conclude that 30–35 per cent of the variance in academic attainment between economic groups is due to differences in their IQ test scores, and suggests that about a third of that proportion is due to the capacity of the most economically advantaged groups to donate superior genes to their offspring, and that two-thirds is due to their competence to develop valued cognitive skills.

Multivariate path analysis is a very powerful technique for examining the relationships between numerical data, and theoretical accounts derived from causal modelling are, at least, more credible than those based on research that avoids quantitative analysis in favour of 'qualitative' observations that, insofar as they rely on what Lazarsfeld (1993) has all too easily castigated as 'impressionistic quasi-statistics', are dismissed without difficulty by those aware of the relationships that actually exist between variables. The Progress at School project made the fullest use of quantitative techniques (Harker and Nash, 1996), including hierarchical linear modelling (Goldstein, 1987), and there is no intention to disparage their value. Nevertheless, the title 'causal sociology' is a polite fiction and it is sometimes necessary to insist that associations between data are not causes and cannot be declared to be so by fiat. All introductions to 'causal modelling' in statistical sociology emphasise in their earliest pages the crucial distinction between genuine causal correlations and contingent correlations but, nevertheless, maintain a formal commitment to a Humean causality in which that distinction cannot be acknowledged. The formal claim, after all, is that if variables are associated they are correlated and that if they are correlated their shared variance is 'explained'. In this way the language of causal relations has become a deeply embedded convention of the field with a definite influence on the forms of substantive explanation developed. Of course, the idea that 'constant conjunctions' demonstrated by correlations represent real relations of causality is not taken seriously, and a large amount of creative energy is actually devoted to devising post-hoc explanatory accounts of the concrete social processes responsible for the generation of observed patterns of associations, but it is in this fashion that 'causal sociology' makes a somewhat illegitimate homage to realist sociology, in which a theory of the causes of a social event, process or phenomenon must gain its substantive explanatory power from its ability to model the mechanism by which it is brought into being.

That associations are not, in fact, explanations, is uncontested, and the term 'variance explained' is, in that sense, one that begs the question, but in the case of many associations the possibility of a genuine relationship of causality is not easily dismissed. Children's test scores cannot determine parental income, but the idea that the prosperity of a family is a partial cause of its children's intellectual development is a great deal more plausible. The substantive theoretical argument constructed around statistical models necessarily depends, in fact, on an appeal to 'reasonableness' and 'plausibility'. In his account of why students from the middle-class rather than the working-class are more likely to leave the educational system with higher qualifications Jencks et al. (1972: 138) argues, for example, that 'they are more likely to have genes that facilitate success in school', 'more likely to have a home environment in which they acquire the intellectual skills they need to do well in school', more likely to 'feel that they ought to stay in school, even if they have no special aptitude for academic work and dislike school life' and, finally, 'may attend better schools, which induce them to go to college rather than drop out'. Jencks et al. make an attempt to calculate the degree of effect due to each of these variables, but the suspicion that there is little more than an informed common sense at work in the construction of this explanatory sociological account is hard to shake off.

In the light of this discussion, and that to follow, it will be helpful to examine Figure 1.1, which presents the pattern of associations between four variables from the Progress at School data – social class, third form ability, School Certificate and Bursary attainment – in the form of a path analysis. The beta weights expresses the associations between the variables included in the model in a standardised form, and in the language favoured by 'causal sociology' the model indicates that prior ability (which many commentators would have no difficulty in recognising as 'IQ') has, by comparison with social class, by far the most significant causal effect on School Certificate attainment. Bursary attainment, in its turn, is overwhelmingly determined by School Certificate performance and only to a very slight independent degree by social class. There is probably no escape from the conclusion that third-form ability must have a major role in any convincing model of fifth-form and seventh-form school attainment, and some implications of that will be faced, but it may first be worth looking a little more closely at the data before reaching the conclusion that social class has no more than a trivial effect on secondary school performance once ability has been controlled.

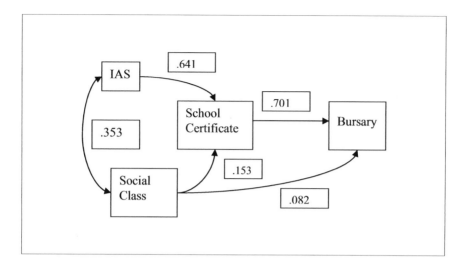

Figure 1.1 Path analysis showing associations between variables affecting bursary attainment

Note: The model shows the beta weights between social class; Intake Ability Score (IAS) based on responses to two standardised instruments, the Progressive Attainment Test (Reading Comprehension) and the Test of Scholastic Abilities, produced by the New Zealand Council for Educational Research (Reid and Elley, 1991; Reid et al., 1981); the principal component from a factor analysis of marks in English, mathematics and science in these three core subjects in the national fifth-form School Certificate examination; and total mark in the seventh-form University Bursary examination. The model indicates that IAS is strongly associated with School Certificate (accounting for 44.1 per cent of the variance) and that social class is only weakly associated (accounting for 2.3 per cent of the variance). It further indicates that IAS has no additional effect on Bursary attainment once School Certificate attainment is controlled, and that social class makes only a negligible additional direct contribution. The total effect, direct and indirect, of social class on Bursary attainment can be calculated as 0.348.

It is not surprising that the criticisms of 'causal modelling' rehearsed above are likely to be shrugged off by exponents of this methodology. Their technical terminology rarely misleads them, their positivist concept of causality is a matter of form, and they can be confident that their research is based on empirical data and analytical procedures open to independent scrutiny. Critics who reject the statement that the correlation of students' IQ with their parents' social class 'explains' a little more than 12 per cent of the variance in IQ must nevertheless account for a correlation of about 0.35 between those variables, and face the unavoidable conclusion that secondary school attainment, over a five-year period, is far more strongly associated with earlier attainment than social class. It is the failure to do that, of course, on the part of so many sociologists of education that is responsible for the great division between so called 'quantitative' and 'qualitative' analysts (Nash, 1998a).

Tabular Flow Models: Boudon

Perhaps the most informed critique, that of a knowledgeable insider, of correlational analysis and its assumptions has been provided by Boudon (1981). *The Logic of Social Action* expresses reservations about the explanatory logic of correlational analysis, which, in Boudon's view, appears to disguise significant relationships apparent in tabular presentations of data, and specifically criticises the syntax of explanation supported by the path-analytic models of so-called causal sociology. In order to *explain* the correlation between class position and educational achievement it is necessary, he maintains, to abandon the schema that suggests that a series of factors interpose themselves between class and educational success with a cumulative effect depending upon their variable weights. In effect, Boudon thus relinquishes the attempt to estimate the contributions of different variables (rendering problematic their very name) on which quantitative sociology is founded. These 'factorial' models, he proposes, should be replaced with 'decision-making' models, in which agents with different social origins are recognised as likely to find in their class position a point of reference from which the advantages and disadvantages of deciding on one educational course or career rather than another are taken into account.

In Boudon's methodological individualism a social phenomenon is only given a satisfactory explanation when what people actually did to bring about that phenomenon is described in such a way that their behaviour, situated within deterministic institutional and social contexts, can be understood with reference to their intentional actions as individuals. This 'action reference' requires an act of understanding on the part of the observer. Boudon's concept of sociological explanation, in fact, follows Weber in making sociological explanations dependent on the intelligibility of action descriptions and supports a discourse in which statistical data and 'interpretative techniques' are regarded as 'complementary rather than opposed' (Boudon, 1981: 147). His observation that 'the description of *another's* actions proposed by the researcher is only really satisfactory when he can convince his reader that, in the same circumstances, he would have acted in the same way' (ibid. 145–6) thus places the test of sociological explanation on the capacity of the 'reader' to understand the purposes of those whose collective actions brought about, directly or indirectly, the event or phenomenon under examination. In this manner, Boudon continues: 'one understands that a poor family is more hesitant to take a risk. I *understand* that relation in the sense that I have hardly any trouble in believing that, in an analogous situation, I would certainly experience the same hesitations'. One might think that poor families would behave in this way, if they do, whether Boudon understood their actions or not, and the capacity of others to understand or accept an explanation cannot be made a condition of its soundness. The Weberian insistence that social processes are *explained* when they are *understood* negates the value of any attempt to specify the distinguishing character of sociological explanation.

Boudon's methodological individualism is unabashedly reductionist: '[t]o *explain* that phenomenon [an observed association presented in a table or represent by a correlation], it must be reduced to the consequences of actions carried out by the agents of the system in question' (Boudon, 1981: 144–5). The emphasis in that sentence is placed by its author on 'explain', but it would go equally well on 'reduced'. Sociological explanations that insist on the reality of the social, even while refusing to embrace all that is sometimes implied by 'methodological individualism' and rejecting a 'deterministic' concept of social structure, can accept the general thrust of this argument. In realist sociological accounts, social class is a structural cause of social differences in educational attainment, but any explanation that failed to outline the mechanisms of the social processes by which differential attainment was generated would, at the very least, be incomplete. This is not a matter of explanatory 'reduction', and it is necessary to address the supposition that accounts of social events, processes and phenomena in terms of the causal powers of social structures, which are held to be paradigmatic of sociological explanations, are rendered superfluous by the 'reductionist' accounts of 'methodological individualism'. One might with more reason argue that without a concept of social structure – the structures of, for example, class position, the distribution of educational qualifications, and access to further education and employment – that the actions of individuals, whether more or less intentional or habit-directed, whose lives are bounded by such real structures could not be explained. It is evident, nevertheless, that methodological individualists prefer to concentrate on rational action, or at least on intentionalist action, rather than on social structures and how people are influenced by them. Far more attention is paid in this field to modelling decisions within the assumptions of game theory than to the examination of social structures and their effects on human practice.

Boudon's interest in decision-making is, in fact, situated within a sociological framework more often criticised for its normative and 'over-socialised' view of the social actor. Thus, Boudon can argue, as is consistent with a concept of 'deterministic' structures, that: '[c]onfronted with a choice the "social" agent, homo sociologicus, can, in certain cases, do, not what he prefers, but what habit, internalised values, and, more generally, diverse ethical, cognitive and gestural conditionings, force him to do' (1981: 156). Dahrendorf's (1968) concept of *homo sociologicus* was introduced to give normative, role-theoretic, sociology a socially determined model actor distinct from the *homo oeconomicus* of economic theory. Yet the presence of *society*, notwithstanding the theoretical language of structural determinism and the uneasy recognition of social conditioning and choice, is barely detectable in Boudon's work, for the investigation of social structure has almost no part in the individually focused research of the game-theoretic tradition that so strongly influences it. What is the occupational structure in a given society? How is it maintained? What are the patterns of thought, of ideology and values that influence the habits and preferences of those who occupy different positions in the economic structure? All of these questions, and others of their kind, which seem preliminary to the development of adequate concepts of social structure, are actually missing from Boudon's sociology, and in place of the expected 'thick description' of social forms and practices there is but the 'thin *condensation*' of the individual actor with unexplained social habits of mind, unaccountable values and unmentioned individual preferences, who is supposed (often against the grain of most empirical evidence) to follow the rational *and hence understandable* course of action. Even as Boudon notes that it is 'one of the essential characteristics of the sociological tradition' to treat the 'objectives and preferences of the actors as variables partly dependent upon the environment' (1981: 160), his mode of practising the discipline directs attention away from the investigation of social structures and their several powers to influence action.

Nevertheless, for all this critique of his position, Boudon's argument that path analysis supports a form of explanatory account with a potential to misrepresent the patterns of decision-making involved is not without substance. It is worth spending a little time on Table 1.1. The strength of the relationship between third-form ability and seventh-form attainment is unmistakable. Rather more than a quarter of all students gain university entrance (UE) Bursary, but the proportion is 58.9 per cent in the case of those in the upper ability quintile and but 3.4 per cent in the lowest ability quintile. It is also plain that middle-class students enter secondary school with attainments far higher than working-class students: 43 per cent of those from professional backgrounds are found in the upper quintile and only 7 per cent in the lower quintile, compared with 10 per cent and 32 per cent respectively in the case of those from low-skilled and non-working backgrounds. The relationship between these core variables, third-form ability, social class, fifth-form attainment and seventh-form attainment, modelled by path analysis, also suggests a negligible effect of social class. Nevertheless, Boudon's point that the structured importance of social class is relatively obscured by path analysis gains support from the observation that, whereas 71 per cent of students with professional origins obtain UE Bursary, the corresponding proportion of those with the lowest social origins is but 41 per cent. In other words, in the upper quintile of the ability distribution, students from professional origins are more likely by odds of 7:4 to obtain Bursary than those from less skilled and non-working origins. Inspection of the table will reveal a more or less consistent association between social class and level of educational attainment. It must be admitted that the variables are not controlled as closely as might be desired by the categorical divisions (the average Bursary mark gained by students with professional origins is higher than that of the lowest social group), but the unmistakable trends are certainly not an artefact of the category system. Unlike path analysis, cross-tabulations do not appear to show the contributions of the separate variables to the generation of differential attainment but an attempt can be made, as in Table 1.2, to model the effect of different influences.

Table 1.1 School attainment by social class and ability (percentages)

Attainment	Prof.	L. prof.	Clerical, farmer	Skilled	L. skilled, non-work	Number
High ability						
Bursary	72	70	58	52	41	579
SFC/SC	21	18	26	29	28	242
Other	7	11	12	16	23	133
None	1	1	3	3	7	29
Ability (%)	43	37	26	15	10	
Mid-ability	47	35	23	19	11	590
SFC/SC	21	24	24	26	15	603
Other	25	35	43	46	56	1305
None	6	6	9	9	17	324
Ability (%)	50	55	63	66	58	
Low ability						
Bursary	7	8	7	5	1	28
SFC/SC	27	8	8	2	3	34
Other	33	66	71	69	64	547
None	33	18	14	24	32	223
Ability (%)	7	8	11	18	32	
Number	310	549	1270	943	1565	4637
Percentage	6.7	11.8	27.4	20.3	33.8	

Note: Students are grouped by ability quintiles ('high ability' denotes the upper quintile, 'average ability' the middle quintiles, and 'low ability' the lowest quintile. Completed school attainment is given by Bursary (at least 150 marks); Sixth Form Certificate or at least five passes in School Certificate; Other (lower) levels of School Certificate award; and no formal school qualifications. Social class is based on the categories of the Elley-Irving (1985) scale of socio-economic status. Higher professional (Prof.), category 1; lower professional (L.prof.), category 2; intermediate (Clerical, farmer); Skilled, category 4; and other (L.skilled, non-work), categories 5 (semi-skilled) and 6 (unskilled with non-working).

Table 1.2 Model of causal influences on access to university: Gains and losses due to ability, school processes and destination choice

Social class	UE bursary	p	Enter uni.	Not enter uni.	Ability predicted	School	Choice	Estimated at uni.
H. profess.	561	(0.95)	533	467	527	+34	-28	17.3
L. profess.	468	(0.85)	348	602	447	+21	-70	23.1
Intermediate	305	(0.80)	244	756	327	-22	-61	32.6
Skilled	213	(0.75)	160	840	217	-4	-53	15.9
Other	114	(0.60)	68	932	140	-26	-46	11.1

Note: Each social class is assumed to contain 1,000 students. The parameter (p) gives the likelihood of students from each social class with UE Bursary gaining access to university. The values are derived from empirical data. The numbers entering (and not entering) university are generated from the information given in the table by the following procedure. The initial step is to calculate the number expected to enter university, given that it can be established that the empirical cut-off point for UE Bursary is an 'IQ' equivalent of 110. Once this datum is known, it follows that an estimate can be made of the number of students in each social class who exceed or fail to exceed the expectation set by their earlier academic performance. The percentage of students from each social class entering university given by the parameter (p) is then applied to estimate the number finally predicted by the model to gain access to university. An estimate of the percentage of students at university from each social class is made from known distributions.

Table 1.2 presents a model in which access to university is controlled by success in the Bursary examination (a realistic assumption in the case of school leavers although a significant proportion of students, particularly Maori, do enter university with poorer qualifications). Each social class has a differential level of success in the examination and a variable likelihood of entering university once qualified to do so. A little more than a quarter of all students gain UE Bursary and the minimal third-form ability level associated with that level of success is 110 points. Table 1.2 shows that of 1,000 students with professional origins 561 obtain at least university entrance, and, on the assumption (based on actual data) that 95 per cent of students from this class fraction so qualified will gain access to university, the number given by the model is therefore 533. As we are interested in exclusion, it will be convenient to note that 467 students from this group will not attend university. Most of these students fail for want of ability: it can be calculated from the ability distribution that 473 students from professional families cannot be expected to be successful in the University Bursary examination, and one is thus made aware that a system of class exclusion, in Bourdieu's discourse, actually disqualifies almost half the children of the professional class itself. Moreover, their additional relative progress at secondary school will add no more than an estimated 34, and in consequence of the differential choice parameter that affects this elite group, 21 qualified students who cannot be expected enter university must be substracted. The success of students of professional origin may be compared, as is traditional, with that of those from the least skilled and non-employed families. This large section of the population, at least a third, sees just 6.8 per cent of its children reach university, where they constitute little more than a tenth of the student body. The model indicates that almost all of the exclusion is due to the level of academic performance demonstrated by these students as third-form entrants, and that only a relatively small additional loss can be attributed to their relative decline at secondary school and to differential decision-making patterns. It is true that the proportions of students from the lowest social classes entering university would almost double were they not affected by relative decline at school and chose to enter university at the same level as those from the professional classes, but that would still leave them, by the conditions of this model, under-represented by a factor of five. Nothing could be clearer from these models than that the most powerful cause of difference in the eventual educational success of different social classes is the earlier level of ability, demonstrated attainment, or academic competence associated with social position.

Internalised (Statistical) Structures: Bourdieu

Whereas Jencks and Boudon are directly concerned with the relationship between specific techniques for the analysis of quantitative data and the substantive explanations these support, it can be seen that Bourdieu's involvement with statistical forms are somewhat different. In Bourdieu's theory the objective structures of social relations given expression in tables of association between social class and educational access have a more fundamental representation in the embodied dispositions generating social practices in accordance with the very 'rules of the game' that bring about the patterns revealed by such collected statistics. This habitus theory has been criticised, with some justification, as circular, but there are other, perhaps more fundamental problems with Bourdieu's sociology, and prominent among them may be included its residual functionalism. The social phenomenon to be explained, for Bourdieu, is the reproduction of the social and cultural system itself, and the explanation requires that in order for reproduction to be effected, if in a transformed manner, societies have in place established practices for the maintenance of the existing system of relations. In Bourdieu's account, this is managed through the formation in social members of socialised frames of perception and thought able to generate the strategic practices necessary for the effective functional reproduction of the system. This theory distances Bourdieu from methodological individualism, for it is social structures operating through habitus that perform the explanatory work, and from 'intentionalism', for it is the habitual, taken-for-granted, routines of people 'following the rules of the game' with no necessary awareness of the socially reproductive functions of their actions, that drive the process. This functionalism makes habitus, with its acknowledged vagueness and indeterminacy, a highly problematic concept to include in explanatory accounts of social differences in education. The theory that working-class children fail because they are trapped in their working-class habitus with inferior forms of 'cultural capital' is not how Bourdieu prefers to express his position, but some such version of his extraordinarily subtle theory is often furnished, and the intentionally abstract and probably no less intentional ambiguities and obscurities of the original texts make it difficult to place the responsibility for such clumsiness of thought entirely on others (Nash, 1990a, 1993b). In fact, it is the lack of precision in the specification of the frames of mind that constitute class habitus in the form they are supposed to have an effect on the mastery of the school curriculum that creates the most serious practical difficulty with Bourdieu's account of the exclusion of working-class children from the educational system.

In his most influential statements, Bourdieu (1976) sees differences in socially conditioned intellectual aptitudes as arbitrary forms of mentality treated by the school as unequal 'gifts of nature' and transformed by its institutional power into actual differences in objective educational qualifications. If he does not fully ally himself with those who dismiss the concept of intelligence as a product of pseudo-science and intelligence tests as ideological artefacts of the technology of class oppression, he nevertheless recognises in the school's 'ideology of giftedness' only arbitrary distinctions of linguistic style and class specific forms of pedagogy. It should be clear that this position lacks conviction, and that the development of literacy-based cognitive skills of a more or less permanent character is the principal form of 'effective cultural capital' acquired by pre-school children in those families, predominantly, but not exclusively, middle-class families, where they are increasingly exposed to systematic practices of literate socialisation specifically designed to further their intellectual development in areas of competency highly rewarded by the educational system. Some implications for a realist interpretation of cognitive differences will be given further discussion.

Class 'Values' in Theoretical Models

It is possible to subject models of explanation to critique at several levels. This chapter has focused on fundamental issues of epistemology and on the practical relation of theories to forms of data analysis but this does not exhaust the possibilities of critical examination. One of the most disconcerting experiences of a reader is to discover that the actual explanatory accounts of concrete phenomenon given by theorists highly critical of each other's epistemological commitments are, more frequently than might seem possible, to all intents and purposes indistinguishable. A telling illustration of this is afforded by the explanations provided of what Boudon calls 'secondary effects'. The tendency of working-class students to select courses leading to occupations with a lower status than those selected by middle-class students, when their school qualifications are the same (a tendency noticeable in the Progress at School data), obviously cannot be explained by reference to earlier differences in cognitive ability, and in the sense that the variance in cognitive ability associated with class socialisation is controlled, this phenomenon may be referred to as a 'secondary effect' of class position (whereas the effects of class socialisation on the development of intelligence may be regarded as a 'primary effect'). Boudon distinguishes two principal theories, or accounts, that have been advanced to account for this specific class-linked phenomenon. First, middle-class and working-class students, at the same level of ability, may have characteristically different occupational preferences as a result of their socialisation into value frameworks with a strong class basis. Second, the different class locations occupied by middle-class and working-class students give them objectively different structures of opportunity costs with a differential effect on their decision-making. Bourdieu's theory, which assumes that practices are generated by deep-rooted frames of mentality acquired as the result of socialisation into social class communities, might be regarded as a value theory, and is certainly criticised as such by Boudon who prefers an opportunity cost theory.

Jencks, for his part, thought the influence of preferences based on distinct values associated with class origin on educational success and destination choice to be overstated. He noted that students with the same test scores gained the same high-school grades regardless of their social origin, and, while he was aware that middle-class students held higher aspirations than working-class students, even when test scores were controlled, he suggested that working-class students probably aspired to working-class occupations because they were reluctant to remain at school, rather than the other way round. Nevertheless, the argument seems strained for it is difficult to explain why working-class students should be more likely to dislike school than middle-class students without introducing some reference to class values. An influential thesis, largely based on ethnographic work, can be cited in support of this position (Corrigan, 1990; Hammersley, 1995), and the subtle processes of interaction, between students and the school, by which 'modes of adaptation' (Woods, 1977) become *forms of identification*, has been explored elsewhere (Nash, 1998b, 1998c). The difficulty here, as Boudon argues, has its origin in the type of explanation supported by the need to interpret factor weights revealed by correlational analysis: the data may very well show, to consider students of average ability, that for every ten of middle-class origin and every ten of working-class origin the majority in each case, eight of the former and six of the latter, aspire to university, that one of the former and two of the latter dislike school and prefer to leave as soon as possible even at the cost of accepting a low-status occupation, and that one of the former and two of the latter have formed aspirations for an occupation in accordance with a preference, which can be recognised as one with a class valuation, for skilled manual rather than mental labour. This sort of 'messy' pattern (but in our studies one very close to reality) is difficult to express in the models used by Jencks by whom, indeed, the concept of 'class values' is left unexplored. The 'classed identity' of the sorts of beliefs that can be recognised as 'values', must be constituted by cultural analysis of an appropriate kind. When that task is carried out, and it is certainly not undertaken by Jencks, it is more easily realised that students are not only and necessarily influenced by the forms of thought common in their own social class – or rather in their class of origin, which for many senior students with a certain level of qualification and established patterns of social intercourse is already not their *own* class – but have available to them, not least, of course, from the deliberate practices of school, other patterns of life.

There is evidence, moreover, to suggest that occupational aspirations and valuations of forms of labour are not necessarily connected (Nash and Major, 1995, 1996, 1997). Working-class students often take a characteristically ambivalent stance towards the valuation they place on the school in relation to mental and manual labour. Occupations granted the highest status are those that demand the longest and most expensive forms of training, and receive the greatest social and financial rewards. There is almost universal recognition in contemporary societies that these occupations include those of lawyer, accountant, medical practitioner, senior civil servant and so on, and they are the focus of many students' aspirations. At the same time, however, working-class students are aware of a different valuation in which the actual labour performed by skilled workers, and the hard-won practical knowledge that makes it possible, is celebrated against the grain of the dominant framework of values even as the hegemony of those values is acknowledged. It is particularly easy for working-class students, who have done no more than pattern their declared aspirations according to commonly recognised valuations, to restructure them should their grades begin to fail or the cost–benefit analysis of a prolonged and expensive course of study appear unattractive as the point of irrevocable decision-making approaches. Jencks's argument, therefore, lacks direct empirical support and appears weak as a generalisable theory.

Boudon's application of decision-theory to this area is intended to provide an alternative explanation to class value or socialised habit theories. The strength of secondary effects, Boudon argues, is not due to preferences derived from distinctive class values, but is the product of a decision-making process that can be modelled in the terms of cost–benefit analysis. Thus, he argues (1982: 191):

> the subject's class of origin (or the class to which a family now belongs) will crucially affect his choices of one or the other option. If their current success is mediocre, the family unit will consider itself 'satisfied' if the child has reached an academic level enabling him to aspire to a social status equal or higher than his own, even if this status is not especially high. A well-placed family unit will on the other hand strive (I ought to add: more often than not) to 'push' the child so that he doesn't fail (even if he doesn't enjoy a greater success).

In essence: middle-class families must encourage their offspring to enter courses leading to the highest levels of professional status or else fail to maintain their status, whereas working-class families are able to accept the 'compromise' of a lower professional destination and still enjoy the satisfactions to be experienced from the relative degree of upward mobility so conferred. Boudon (ibid. 102) speculates, moreover, that this process of decision-making sometimes takes an explicit and self-conscious form:

> the notion of mathematical probability is itself implicit in reasoning which runs as follows: 'I have little hope of obtaining the aggregation – though one can never be sure; I have a reasonable chance of getting a CAPES and at worst I could always use my first degree to get an appointment as an assistant teacher.'

This is not a difficult argument to follow and the point has been made by others. Collins (1979: 170), for example, suggests that: 'For those of lower social origin, a position as a technical specialist in the middle ranks of a bureaucratic organisation is an acceptable goal, although it may not be for the upper-middle-class person seeking elite status.'

Nevertheless, there are serious weaknesses in Boudon's argument that the distribution of educational qualifications to students of different social origins shown in tables provides evidence that secondary effects are caused by opportunity cost decision-making rather than class values. In Table 1.1 it will be noted that, in the highest ability quintile, students from professional families have a much greater likelihood of gaining Bursary than those from low-skilled and non-working families: it will also be noted that there is less difference in the proportions of students from these classes gaining the lower level of qualification at sixth form. Boudon suggests that if class values were a major influence on the decision to pursue educational qualifications the effect would be consistent and not made most evident at particular stages in the structure of an educational career. The argument is, once again, one where formalism has the capacity to misrepresent reality. In fact, class-based preferences and modes of thought do seem to become important in the process of mediation as the point of final decision-making about post-school destination draws nearer (Nash, 1997c, 1999). It is in this respect that certain areas of concordance in theories that appear to be distinct and, indeed, contradictory may be noted.

In Bourdieu's accounts of the processes by which students of different social origin tend to reproduce existing patterns it is the unreflected actions of socialised actors that provide all the sociological explanation necessary. Yet such are the ambiguities inherent in Bourdieu's approach that he is fully prepared to introduce modes of explanation of particular phenomenon that seem entirely compatible with those advanced by Boudon. Thus, Bourdieu (1990: 43–4) argues, in relation to the increase in the amount of education consumed by working-class students, that:

> everything suggests that workers who ... hardly made any use of secondary education, began to do so. because the school-leaving age was raised to sixteen ... but also because, in order to maintain their position, which is not the lowest, and to avoid falling into the sub-proletariat, they had to possess a minimum of education.

The arguments are: (i) from Boudon, families from all social classes strive to maximise their consumption of education up to the point where it is no longer cost-effective to do so; and (ii) from Bourdieu, upper working-class families have begun to consume more education as far as it is necessary (a functionalist necessity) in order to maintain their relative social and economic standing. These explanations, even if they can be distinguished, are certainly not incompatible. Boudon regards the whole process as one that can be explained by a model that assumes actions to be made in accordance with economic rationality (even while being indifferent to the actual character of decision-making), while Bourdieu holds the reverse position that the practices of a group that serve to effect its reproduction are effected, by and large, by habitual behaviour that is to be explained as the product of a form of socialisation into the practices of the group made necessary by the structural imperative of system reproduction.

Not only are substantive explanations of particular social phenomenon from rival theories sometimes identical, they frequently share the property of being closed to the test of empirical demonstration. Boudon presents a scientific model that assumes rational economic action while being indifferent to people's actual decision-making practices. The purpose of economic modelling is to provide an explanation of economic behaviour in populations and, although based on an ideal typification of people as rational economic actors, makes no necessary reference to the actual decision-making processes of individuals. The implication of this is that evidence from studies of decision-making is strictly irrelevant – Boudon's illustration of the argument with comments from a (hypothetical) self-aware speaker is to that extent misleading and cannot be advanced either as support for or against such economic models. In the world of economic management models are found to be useful in so far as they succeed in predicting the performance of a specified economic sector, and the fundamental assumption that people will, on the whole, attempt to maximise their gains and minimise their losses is given. The psychology of game theory has accumulated a body of useful evidence relevant to these issues, but economic science operates quite independently of this field, and the fundamental assumption of its models, that people may be regarded as rational economic actors, even if far from always accurate, seems not to detract from their practical utility as predictive tools. The value of models is tested by pragmatic considerations and in as much as one model may be superior to another it is not because they do not share the same view of economic behaviour. These are the considerations Boudon offers in favour of his models of access to education and social inequality: their value rests in their capacity to form the functions of a tool, resembling those of macro-economic theory, enabling policymakers to predict the consequences for social inequality of an increase in the output of an educational system. It may be unfortunate that their capacity to do this is extremely limited: for all they show is that it is the *relative* rather than the absolute distribution of educational qualifications to social classes that determines access to further education and the labour market. Moreover, although it is possible to argue, as Boudon does, that sociological models may assume an economic rationality that need not reflect actual decision-making processes, it is difficult to admit the worth of theoretical accounts so frankly indifferent to the real determinants of social practice.

This does not mean that Bourdieu's account of secondary effects is any better placed with regard to empirical testing. The fundamental assumption, that social structures are maintained as the result of social members following the taken-for-granted 'rules of the game' common in their communities, has been sufficiently discussed and the analysis of values, preferences and actual decision-making, although essential to realism and the study of habitus, is to that extent irrelevant to the structural form of the explanation offered. There is thus an identified phenomenon in secondary effects for which two theoretically incompatible accounts have been advanced neither of which can actually be supported by evidence in such a way that the dispute between them can be resolved. Moreover, although apparently in fundamental disagreement their proponents are entirely capable of providing surprisingly similar explanation sketches of the generative processes causing the phenomenon. The debate is clearly on the grounds of theory, but it is a debate, nevertheless, that ought to be subject to an analysis willing to accord some respect to empirical data. Many conclusions might be drawn from this analysis, and in the context of this discussion it will be noted that the fundamental reason for the coming together of these theorists, actual if not admitted, is due to the attractive force of reality that drags almost any modelled account closer to the problem that actually exists and demands to be explained in terms of generative processes. There is another comment to be made: in comparison with the importance of differences in school attainment that seem without doubt to be based on cognitive differences detectable in early childhood, the sources of variation examined by Boudon as secondary effects appear, after all, to be relatively minor.

A Realist Interpretation and Cognitive Differences

The evidence that completed secondary school attainment is overwhelmingly influenced by the level of ability demonstrated by students at their entry to secondary school, five years earlier in the case of those who attain a Bursary qualification, has implications for a causal model of social differences in educational attainment that merit serious consideration. It very strongly suggests that what happens at secondary school has little additional effect in creating the patterns of difference observed and that they must, to the extent that their origin lies in the educational system at all, be formed at an earlier point. According to the data presented in Tables 1.1 and 1.2, Boudon's thesis that secondary effects are a more significant cause of educational inequality is not supported in contemporary New Zealand. In fact, as the relative differences associated with social class in the cognitive skills of children may be detected before they attend school on reaching the age of five, the hypothesis that the root causes may be outside the educational system is not easily dismissed by serious workers in this area. The most that can be argued, it seems, is that the relative progress of middle-class students is perceptibly better than that of working-class students and that the schools are effectively powerless to interrupt this process. Sociology of education once took for granted the importance of IQ and its association with social class in accounts of social differences in educational attainment, but the challenge of the last 20 or 30 years to that assumption may have become so widely accepted as to pose an actual obstacle to our interpretation of data that should be incorporated in causal models of social differences in access to education. Attention directed towards school and classroom processes will no doubt remain an important area of study, but the evidence that schools are greatly involved in the overall production of social differences in attainment is, at best, rather slender.

The most acute problem for the interpretation of the models of the Progress at School data, reported in path analysis and tabular format, is that of the status to be afforded the tests used to assess attainment on third-form entry. One of the tests was designed as a test of reading comprehension and the other, developed in the psychometric tradition of verbal intelligence measurement, as a test of 'scholastic abilities'. Contemporary test theory minimises the theoretical differences between what were once regarded as conceptually and practically distinct instruments and, indeed, when items of exactly the same sort are included indifferently in tests designed to test 'IQ' and 'attainment', as Jencks knew to be the case, the argument for a fundamental distinction between the two concepts in practice is hard to maintain. There are implications of this, however, that need to be faced. If the competencies involved in obtaining high scores on IQ-type tests are more or less those involved in doing well at school, then certain specific objections to such tests may lose much of their force. The most popular critical argument, for example, is that IQ-type tests are biased in such a way that middle-class children are advantaged and working-class children disadvantaged with the result that a fundamentally spurious association is observed between social class and tests that purport to measure important cognitive skills. This is, in effect, the substance of Bourdieu's argument that the cognitive skills favoured by the school should be recognised as an artefact of a class-cultural system of mentality, a form of symbolic violence, with no legitimate claim to superiority. A library has been written on these arguments and there is nothing to be gained from reviewing them here. The most effective form of refutation to this view is likely to be afforded by the demonstration that IQ-type tests, despite being extremely problematic in almost all theoretical and practical respects (Nash, 1990b), have certain robust properties as tests of specialised cognitive performance. A recent Danish study (Grandjean et al., 1997) of 917 seven-year-old children from the Faeroe Islands will illustrate the point as well as any other. The object of the research was to monitor the effects of mercury in the systems of pregnant mothers, due to the ingestion of meat from whales affected by polluted waters, on the intellectual development of their offspring. It was found that the amount of methylmercury detected in the children's tissues before birth proved to be correlated significantly with their eventual performance on a number of IQ-type tests, including language, attention and spatial perception, sufficient to impair performance by three or four points. It is very difficult to shrug off this kind of result, which has nothing to do with social class bias in the test instruments, and, if it contributes to the reduction of levels of toxicity in the natural environment, represents an entirely unobjectionable use for such tests of intellectual functioning. Sociologists rarely trouble to conceal their scepticism about IQ tests and attainment tests alike, and with good reason, but evidence of this kind weighs heavily in the balance. It can only be hinted at here, but there may be a case for recognising that certain cognitive skills are not constituted by the class arbitrary but are, in fact, necessary to the mastery of any effective form of pedagogy and curriculum in which the skills of literate communication and the concepts of a realist science (all of which are essential to a worthwhile education) are given central importance. We may need to pay as much attention to the 'educationally necessary' as the 'culturally arbitrary'.

The central concern of the sociology of education, if social difference in educational attainment is its central concern, seems to require a very much closer attention to the processes of intellectual development than has been given hitherto by mainstream research in our discipline. Despite the important contribution of Bernstein (1990) and the substantive tradition of empirical work sustained by his influence, the sociology of cognitive development, a process that takes place largely in the home, remains a peripheral matter when everything suggests that it should be central. The structures of social class, specified as family resources of wealth, 'cultural capital' and social assets, should be recognised as effective causes of the differential cognitive and non-cognitive habits of mind and body that enable middle-class children, as a group, to make much better progress through the educational system than working-class children. But such a realist account of social differences in the education will remain unconvincing until it has united with social and developmental psychology to describe and analyse the actual processes of interaction by which effective skills of literate cognition are developed. Several studies of natural language development have made significant contributions in this area, but there is certainly room for additional research. For all the many ethnographic studies of classrooms and schools it is hardly possible to think of an attempt to explore what seems to be the real site of cognitive development, the family, by systematic and statistically controlled ethnographic research. Exactly how do the pre-school children of the upper professional class come to have so high a level of demonstrated ability? If the difference is not genetic, and Flynn's (1984) models suggest this to be unlikely, then their superiority must be due to environmental differences, and the only ones that seem remotely plausible are family-based early childhood socialisation practices.

There is evidence from New Zealand research, worth mentioning in this context, that the literacy-related skills of pre-school children have increased in the last decades of the twentieth century. Clay (1981) found in the late 1960s and early 1970s that the ages at which 50 per cent of children could 'handle books' and 'locate words' (under standardised conditions) were, respectively, five and a half and six years, but, some 20 years later, Wylie, Thompson and Hendricks (1996) reported that the first of these two proficiencies was demonstrated by 87 per cent and the other by just over a half of the 'near fives' in their sample. Moreover, according to their mothers, these children had gained their skills largely from home rather than the pre-schools they attended. Whereas almost nine out of ten of the most highly qualified mothers declared that they read to their child at least once a day, the corresponding ratio for the least- qualified mothers was not quite one in two. It will not be irrelevant to note that the authors of this report also found that the behaviour of four out of five of those children whose mothers had gained the highest school qualifications was described, by fieldwork researchers, as 'quick', 'confident' or 'matter of fact', compared with barely more than one in two of those whose mothers held no school qualifications. Nevertheless, despite the mounting evidence that class variation in literacy-related early childhood socialisation practices is likely to be the major source of the progressive differential access to education associated with social class (McGee and Silva, 1982; McGee, Williams and Silva, 1988), there remains some reluctance to link such differences in the transmission of 'cultural capital' to the generation of actual cognitive skills of a non-trivial kind.

Conclusion

The Progress at School project, like the earlier Access and Opportunity in Education project, was structured by a 'family resource framework' that might best be described as an explanatory sketch, or a set of connected hypotheses, for the purposes of directing the research and interpreting empirical data of both a quantitative and ethnographic kind (Nash, 1997a). After some practice it has been found possible to express this framework in a sentence. It is supposed that: the economic class structure generates social classes; that families are located in the class structure; that as a result families have access to resources (financial, educational and social); that families are engaged in long-term actions with the strategic purpose (broadly known to them) of enabling their offspring to maintain their economic, cultural and social position; that schools are involved in this process of differentiation by affording recognition to the skills acquired through a literacy-focused socialisation (a recognition that is not arbitrary but in all essential respects given by the nature of the techniques necessary to gain an adequate scientific knowledge of social and physical reality); and that the social relations and processes referred to in this sketch can be studied through a 'numbers and narratives' methodology in which the constraining and enabling aspects of the economic, cultural and political structures that affect families, schools and students, and call forth from them such a complex and creative set of responses, may be modelled. This framework is an expression of our struggle to bring the theses of realism to the investigation of educational inequality (Nash, 1997c, 1997d).

The specific techniques of path analysis, and of correlational analysis more generally, should not be ignored by studies with access to quantitative data on social differences in educational attainment. At the same time, Boudon's argument that the mode of presentation of the data, what he calls the syntax of explanation, has a non-trivial significance in constructing causal accounts of social differences in education should be admitted as one with considerable force. This does not commit realists to the 'methodological individualism' of Boudon's empiricism, or to accounts in terms of a model *homo sociologicus* acting within deterministic social structures, but neither are realists committed to the habitus-driven agent of an ultimately functionalist, and probably formally determinist, theory of social and educational reproduction. Both path analysis and system-flow models represent how, given their largely class-generated resources and cognitive skills, students attain educational qualifications, and make decisions about how to utilise their exchange value after the completion of schooling. Flow-models do seem to give a more precise indication of the underlying activity than path-analytic models, and certainly make it easier to see where the differences are being made. In the forms of explanation associated with both modes of analysis, however, the fundamental mechanism in the generation of social inequality in attainment is shown to be differences in intellectual skills developed, in the case of the data reported in this chapter, at least before secondary school, and, drawing on a wider body of knowledge in our field, in early childhood.

There is, in fact, a crisis in contemporary sociology of education due to the fact that the most widely accepted theories do not acknowledge the overwhelming empirical evidence that by far the greatest proportion of the observed variance in educational attainment and access to education associated with social class does not have its origin in the educational system, which, as Bourdieu puts it, need merely fail to interrupt the processes of socially differentiated cognitive development in order to perform its functional role as an agent of social and cultural reproduction. Bourdieu's central concept, habitus, is most usefully interpreted as an invitation to observe and analyse the experiences of social agents in order to gain knowledge of the ways in which social structures have their effect on practice. As a methodological injunction this, in fact, points directly at what a realist sociology of education, for which there is no explanation without a detailed account of the socially structured human practices that generate observed statistical patterns, attempts to do. It is the generative power of social class – conceptualised as a set of structures of social relationships – that may be stated, with an irreducible degree of truth, to be the major cause of socially differentiated educational attainment. And it is in no sense inconsistent with this assertion to demand further research into the actual mechanisms by which intelligence – intelligence of a particular kind, but if words mean anything, intelligence – is generated and sustained by family socialisation practices of a more or less specific character. Eysenck (1979) noted that middle-class children were eight times more likely than working-class children to reach the IQ level (122.5) he thought necessary for successful university completion, and it is salutary to note that our New Zealand data shows that ratio to be very little reduced. Research into this area might be a task for another generation of sociologists of education, but it is work that one may hope will be done.

References

Archer, M. (1995). *Social Theory: The Morphogenetic Approach* (Cambridge: Cambridge University Press).

Bernstein, B. (1990). *Class, Codes and Control 4: The Structuring of Pedagogic Discourse* (London: Routledge & Kegan Paul).

Boudon, R. (1981). *The Logic of Social Action: An Introduction to Sociological Analysis* (London: Routledge & Kegan Paul).

Boudon, R. (1982). *The Unintended Consequences of Social Action* (London: Macmillan).

Bourdieu, P. (1976). The school as a conservative force: Scholastic and cultural inequalities. In R. Dale, G. Esland and M. MacDonald (eds), *Schooling and Capitalism* (London: Routledge & Kegan Paul/Open University Press).

Bourdieu, P. (1977). *Outline of a Theory of Practice* (London: Routledge & Kegan Paul).

Bourdieu, P. (1990). *In Other Words: Essays towards a Reflexive Sociology* (Cambridge: Polity Press).

Bunge, M. (1979). *Ontology II: A World of Systems* (Dordrecht, The Netherlands: Reidel).

Clay, M. (1981). *The Early Detection of Reading Difficulties*, 2nd edn (Auckland, Heinemann).

Collins, R. (1979). *The Credential Society: An Historical Sociology of Educational Stratification* (New York: Academic Press).

Corrigan, P. (1990). *Social Forms/Human Capacities: Essays in Authority and Difference* (London: Routledge).

Dahrendorf, R. (1968). *Essays in the Theory of Society* (London: Routledge & Kegan Paul).

Elley, W. and Irving, J (1985). The Elley-Irving socio-economic index: 1981 census revision, *New Zealand Journal of Educational Studies*, 20(1): 115–28.

Eysenck, H.J. (1979). *The Structure and Measurement of Intelligence* (Berlin: Springer).

Flynn, J.R. (1984). Banishing the spectre of meritocracy, *Bulletin of the British Psychological Society*, 37: 256–9.

Goldstein, H.I. (1987). *Multilevel Models in Educational and Social Research* (London, Oxford University Press).

Grandjean, P., Weihe, P., White, R.F., Debes, F., Araki, S., Yokoyama, K., Murata, K., Sorensen, N., Dahl, R. and Jorgensen, P.J. (1997). Cognitive deficit in 7-year-old children with prenatal exposure to methylmercury, *Neurotoxicology and Teratology*, 19: 417–18.

Hammersley, M. (1995). *Social Research and the Problem of Educational Inequalities: A Methodological Assessment* (London: Falmer).

Harker, R.K. and Nash, R. (1996). Academic outcomes and school effectiveness: Type 'A' and type 'B' effects, *New Zealand Journal of Educational Studies*, 31(1): 143–70.

Jencks, C., Smith, M., Ackland, H., Bane, M.J., Cohen, D., Gintis, H., Heyns, B. and Michelson, S. (1972). *Inequality* (New York: Basic Books).

Lazarsfeld, P. (1993). *On Social Research and Its Language*, ed. R. Boudon (Chicago: University of Chicago Press).

McGee, R. and Silva, P. (1982). *A Thousand New Zealand Children: Their Health and Development from Birth to Seven* (Wellington: Medical Research Council).

McGee, R., Williams, S.M. and Silva, P.A. (1988). Slow starters and long-term backward readers: A replication and extension, *British Journal of Educational Psychology*, 58: 330–37.

Nash, R. (1990a). Bourdieu on education and social and cultural reproduction, *British Journal of Sociology of Education*, 11(4): 431–47.

Nash, R. (1990b). *Intelligence and Realism: A Materialist Critique of IQ* (London: Macmillan).

Nash, R. (1993a). *Succeeding Generations: Family Resources and Access to Education in New Zealand* (Auckland: Oxford University Press).

Nash, R. (1993b). Extended review, contribution to review symposium on Richard Jenkins's 'Pierre Bourdieu', *British Journal of Sociology of Education*, 14(3): 318–22.

Nash, R. (1997a). Deficit theory and the family resource framework: Parkyn revisited, *New Zealand Journal of Educational Studies*, 32(1): 13–24.

Nash, R. (1997b). *A Year in the Sixth Form* (Palmerston North: ERDC Press).

Nash, R. (1997c). Radical sociology of education: A contribution to the agency/ structure debate, *Sites*, 34: 36–52.

Nash, R. (1997d). *Inequality/Difference: A Sociology of Education* (Palmerston North: ERDC Press).

Nash, R. (1998a). Commentary: A realist approach to school composition effects: a response to Thrupp's 'How school-mix shapes school processes', *New Zealand Journal of Educational Studies*, 33(2): 223–30.

Nash, R. (1998b). Progress at school: Modes of adaptation and realist sociology, *New Zealand Journal of Educational Studies*, 33(1): 67–79

Nash, R. (1998c). Radical structuralism in the sociology of education: A realist critique, *New Zealand Sociology*, 33(1): 97–143.

Nash, R. (1999). *School Learning: Conversations for the Sociology of Education*, Delta Studies in Education (Palmerston North: Massey University College of Education).

Nash, R. and Harker, R.K. (1998). *Making Progress: Adding Value in New Zealand Education* (Palmerston North: ERDC Press).

Nash, R. and Major, S. (1997). *Inequality/Difference: A Sociology of Education* (Palmerston North: ERDC Press).

Reid, N.A. and Elley, W. (1991). *Progressive Achievement Tests of Reading, Teacher's Manual* (Wellington: NZCER).

Reid, N.A., Jackson, P., Gilmore, A. and Croft, C. (1981). *Test of Scholastic Abilities* (Wellington: NZCER).

Smith, D. and Tonlinson, S. (1989). *The School Effect: A Study of Multi-racial Comprehensives* (London: Institute of Policy Studies).

Woods, P. (1977). *The Divided School* (London: Routledge).

Wylie, C., Thompson, J. and Hendricks, A.K. (1996). *Competent Children at 5: Families and Early Education* (Wellington: Report to the Ministry of Education, NZCER).

Chapter 2

Numbers and Narratives: Further Reflections in the Sociology of Education

A Structure–Disposition–Practice Model

A definitive problem for the sociology of education is given by the continued existence of inequality/difference in social access to education (Halsey, 1975). Significant variations in the levels of examination performance and entry to tertiary education associated with social class and ethnic origin have been demonstrated in all countries where appropriate investigations have been carried out (Shavit and Blossfield, 1993). The challenge for the sociology of education is to construct a framework within which models with a reasonable semblance to the complex social processes that generate observed inequalities in educational opportunity might be constructed. Any report into the extent of variation in educational access requires quantitative expression, but it equally requires an explanatory narrative, and it is in this sense that a methodology of 'numbers and narratives' may be defended. The realist framework developed in this chapter has its origin in a programme of empirical research into access and opportunity in education carried out in New Zealand for more than a decade (Nash and Harker 1998; Nash 1999a). The research has stimulated an intense theoretical analysis of models of inequality/ difference and reached a position that might, with tolerable simplification, be described as a form of elaborated sociological common sense. The present chapter will offer some necessary further elaboration. In fact, the structure–disposition– practice (SDP) model is proposed as no more than a systematisation of a standard form of sociological explanation (Sorokin, 1998). It will become evident that the discussion is heavily indebted to Bourdieu's (1986) development of a theory of practice, but the scheme is unlikely to be recognised as Bourdieusian, and the phenomenological discourse of that approach is explicitly rejected. The realist stance adopted here is, however, intended to be broadly compatible with both the tenets of scientific realism (Bunge, 1980) and critical realism (Bhaskar, 1993), which represent the two leading realist positions in contemporary philosophy of science. The outline of a materialist theory of measurement is taken directly from Berka (1983) whose position may be regarded as an almost paradigm form of scientific realism. The thesis presented in this chapter, therefore, is thus not in any sense an eclectic and unprincipled borrowing, and adopts a position that now might be considered mainstream in the philosophy of science.

Scientific realism rejects the standpoint of 'positivist' science, with its Humean negation of causality, its construction of models in terms of laws with no necessary reference to mechanism, and its indifference to the essence and substance of things, as inadequate to a satisfactory explanation of physical and social events and processes. A scheme competent to provide an account of mechanism and process must be constructed in terms of system properties, individual dispositions and individual action within recognised social practices, in such a way that the effective linkages between these levels may be demonstrated. It is clearly necessary to this integration to describe the relationships between the levels of system properties, individual dispositions and the practices that structure action in appropriate concepts, and also to develop adequate techniques of quantification. The causal relationships, for example, between familial class position, parental desire to stimulate children's intellectual development and the adoption of a specific social practice have all to be demonstrated by practical observation and theoretical argument of a kind appropriate to the events and processes studied. In this fashion, the SDP scheme seeks to construct a theoretically informed account in which the quantitative and qualitative methodological elements of social research are recognised and included in an explanatory narrative of social process (Nash, 1999b). The SDP scheme also implies that, in as much as the middle term 'disposition' refers to properties of the individual, the achievement of disciplinary independence adopted by sociology through the conflation of psychological and social properties is misconceived (Archer, 1995). In this dual manner, in seeking to integrate 'numbers and narratives' and to place the individual at the centre of its explanatory framework, the scheme aims to generate *realistic* accounts of the causes and consequences of social processes.

A programmatic case must be argued in which procedures for the identification and quantification of variables at each level of the explanatory scheme may be fashioned. The problematic aspects of quantitative research have been well canvassed, but it may be useful to review some of the objections often raised to 'causal' statistical modelling and its ability to deliver convincing accounts of social process. Many of these problems have their origin in the theory of measurement and, although the discussion is highly abstract, the critique developed by Berka (1983) is invaluable as a source of insight into the origin of the strains that inevitably result from conceptual disorder in this area. The concept of statistical explanation is a no less fundamental source of misunderstanding. Salmon (1975) has presented the most accomplished defence of the theory of statistical explanation, and it is thus appropriate to critique the substantive and complex issues in that context. These two elaborate arguments require distinct sections to expound their genuine complexities in an adequate critique. There are certain general comments, however, on the influence of the conventional and bureaucratically supported 'at risk' positivism as a source of support for normal science in this field that may be reviewed at this point.

The standard form of 'quantitative' sociological research is designed to establish correlations between indicator variables of social properties in order to construct causal models of the processes and events subjected to investigation. School attainment, for example, is almost invariably correlated with number of books in the home, but not with number of books in the school library; with mother's education but rarely with teachers' education; and with parental aspirations, but not so much with teachers' expectations. These associations, and so many others of their kind, appear to set the parameters within which an explanatory narrative of educational inequality may be constructed. The statistical model seems both to provide information about 'where the action is' that 'makes the difference', and to allow the identification of 'at risk' individuals with the possibility of intervention at that level. The goal of such research is an explanation capable of demonstrating what actions, by what people, and at what sites, are actually involved in the generation of the social processes or events ('outcomes') that are the particular object of investigation. So far so good.

The theoretical derivation of variables within such models is, however, often more problematic than is generally realised. The Coleman Report (Coleman, 1966) for example, identified family, school and peer variables but in such a fashion that there was considerable overlap between them. Hunushek and Kain (1972) were able to show that, as a consequence of this, the regression analyses were subject to a marked order effect. In this way, the effect of School variables *after* entry of Family and Peer variables was 0.212, whereas the effect of School variables fell to 0.081 when entered *before* Family and Peer variables. One of the principal causes of this so-called multicollinearity problem is the practice of constructing composite indices in which structural (resource) variables, dispositional variables and practice variables are combined in a single indicator. Cox and Jones (1983), for example, employ indicators of (i) mother's health and stability and (ii) her level of interest in educational development (both dispositional), but include the first in a set of 'material' circumstances and the second in a set of 'cultural' circumstances. There is rarely any attempt in such research to adopt a causal SDP scheme and, when variables are formed into sets, both the classification scheme and the allocation rules typically have an untheorised and ad hoc character. It is commonplace in the literature to be advised that statistical effects should not necessarily be taken at their face value, which, of course, is to say the value they have in the model, without the least hint that this admission brings the entire procedure into question. By what rule is one to know which values are to be trusted and which are not? Amer (1972), for example, discussing the Coleman Report, notes that an increase of 1 standard deviation (SD) in teacher salaries is associated in with a 0.2 SD increase in student attainment, and points out that it would be foolish to conclude on this evidence that a tenfold increase in teachers' pay would produce a generation of geniuses. Lauder and Hughes (1999), in similar vein, observe that working-class students appear to perform better in middle-class schools (where they receive fewer positive comments than those at working-class schools), but nevertheless reject the conclusion that teachers should desist from encouraging their working-class students. This is, no doubt, entirely sensible advice, but it reveals a problem that statistical modelling has never been able to resolve within its own terms. These difficulties have become particularly acute with the widespread adoption of 'at risk' positivism within the field of education.

The conventional form of quantitative analysis and explanation, widely used for the purposes of policymaking and state management, has given rise to a kind of shorthand in which behaviour is typically explained by 'risk factors'. The limitations of this kind of explanatory narrative should be self-evident. As an explanation of a social practice, to say that those who adopt it do so because they are the kind of people *who probably will do so*, takes one no great distance towards understanding *why* recognisable forms of practice have emerged, why *these* individuals (rather than others with similar 'at risk' characteristics) are affected, or why they happen to number 10 per cent or 20 per cent, and not some other figure. The related notion that all students from a particular group, identified, for example, by its social or ethnic origin, are each equally 'carriers' of a specified weight of disadvantage, a virtual handicap, is a further common error. Those at home with this discursive framework, nevertheless, often allow the apparent practical utility of such accounts to obscure their fundamental weaknesses. Nash and Harker (1998), for example, offer models of progress at school based on logistic regression. The best that can be achieved is an 80 per cent prediction rate in each direction. This means that the prediction was falsified in 20 per cent of cases: about one-fifth of those students who were expected to decline did not do so, and likewise one-fifth of those who were expected to improve failed to do so. Provided that interventions based on such predictions are innocuous when delivered to those incorrectly identified by the model, this degree of error may have no practical consequences, but that benign assumption cannot always be made. In that case, where the structural and dispositional causes of practice are misrecognised, it is also likely that the significant ethical considerations involved will be ignored. The location of such predictive models within a formal SDP heuristic might act as a corrective to the conventional positivist interpretation that contributes strongly to their potential for abuse.

The SDP explanatory scheme is also likely to offer the most satisfactory response by sociology to the emerging tradition of economic reductionism. Mayer (1997: 8), a particularly influential figure in this field, regards the 'true effect' of social class as 'the effect controlling all parental characteristics, both observed and unobserved, that influence the parents' income and the children's outcomes'. Mayer points out that 'the fact that poor children fare worse than rich children does not suffice to prove that low parental income per se hurts children', and notes that children with certain attributes 'do well even when their parents do not have much money' (Mayer, 1997: 3). It may seem absurd to argue that a set of dispositions and practices cannot be derived from class position on the grounds that such a lived culture, in that sense, is not adopted by *all* members of a social class and not *only* by them. These notions obviously represent a failure of the sociological imagination on a gigantic scale, but they seem to have a compelling attraction for policymakers, with implications for the future of social research that merit serious attention. It is interesting to consider the quest for the 'true effect' as a means to discover the actual behaviour involved in the generation of the outcome investigated and therefore 'realist' in its direction. The problem with such an approach, however, lies in its refusal to acknowledge the concept of social practice; its failure to recognise that links between structures and practices are not contingent merely because they are not necessary; and its insistence on setting structure, disposition and practice variables in a relationship of competition – all of which effectively negates the possibility of exploring the causal connections posited by SDP models between these distinct levels.

All statistical methods, whether they seek to estimate the proportion of variance explained or to provide estimates of the odds associated with each variable, depend on more or less tacit background assumptions about variables, their measurement status and how the associations between them should be interpreted. This process is not primarily a technical matter, of course, and inevitably introduces an extra-theoretical dimension that need not be left to an unarticulated common sense. It is certainly true that realism need have no quarrel with informed common sense in the explanation of social events. As Sayer (1992: 277) has remarked:

> Whatever the faults of common sense, it is at least adapted to a wide range of contexts – wider, in most cases, than are scientific theories. Consequently, when social scientists, 'rediscover' formerly overlooked aspects it is sometimes found that they were recognised in everyday knowledge all along. Naturally, this hardly improves social science's reputation. If common sense is criticised for being unexamined, then we should examine it rather than ignore it or uncritically absorb it.

At the same time, it is one of the responsibilities of sociology to extend and elaborate that common sense. In our substantive field, it is more than likely that the common-sense view that the political–economic division of labour generates class-located families with differential material and symbolic resources that consequently enable them to achieve educational success more or less as in direct ratio to those resources is actually correct (Nash 1993; Reay 1998; Lareau and Horvat, 1999). Resistance to this model, based largely on a principled rejection of so-called deficit theory, is understandable, but it may be necessary to re-engage with the ideas in a fully articulated theoretical discourse. The contribution of an SDP scheme may offer the best hope of developing integrated models of the generation of inequality/difference in education within such a broad theoretical framework. The likelihood of that hope being realised depends, at least in part, on our ability to achieve a greater degree of clarity on the question of measurement.

What is Quantifiable?

Berka (1983) has developed a materialist theory of physical and extra-physical measurement based on a rigorous critique of conventional measurement theory. His fundamental premise is that the accepted conception of measurement in the social sciences is too wide. Measurement is an operation that must always be based on the actual nature of the object of measurement in so far as its properties have been established by science. The essential concept of measurement theory is 'magnitude', which must be constructed by specific theoretical and practical investigations. Measurement is achieved by mapping an empirical relational system onto a numerical relational system, and before an object can be measured it is necessary to demonstrate that these necessary operations are actually possible. The first stage in the process of measurement is, therefore, the delimitation of the various properties of the measured object in their qualitative and quantitative aspects. Berka insists on the conceptual distinction between the 'measured object' itself and the conceptual 'object of measurement'. When the length of a stick is measured there is a measured object (the stick) and an object of measurement (the length). It is improper to say that numerical values are assigned to metrical concepts – for example, to the concept of length – since the measured object is simply a stick (not the concept of 'stick'), and the object of measurement is the length of the stick (not the concept of 'length'). Berka notes that some things have strongly quantitative properties – those that admit discernment of degrees and sizes – whereas others have weakly quantitative properties that admit distinction only by degrees. The numbered magnitude 'one metre' is thus an equivalence class of all objects having the same length as a certain model object, and the magnitude 'metre' stands for the name of the equivalence class. Many different sorts of magnitudes may be distinguished: including linear magnitudes (height, breadth, distance, focal distance and so on); scalar magnitudes (heat, work, energy); vector magnitudes (momentum of force) and dimensionless magnitudes (radian, decibel). Berka points out that the central problem for extra-physical measurement – the most often required in the social sciences – is how to extend the concept of measurement without a measurement unit. The conventional solution, to use standard deviation units, so far from being a genuine solution, simply bypasses the fundamental issues involved and constitutes a source of confusion.

The conventional theory of scales (Stevens, 1951), once taught to all students of statistical methods, recognises four so-called levels of measurement: nominal (naming by numbers); ordinal (rank ordering); interval (equal interval units) and ratio (equal interval units and a scale zero). This approach is criticised by Berka in a detailed and rigorous argument that can be summarised only briefly in this chapter. Naming by numerals (the numbering of bus routes and football players' jerseys, for example) does not constitute measurement in any sense, and the so-called nominal scale should thus be excluded entirely from the discussion of measurement. The distinction between ordinal and interval measurement, furthermore, is unsound because all ordinal scales can be converted to interval scales by a more or less arbitrary procedure (as in the conversion of centigrade to kelvin), and therefore the distinction cannot be maintained. In this way, the system of classical scale types is reduced to two, namely non-metric and metric, which can then be connected to the associated methods of scaling and measuring. The former operation has a central importance in extra-physical measurement: 'in psychology, sociology and other social-scientific domains, by scaling one signifies the actual process of measurement, more precisely, the process of the so-called qualitative measurement that only leads to scale values of non-metrical scales' (Berka, 1983: 101). Scaling should be recognised as an independent method, a form of quasi-quantification that provides a form of practical measurement in appropriate situations. In this context, Berka makes an obvious but crucial conceptual distinction between the *scale of a measuring device* and *so-called scales of measurement*. This may seem self-evident, but there is a great deal of confusion in this matter, and many writers are incapable of distinguishing between the conceptual scale and the gauge of a measurement instrument.

The twin legitimating concepts of standard 'measurement' theory in social science – reliability and validity – are subjected to a searching critical examination. The question of reliability, which conventional practice, as Berka dryly observes, has confused with repeatability, should be dealt with as a matter of error in the measurement device, and as such poses no serious epistemological difficulties. The essential question for psychometrics, the dominant theory of extra-physical measurement in all social sciences, is hence that of validity, which is a question of meaning to be resolved by philosophical enquiry and therefore not one open to a 'technical' solution. Berka demonstrates that the technicist approach to validation adopted by psychometrics is arbitrary and untenable. After a detailed analysis of the conventional processes, he observes, in a penetrating comment, '[i]t is then asserted of a certain measurement (measuring procedure, tool, result, and the like) in an apparent tautological formulation, that it is valid exactly when it indeed measures what we think (expect) it does' (ibid. 203). The origin of these difficulties is, needless to say, transparently clear to this author. Whether a property can be quantified or not depends not on the assignment of numerals, which may always be materialised, but on the objective reality of the corresponding entities or processes. 'To comprehend the assignment of numerals as an instance of quantification,' he comments (ibid. 103), 'means to conventionalise this concept to such a degree that there would cease to exist any difference between what is measurable and what is not measurable and what is quantifiable and what is not quantifiable'.

This tight summary of a complex book-length thesis, inadequate as it must be, may suffice to support the argument that properties included in an SDP scheme cannot be subjected to quantification within the naive practices of conventional measurement theory. On the contrary, in a sociological account that recognises system properties ('structure'), intervening dispositions and practice ('action'), the construction of variables and the operations of measurement (or scaling) should be informed by Berka's materialist analysis. The following section on statistical explanation will carry the discussion forward.

The Identification and Quantification of SDP Properties

The empirical variables included in a statistical model of the causes of social differences in education should be identified by their ontological character as properties of social organisations, properties of people, and units of behaviour that can be related to social practices. This scheme should not be confused with the conventional distinction between 'sociological variables' (social class, family structure, ethnic status, etc.) and 'psychological' variables (personality type, self-concept, etc.), as if these disciplines could be identified with the nomonological status of the variables they recognise, but as one founded on the distinct properties of social entities and physical beings. The approach represents a sharp break with the standard theory of measurement, its positivist theory of meaning, its circular concept of 'validity', and its tautological concept of 'reliability'. If significant progress is to be made in this area it will require first the adequate conceptualisation of the variables distinct to the description of the real properties involved in the causal process.

The Properties of Social Systems

Social systems are complex and stratified entities with properties distinct to their individual kind. The system properties of a social organisation are just those that enable it to carry out its particular functions. The definitive properties of a school are those of its means of organising, transmitting and evaluating knowledge (Bernstein, 1971), and indicators of an appropriate kind to assess these properties may more or less readily be constructed. The provision of school classes, the basis of their composition and their levels of performance are evidently open to demonstration and quantification. It will be useful at this point to distinguish between aggregate properties and real system properties. Aggregate properties are commonly used in the sociology of education to indicate aspects of the social constitution of an organisation. Coleman, for example, included the percentage of lower-class students enrolled as an indicator of what he called peer effects. The entire school composition (school mix) debate is concerned with the effects associated with aggregate indicators of student attainment or social origin (Thrupp, 1999). It is precisely because aggregate properties are not emergent system properties that it seems necessary to search for the social processes likely to be involved in a context where it is still uncertain that the observed effect is actually something more than an artefact of measurement error (Goldstein and Thomas, 1995). The existence of a real property is always a matter to be established by appropriate forms of demonstration. The relationship between an indicator and the object of measurement, moreover, can only be demonstrated by an appropriate form of argument. Those forms of nominalism that suppose, for example, that a concept of 'school ethos' is established by operational procedures, that is by the construction of a more or less plausible indicator (such as a litter and graffiti count), are inconsistent in this respect with scientific realism. A commitment to realism thus places a considerable responsibility on sociologists to describe in an adequate concept the nature of system properties included in explanatory models.

It may be worth noting in this context that the status of ethnic identity, social class origin and so on, routinely assessed in sociological studies, are properties of the individual by virtue of his or her membership of a collective entity. Membership of a group is a collective property. The status of citizen, trade union member, religious membership and so on involves a relationship with others who constitute that social entity and so generate through their collective action its real system properties. To be middle-class, for example, is not to be regarded as a true dispositional property of an individual. The resources and capacities given by class location are, however, real things that may be quantified according to their inherent and individual character. In the sociology of education, parental occupation, income, educational level and specific resources (books, computers, etc.) are all commonly used indicators of the socio-economic status or social class of a family. The reality of social class is, of course, not demonstrated by such indicators, but must be established by an analysis of the system of social relations that confer different degrees of control over economic, political and cultural resources, in such a way that a particular form of social stratification is realised in a society.

The Properties of (Socialised) Individuals

The term 'disposition' is used in the SDP scheme to cover a wide range of acquired personal states, including those states of mind recognised as beliefs, which are conceived as habits embodied in a more or less durable manner. Academic self-concept, broadly understood as the belief in one's ability to achieve a satisfactory level of success at school; aspirations, which, if they are to be effective in structuring action, must always be rooted in the sedimented and habituated self; and the decision to cooperate with schooling, are all dispositions in the sense adopted. The concept of disposition in this scheme is derived in the first instance from Bourdieu's concept of habitus as the embodiment of cultural structure responsible for the generation of practice. It seems preferable, however, to use the more general term. As Bourdieu (2000: 146) remarks, admitting this general sense, 'to deny the existence of dispositions is to deny the existence of learning and knowing'. Furthermore, if 'to speak of dispositions is simply to take note of a natural predisposition of human bodies' (ibid. 136), then there should be no objection from this quarter to the adoption of the term in that sense. This reference of disposition may, in fact, be too wide, but there is a need for an inclusive term and disposition may suffice. It should be noted, however, that the usage does not necessarily imply acceptance of the neo-behaviourist arguments associated with Ryle (1984), where disposition is also a term of art, although it is interesting that Bourdieu (2000) has recently begun, in his eclectic and synthetic manner, to engage with these ideas. It is clearly necessary to recognise the physical characteristics of individuals and their cognitive and moral qualities, and comprehensive technologies exist for the assessment of individual properties. There is no insurmountable difficulty in enumerating material and material goods and in quantifying knowledge and skills.

The quantitative assessment of dispositions, which being embodied are necessarily individual, and yet have a social character in as much as they have been acquired through socialisation, must be achieved with respect to the same principles. Aspirations, a belief in one's ability to succeed, and acceptance of the institutional order, are all typical of the weakly quantifiable individual dispositions of the stratified self that the middle term of the SDP model must deal seek to assess. The construction of a normally distributed scale of self-concept, defended by the theory that academic self-concept is a property of individuals with that character, is probably not necessary within a realist framework, but the idea that people vary in the sense they have of being able to achieve their aspirations through their own efforts, is doubtless a real disposition of interest to the study of human practice. The use of instruments designed to provide an indication of this belief and its strength may thus be defended, but always with due regard to Berka's comments on the technicist concepts of 'reliability' and 'validity'. In the psychological domain, where the influence of psychometrics still dominates, it is crucial to specify the object of measurement, which is not a concept but the property of a thing. Reading is thus an attainment that can be tested on standard instruments. What is so measured – if that is even the appropriate term to use – is reading, in its specific forms of comprehension, vocabulary and so on, rather than the concept of 'reading ability'. In the same way, the 'meaning' of a test of whatever kind must always be sought in the test-text and not in its pattern of correlation with other variables. The question of what the object of measurement is – in the wrong-headed term favoured by psychometrics – can be settled only by conceptual enquiry. What matters is whether the existence of the dispositions identified is revealed by the indicators used for that purpose. That is not a question to be settled by some technical operation, but one to be resolved by philosophical enquiry directed towards the practical end of establishing the character of reality in that area. It goes without saying that the attribution of a psychological disposition should be based on observation and not conferred by fiat in order to solve the problem of social reproduction by taken-for-granted action within the 'rules of the game'.

Action within Social Practice

A practice is a recognised way of doing something within a social group. Practices are themselves social properties. The social conditions that give rise to practices, their history, and the ways in which they function to sustain (or undermine) the social order are all crucial elements of sociological enquiry. It is possible to distinguish an hierarchy of practices 'bringing up children' (parenting), which includes the processes of emotional, intellectual and moral development in their various recognised character as 'keeping them safe', 'teaching right from wrong' and so on. There is no set of procedural rules by which the existence of a recognised social practice can be demonstrated. At the same time, it is certainly possible to identify, at their respective sites, bedtime stories, ability streaming, 'wagging' school and so on as distinct practices that may be studied as such in terms of their historical and current conditions of maintenance. The knowledge required to identify an action as one located within a recognised social practice can be acquired only by a process of observation and analysis (Macintyre, 1984). Social practices, action within their forms, the dispositions of mind that generate such action, and the properties of social organisations recognised in this account as structural, are actually and analytically distinct. One of the central tasks of sociology is to identify the contours of the social practices that make up the repertoire of socialisation in a given society. These matters are, in fact, the principal objects of Bourdieu's sociology.

Indeed, it could be argued that the entire purpose of sociology is to analyse the origins and consequences of social practices. Bourdieu's (1990) remark that it is because agents never know completely what they are doing that what they do has more sense than they know – an echo of Foucault's comment that '[p]eople know what they do; they frequently know why they do what they do; but what they don't know is what what they do does' (Dreyfus and Rainbow, 1982: 189) – expresses the same concern that Boudon (1982) attempts to investigate as the unintended consequences of social action. Bourdieu begins with the observed fact that societies, by and large, reproduce their constitutive social structures from generation to generation and maintains that this is effected by collective strategies without the necessity for any self-conscious action directed towards those larger ends. As people follow the 'rules of the game' normative within their society, which they do more or less 'automatically' through the generative habitus, they effect 'strategies' that reproduce existing social patterns. What is habituated is behaviour, of course, not as a stimulus-response habit, but as an organised sense of what should be done – and how it should be done – in particular circumstances. The informed critical response to Bourdieu's work is increasingly based on the realisation that habitus conflates conceptual distinctions necessary to the development of a coherent theoretical account of social practice (Calhoun, LiPuma and Postone, 1993; Shusterman, 1998; Alexander, 1995). There is certainly more than a hint in Bourdieu of the functionalist argument of last resort in which such practices both emerge and are maintained in order to ensure that the demonstrated relations of social domination are not successfully challenged. Such indefensible functionalism is, however, not a necessary characteristic of SDP models (Pettit, 1993).

A social practice in this sense is not a quantifiable entity, but practices are open to description, and their degree of adoption within a group may be given quantitative expression. The number of classed families in which bedtime stories, for example, is a recognised social practice is an aspect of social reality – a social fact – that may be counted within the limits imposed by what is possible within a specific investigation. The quantification of units of individual behaviour within practices is far from unproblematic, of course, but the standard techniques of empirical research can often be adopted by a realist methodology conscious of its theoretical assumptions. The reason why some students make progress at school where others with the same prior ability do not, for example, may be explained at that level by the fact that the former, compared with the latter, attend school more frequently, listen to their teachers more attentively, give more time to their homework, conform more readily to school regulations, and so on (Nash and Harker, 1998). The actions of others, teacher and parents in particular, are reciprocally involved in the maintenance of the practices within which such actions are situated. It is often, in fact, a relatively simple matter to devise observation schedules of one kind or another from which indicative scales of behaviour can be constructed. Counting is simply counting and, within limits, the more accurately the operation can be carried out the better: the kind of pseudo-counting sometimes legitimated as 'qualitative' ('more boys than girls were absent') is simply less precise than the 'quantitative' version ('35 per cent of boys and 10 per cent of girls were absent') and should not be legitimated by a claim to methodological privilege. Individual practices, which always have a social form, are not the only kinds of practice with which sociology is concerned. The school, for example, selects and instructs its students, qualifies some and excludes others, and so on, and such institutional practices are also open to quantification in an appropriate form. The discussion of the concept of statistical explanation will give further elaboration to these points.

Statistical Explanation

Systems to system level causal relations provide the paradigm case of sociological explanation. Durkheim regarded this as defining the field of sociology and in his approach social facts are always to be explained by other social facts (Schmaus, 1994). The relationships between, for example, the housing supply and drunkenness (Engels, 1935), the marital dowry system and female infanticide (Harris, 1979), and unemployment and school retention rates (Bauman, 1998), are simply a few of the endless examples that could be given in illustration of models in which social facts are explained in terms of other social facts. Several applications of statistical laws, considered as regularities, are very powerful. The nineteenth century saw the development of methods of analysis that could be used for the greater advancement of society. Jevons's (1883) discovery, for example, that the average rate of infant death in England was 70 per 1,000, and 104 per 1,000 in Liverpool, might be taken as a demonstration that in that city an additional 34 infants in every 1,000 died, when they need not have done by the standards of the nation as a whole. It is not possible to know which of the 104 they were, or even to know why they died, from this information alone, but few could doubt that these deaths were caused by the particularly poor sanitary conditions in that city, or that the rate could be reduced by improvements in public health. There is nothing objectionable in this form of argument. It is often possible to construct equations where the relationship is modelled by the form, 'for each unit of increase in variable a there is observed a decrease of y units in variable b', which sometimes have a high degree of predictive efficiency. The relationship between unemployment and school retention rates, for example, readily lends itself to this mode of statistical analysis. It has already been shown that the interpretation of such models is, however, by no means unproblematic. Their justification by appeal to the concept of statistical explanation requires an additional discussion.

Perhaps the most influential attempt to provide the concept of statistical explanation in social science with philosophical support has been offered by Salmon in a sophisticated application of Hempel's (1968) deductive-nomological system. The most accessible summary of Salmon's (1975: 160–61) complex position and its implications, which even then needs to be quoted at length, is stated in this response to a critic:

> it seems to me, when we ask why *this* boy (Johnny Jones) is delinquent, an adequate explanation of that fact will, by implication, be an answer to the question of why any arbitrarily selected member of the class of delinquent boys exhibits that attribute … Thus, to explain Johnny's delinquency, I maintain, one must provide a partition of the entire class of boys in terms of (ideally all) factors statistically relevant to the occurrence of delinquency, along with the associated probability value for each subset of the partition. In addition, of course, Johnny must be referred to the compartment to which he belongs. But the fact that he is referred to a compartment in which the possibility of delinquency is low … does not detract from the value of that explanation. If an explanation of delinquency makes delinquency more probable for some classes of boys, it *must* also render it less probable for other classes of boys. [Original emphasis]

Salmon argues in this passage that a statistical explanation of an 'outcome' applies to all those in the relevant population whether the 'outcome' is positive or negative. If a clever middle-class boy fails at school then his failure is explained by the fact that he is a clever middle-class boy: the odds of him failing were, say, 10 in a 1,000 compared with 950 in a 1,000 for a low-ability working-class boy, but that has no bearing on the status of the explanation provided. These models treat individuals as units operating within the realm of probable action. The explanation is not of individuals in any real sense, but of groups understood as being composed of identical individuals. As they are assumed to be identical in all relevant respects, the variables of the model can be applied universally. But this conclusion is at odds with realist common sense: the achievements of a successful student may demonstrate the effects of the variables included in the model to their precisely calculated extent – it is by definition so – but whether probably it is actually so is an entirely different matter. Without a careful analysis of individual cases, what they did and what happened to them is absolutely unknown and therefore unexplained (Nash, 1999c).

Salmon's scheme can be related directly to the statistical model of the effect of individual (socialised) dispositions on relative progress and decline at school. There is a partition of the class of students in terms of the factors known to be relevant to their progress or decline at school with the odds for each subset, and the subset to which each student belongs is known. Nash and Harker (1998) show, for example, that a student of average ability and social background, with high aspirations, a good self-concept and positive perceptions of school, is about 30 times more likely than a similar student with low aspirations, a poor self-concept and negative perceptions of school to show significant relative progress at school rather than significant decline. The explanation of relative progress at school is given in terms of high aspirations, positive academic self-concept and favourable perceptions of teachers. Yet many students with these characteristics merely maintain their relative position and a few actually demonstrate a decline in relative progress. On Salmon's argument this divergence from prediction is explained in terms of the statistical model, and the odds of an event occurring, or not occurring, are irrelevant to the validity of the explanation. Many people, however, will be dissatisfied with such an account. They will suspect that there is a special story, involving some variable or variables not included in the model – absence from school due to illness, or something of that sort – that will make sense of the observed pattern. Interestingly, this is exactly the role given to case studies by normal science in this paradigm. Cox and Jones (1983: 129), for example, invariably make their case studies support their model by showing that, on individual examination, 'unexplained' results can be accommodated by detailed observation of their particular circumstances. The story of the boy from an objectively classified 'disadvantaged' background who achieved good results at school because his unemployed father (whose status in that respect had contributed to the classification) took an 'active interest' in the boy and engaged him with 'books and constructive play materials' is a representative example of the genre. The fact is that researchers in this tradition typically use their 'thumbnail' case studies both to illustrate how the model succeeds when it does so, and to show that it *really* succeeds even when it fails. One may note, moreover, that they employ a taken-for-granted SDP model for that purpose. Salmon further argues that an adequate explanation of why any given student makes progress will also be an answer to the question of why any arbitrarily selected student makes progress. This notion also seems to have little practical worth. A student might have made unexpected progress because he/she was moved from a class where he/she was incompetently taught to a class where he/she was competently taught, but this might be such an unusual occurrence that it does not form part of the statistical model, and in that case it obviously cannot apply to any arbitrarily selected student or, indeed, to any other student at all. The formal objection to this criticism is that it is beside the point because it ignores the assumption stated in the model that all relevant variables should be included: but that is the issue most at stake, because in the practice of social research the assumption is almost never valid.

These aspects of Salmon's argument do not convince. First, it is counter-intuitive to suppose that the failure of a student with the characteristics of success failed for those reasons, that is because 10 in a 1,000 do and this case happens to be one of the few, and, second, the explanation of Johnny Jones's delinquent status surely need not be the same as the explanation of why Billy Brown, an arbitrarily selected boy, is also a delinquent. In a realist scheme, to suppose that a student with the characteristics of success actually failed because he/she happened to be one of the few in that category with a probability of failing is no explanation at all. This is, indeed, the equivalent of saying that he/she failed 'against the odds'. To reject that argument seems to imply, however, as Salmon has realised, that the reciprocal explanation of success must also be rejected, for it has the same status. A student with high aspirations, positive self-concepts and favourable perceptions of teachers succeeds because students with these characteristics have a high probability of doing so. The statistical explanation of success and failure is consistent: it explains both, and for the same reason. The problem lies not with Salmon's impeccable logic, but with the concept of statistical explanation itself and with its practical application, particularly in social science where the necessary conditions of the model, the identification of all relevant variables being the most obvious, are impossible to satisfy. The realist explanation, in the illustration discussed, is that high esteem, high aspirations and acceptance of school are among the causes of relative educational success, and so when these dispositions are associated with success for an individual the explanation is probably true (but should always be confirmed if necessary by investigation at that level), and when an individual with such dispositions fails, the special reasons for that failure should be sought. The need for statistical explanation is actually driven by the theoretical demand for an explanation that can be accepted as useful and true for groups regardless of whether those explanations are also useful and true for each individual in those groups. The problems of reconciling explanations of group behaviour and individual action, however, are not satisfactorily resolved by non-realist and neo-positivist solutions.

Conclusion

The SDP scheme is not offered in any respect as a novel solution to the problems of theory and methodology that beset the sociology of education. It should, on the contrary, be recognised as the formalisation of a commonplace approach to the construction of sociological explanations. There may, nevertheless, be some merit in restating the case for a common-sense and realist approach to these matters. Statistical methods are able to provide essential information about sources of variance in the behaviour of students and, through multivariate analysis, provide an investigator with a shrewd idea of the various social processes through which it has been generated. It remains true, however, that the interpretation of statistical patterns without any direct knowledge of the social processes by which they were generated lacks the evidence required by a deep explanation. Although it is not always easy to identify the social processes responsible for specific system effects, an integrated realist approach is more likely to reveal what is happening at that level than research legitimated as 'quantitative, or even 'evidence-based', where that excludes associated contextual investigations of social process. The taken-for-granted theory of measurement in social science, which gives support to operationalism and nominalism, is fundamentally anti-realist. The theory of statistical explanation associated with it, moreover, is equally inconsistent with a realist concept of explanation. Some final remarks on the methodological separation of numbers and narrative will be offered.

The division between so-called qualitative and quantitative research is accepted far more readily in the sociology of education than ought to be the case. It is obvious that the rupture is sustained by an incoherent conceptual distinction (for the terms 'qualitative' and 'quantitative' are not semantic antonyms), and it continues to inhibit principled attempts to develop integrated 'numbers and narratives' models of educational research. The argument of this chapter has focused on problems of statistical models and their interpretation, but the dogmatic celebration of 'qualitative' in contrast to 'quantitative' approaches is as much an indulgence as the reverse position. Ethnographic analyses, narrative accounts of practice at specific sites, and in-depth case studies of individuals and groups in their social context are all essential to research within an SDP model. These methods provide the only access we have to forms of action within social practices. What may be called the linkage problem is, however, acute and very difficult to resolve. How are system effects, only detectable by statistical analysis – school composition effects are a paradigm example – to be causally linked to the social processes at different sites at which they are generated?

The most obvious procedure in the investigation of social processes that give rise to system to system level effects is to carry out methodical observations at the sites where such effects seem to be generated. If something is happening, then it ought to be possible to find out what it is by observation at the sites likely to be involved. The whole problem, however, is more difficult than it might seem. Classroom observation, in particular, is in one sense all too easy and in another frustratingly difficult. One sees so much going on and yet one often cannot see what is happening as a result. It is extremely difficult to be certain that this or that observed behaviour, which must be located in its specific practice, is important in generating an effect isolated for explanation, and there is always the logical possibility that a study might miss the mark entirely. Many processes that take place in classrooms, and that can be observed continually in the interactions of teachers and students, need have no necessary causal effects on attainment, despite the imperative demand of theory or even the compelling – and in this context ironically – empirical authority of immediate experience. The difficulty is simply this: although the behaviour responsible for the effects we can detect is undoubtedly happening, before our very eyes as it were, we do not know what that behaviour is and ethnographic accounts, simply because they are ethnographic, are unable to provide the insight required (Nash, 1998). The issues are clearly ones of theory and methodology that require investigation at that level. There is, in fact, an ineluctable discontinuity, a difference of level, between behaviour that can be observed in schools and the effects of that on some 'outcome' that can only be detected by statistical analysis. As Bourdieu appositely remarks: 'The perfectly commendable wish to see things in person, close up, sometimes leads people to search for the explanatory principles of observed realities where they are not to be found (not all of them, in any case), namely, at the site of observation itself' (Bourdieu et al., 1999: 181). The further discussion of this matter must be left for another occasion, but it may be noted in passing that there is little point in carrying out studies, legitimated as 'qualitative' research in deference to an entirely fallacious methodological principle, when the questions they seek to answer are better investigated by methods that do not eschew quantitative analysis as a matter of preference. The task of demonstrating the linkage certainly requires more than the description of social processes at some site accompanied by a more or less plausible suggestion that they could be involved in the generation of an effect detected at the system level.

This chapter has raised serious issues for the practice of a sociology of education that attempts to provide evidence of the linkages between the stratified entities of the social world. Statistical models that recognise system properties (structure), individual disposition, and action within social practices need to be interpreted as specific levels within a fully articulated SDP explanatory scheme. It is necessary to devise indicators appropriate to each level (as it might be, parental occupation, aspiration, hours spent on homework and so on) that might then be interpreted according to what is known about the actual social processes involved. A realist concept of sociology and variable construction is important in these respects. It is particularly unhelpful to include variables at all levels, as it might be, parental income, 'need for achievement', and bedtime stories, in a composite index of 'family background', with the inevitable result that these indicators more or less cancel each other out. Yet it is actually common to see variables at one level presented as if they were in competition with those at another for the proportion of variance 'explained'. It is manifest nonsense to propose a model of school attainment where social class (indexed by parent occupation), student aspirations (indexed by a conventional scale) and student practices (indexed by number of completed assignments) have the same nominal status, with an 'accidental' relationship to each other, and worthy of notice only in so far as it raises the technical problem of multicolinearity. The debate about the significance of social class and ethnicity as causes of variance in educational attainment, for example, is beset with technical and political issues that are extremely difficult to resolve within a nominalist framework. A realist is able to accept that the dispositions and forms of behaviour associated with social class and ethnic origin may be similar, is able to construct indicators of an appropriate kind to test that hypothesis, and equipped to investigate the far more complex historical and sociological question of where the distinct structural derivation of the practices involved should be located. The practical–political aspects raised by this analysis are significant, even if they have not taken centre stage in the exposition, and this will provide an appropriate point to conclude with the suggestion that the adoption of an SDP explanatory scheme has the potential to take the sociology of education a step further towards our collective goal to understand and interrupt the process that generate inequality of educational opportunity.

References

Alexander, J. (1995). *Fin de Siècle Social Theory: Relativism, Reduction, and the Problem of Reason* (London: Verso).

Amer, D.J. (1972). School and family effects on black and white achievement: A reassessment of the USEO data. In F. Mosteller and D.P. Moynihan (eds), *On Equality of Educational Opportunity.* Papers derived from the Harvard University Faculty Seminar on the Coleman Report (New York: Random House): 168–229.

Archer, M. (1995). *Social Theory: The Morphogenetic Approach* (Cambridge: Cambridge University Press).

Bauman, K.J. (1998). Schools, markets, and the family in the history of African-American education, *American Journal of Education*, 106: 500–531.

Berka, K. (1983). *Measurement: Its Concepts, Theories and Problems* (Dordrecht, The Netherlands, Reidel).

Bernstein, B. (1971). On the classification and framing of educational knowledge. In M.F.D. Young (ed.), Knowledge and Control: New Directions for the Sociology of Education (London: Collier-Macmillan): 47–69.

Bhaskar, R. (1993). *Dialectic: The Pulse of Freedom* (London: Verso).

Boudon, R. (1982). *The Unintended Consequences of Social Action* (London: Macmillan).

Bourdieu, P. (1986). *Distinction* (London: Routledge).

Bourdieu, P. (1990). *The Logic of Practice* (Cambridge: Polity Press).

Bourdieu, P. (2000). *Pascalian Meditations* (Cambridge: Polity Press).

Bourdieu, P. et al. (1999). *The Weight of the World: Social Suffering in Contemporary Society* (Stanford, Calif.: Stanford University Press).

Bunge, M. (1998). *Social Science Under Debate: A Philosophical Perspective* (Toronto: University of Toronto Press).

Calhoun, C., Lipuma, E. and Postone, M. (eds) (1993). *Bourdieu: Critical Perspectives* (Cambridge, Polity Press).

Coleman, J.S. (1966). *Equality of Educational Opportunity* (Washington, DC: United States Department of Health, Education and Welfare).

Cox, T. and Jones, G. (1983). *Disadvantaged 11-year-olds* (Oxford: Pergamon Press).

Dreyfus, H.L. and Rainbow, P. (1982). *Michel Foucault: Beyond Structuralism and Hermeneutics* (Brighton: Harvester).

Engels, F. (1935). *The Housing Question* (London: Martin Lawrence).

Goldstein, H. and Thomas, S. (1995). School effectiveness and 'value added' analysis, *Forum*, 37(2): 36–8.

Halsey, A.H. (1975). Sociology and the equality debate, *Oxford Review of Education*, 1(1): 9–28.

Harris, M. (1979). *Cultural Materialism* (New York: Random House).

Hempel, C.G. (1968). Fundamentals of concept formation in empirical science, *International Encyclopaedia of Unified Science*, vol. XI, no. 7 (Chicago: University of Chicago Press).

Hunushek, E.A. and Kain, J.F. (1972). On the value of 'Equality of Educational Opportunity' as a guide to public policy. In F. Mosteller and D.P. Moynihan (eds), *On Equality of Educational Opportunity*, papers derived from the Harvard University Faculty Seminar on the Coleman Report (New York: Random House): 116–45

Jevons, W.S. (1883). *Methods of Social Reform and Other Papers* (London: Macmillan).

Lareau, A. and Horvat, E. McN. (1999). Moments of social inclusion and exclusion: Race, class and cultural capital in family–school relationships, *Sociology of Education*, 72(1): 37–53.

Lauder, H. and Hughes, D. (1999). *Trading in Futures: Why Education Markets Don't Work* (Buckingham: Open University Press).

Macintyre, A. (1984). After Virtue: A Study in Moral Theory, 2nd edn (Notre Dame, Ind.: University of Notre Dame Press).

Mayer, S.E. (1997). *What Money Can't Buy: Family Income and Children's Life Chances* (Cambridge, Mass.: Harvard University Press).

Nash, R. (1993). *Succeeding Generations: Family Resources and Access to Education in New Zealand* (Auckland: Oxford University Press).

Nash, R. (1998). Commentary: A realist approach to school composition effects: A response to 'How school-mix shapes school responses' [M. Thrupp], *New Zealand Journal of Educational Studies*, 33(2): 223–30.

Nash, R. (1999a). Realism and explanatory models in the sociology of education: A New Zealand study, *British Journal of Sociology of Education*, 20(1): 107–25.

Nash, R. (1999b). What is real and what is realism in sociology?, *Journal for the Theory of Social Behaviour*, 24(9): 445–66.

Nash, R. (1999c). *School Learning: Conversations with the Sociology of Education*, Delta Studies in Education 3 (Palmerston North: Delta Press).

Nash, R. and Harker, R. (1998). *Making Progress: Adding Value in Secondary Education* (Palmerston North: ERDC Press).

Pettit, D. (1993). *The Common Mind: An Essay on Psychology, Society and Politics* (Oxford University Press: Oxford).

Reay, D. (1998). *Class Work: Mothers' Involvement in Their Children's Primary Schooling* (London: UCL Press).

Ryle, A. (1984). *The Concept of Mind* (Chicago: University of Chicago Press).

Salmon, W.C. (1975). Reply to comments [on 'Theoretical explanation', pp. 118–45]. In S. Körner, (ed.), *Explanation* (Oxford: Blackwell): 160–184.

Sayer, A. (1992). *Method in Social Science: A Realist Approach*, 2nd edn (London: Routledge).

Schmaus, W. (1994). *Durkheim's Philosophy of Science and the Sociology of Knowledge: Creating an Intellectual Niche* (Chicago: Chicago University Press).

Shavit, Y. and Blossfield, H.P. (eds) (1993). *Persisting Inequality: Changing Educational Attainment in Thirteen Countries* (Boulder, Col.: Westview Press).

Shusterman, R. (ed.). (1998). *Bourdieu: A Critical Reader* (Oxford: Blackwell).

Sorokin, P. (1998). *On the Practice of Sociology* (Chicago: University of Chicago Press).

Stevens, S.S. (ed.) (1951). *Handbook of Experimental Psychology* (New York: Wiley).

Thrupp, M. (1999). *Schools Making a Difference: Let's Be Realistic! School Mix, School Effectiveness and the Limits of Reform* (Buckingham: Open University Press).

Chapter 3

Social Explanation and Socialisation: On Bourdieu and the Structure–Disposition–Practice Scheme

Introduction

The enormous expansion of educational provision throughout the twentieth century, in all developed states, has been accomplished while leaving relative social differentials in school attainment and tertiary-level access largely unaltered (Shavit and Blomfield, 1993). All the efforts of policymakers to uncouple the link between social class and educational attainment have largely been frustrated by complex processes that the sociology of education struggles to model in its explanatory narratives. The causes of 'inequality of educational opportunity', to use the term Coleman (1991) has made a synonym for inequality/difference in educational attainment, are obviously multiple, and the importance of statistical models, with their estimates of the relative importance of discrete variables, will always be recognised in the discipline. The most influential theories of inequality/ difference in the sociology of education, however, take little from statistical investigations, other than the apparent immutability of their findings, and argue that schools are, perhaps inevitably, agents of social and cultural reproduction (Nash, 1997). Bourdieu's contribution to the sociology of education, which is for him the study of symbolic meaning and its social distribution, has been welcomed by sociologists who recognise its radical conception of the school as a conservative force. Charlesworth (2000), for example, a close observer of contemporary working-class life, endorses this argument completely and notes how little the reproductive function of the school has changed since the first publication of Bourdieu's thesis almost 40 years ago. Bourdieu's work enjoys a status unparalleled in contemporary sociology, particularly in the area of cultural studies, and criticism of his approach, in this increasingly well-defended field, is often perceived as unwelcome. This is perhaps even more likely given that, as Robbins (2000a: 190–91) has pointed out, the characteristic style of Bourdieu's academic production is such that criticism is virtually obliged to assume an *ad hominem* form. The purpose of this chapter, it may quickly be said in this context, is not so much to criticise Bourdieu as to investigate the explanatory capacity of theories of reproduction at this level of generality that rest on socialisation.

The critique might be regarded as sympathetic to the Bourdieusian project in as much that it will support, within a realist sociology, the basic structure–

disposition–practice (SDP) explanatory scheme adopted by Bourdieu's sociology. Bourdieu's theory, of course, requires that agents acquire through socialisation a habitus that is the embodiment of generative social structures, and this is the basis for a specific use of socialisation theory (Howson and Inglis, 2001; LiPuma, 1993; Shusterman, 1998). The SDP scheme is, in fact, more common than otherwise in social theory. In the most summary form, it is an explanatory account that describes how social structures give rise to characteristic dispositions that enable the competent performance of social practices. This scheme, which will be discussed more fully in a later section, is entirely defensible and, indeed, might be recognised by a realist sociology as the ideal form of explanation, but it raises matters of theory and methodology that will reward examination (Nash, 2002). Although socialisation theories, particularly those of Freud (1922) and Mead (1934), are generally familiar to social scientists, what can be *explained* by reference to the fact of socialisation requires some attention. In themselves, theories of socialisation deal with the conditions of acquisition of social identity, they explain how social identities are formed, but the incorporation of *socialised agents* in sociology, although resting on foundations established by socialisation theory, has a different status.

The pages of social theory are actually replete with paeans of praise to the power of habit in human conduct to perpetuate social patterns. Dewey (1983), Husserl (1970), Merleau-Ponty (1974), Schutz (1972), Sorokin (1962, 1998), Parsons (1954), Elias (1972), Harré (1982) and Bourdieu (2000) may be included as only a few of the most influential among the many who have given socialised habit a central place in social explanation. The conviction that habit underpins the stable routines of everyday life, however, cannot be granted the status of a general theory, and explanations in these terms of particular events need to be considered on their merit. When Davis and Dollard (1940), to take an early example, stress the importance of habit in the conduct of social life, what interests them is not so much how agents become socialised beings, but the fact that a set of semi-automatic responses applicable over a wide range of everyday contexts provides an explanation of how social patterns are maintained. When they insist that, '[m]en behave differently as adults because their cultures are different; they are born into different habitual ways of life, and these they must follow because they have no choice' (ibid: 4), they seek to explain the stability of social processes and why they are so resistant to change. How such accounts are to be tested, of course, presents a serious methodological problem. A theory that posits, for example, that class differences in education are caused by the habituated practices of agents at relevant sites of practices – teachers in schools, parents in homes, and so on – thus effectively ensuring the reproduction of the entire system, would surely raise more questions than it answers. It is hardly necessary to demonstrate that something very much like this is frequently offered as a Bourdieusian theory of the reproduction of educational inequality. Branson and Miller's (1991: 42) summary account – '[t]he working-classes are trapped in their habitus through cultural impoverishment and cultural difference' – has become the standard narrative. Apart from the fact that this determinist formulation ignores the habitus of the middle class, not least the cognitive habitus that is all too probably the real basis of their relative success, the explanation at this level of abstraction has no substantive content. Some of the difficulties with this as a general theory, as an explanation of the social causes of *inequality/difference*, are immediately evident. In the first place, the same explanation would hold whether the observed pattern was characterised by a twofold or a tenfold class difference in educational access. It would also appear to be virtually worthless for all practical purposes unless the specific practices of specific groups of agents were known, ideally with some indication of their respective importance, and presented within an explanatory narrative in such a way that its claims could be tested. The difficulties of achieving this within Bourdieu's theory of reproduction are proving to be rather formidable. The theoretical problem is posed in an acute form, as the following discussion will demonstrate, by the opposition of structural and phenomenological approaches to sociological explanation.

Mediating between Agency and Structure

The influence of structuralism, which insists that ways of life, or 'cultures' in that sense, are informed by deep principles that create homologous relations between practices in separate domains – economic, political, cultural (that is religious, artistic, educational and so on) – in such a way as to impose a coherent symbolic order on the cultural as a whole, is fundamental to Bourdieu's sociology. One of the theoretical purposes of habitus is to effect the mediation between structural principles and cultural practice within and across specific fields, and Bourdieu's break with structuralism is, therefore, not so thoroughgoing that the master concept of culture as an organised whole is abandoned. It would be surprising if it were. Many anthropologists regard the search for structural principles as the entire point of their discipline. Barley's (1983) amusing introduction to anthropological fieldwork – among the Dowayo people of the Cameroons – is particularly instructive: 'One is seeking to describe what sort of a world the Dowayos live in, how they structure it and interpret it. Since most of the data will be unconscious, this cannot simply be approached by asking about it' (ibid. 127). Barley was elated to discover, by laborious investigations, that a mental model derived from the growth of their basic food crop apparently structured many aspects of Dowayo practice. As he writes: '[a] series of parallels is established by the culture between various stages of the millet cycle and the sexual processes of women' (ibid. 130). These coded relations take the form of grand metaphor that helps to organize life in a way not formally known to members of the society who, although aware of what is required and what is not in the ritual order of their lives, seem to possess little or no understanding of its underlying principles. Once the code has been revealed, however, it is possible to make sense of otherwise seemingly unrelated social conventions and practices. What degree of control these structures impose on human action is a matter of intense discussion (Godelier, 1986). Bourdieu (1990: 9–10) further accepts the structuralist position, which is clearly functionalist in this respect, that 'types of behaviour can be directed towards certain ends without being consciously directed to these ends, or determined by them', and states that '[t]he notion of habitus was invented for this paradox'. Bourdieu was not, as he often said, a structuralist, and had he not been acutely dissatisfied with its orthodox formulations the concept of habitus might not have been introduced, and yet this itself demonstrates his acceptance of its problematic. All this makes the concept of 'strategy' in his theory another demanding area blurring, as it does, the distinction between determinism and non-determinism. The importance given to this form of analysis in social theory, not least in the field of education, is critical. Bernstein's (1996) contribution to the sociology of education is impossible to understand unless its structuralist origins are recognised (Davies, 1994). If these principles *control* practice, as Lévi-Strauss argued, then what is the mediation between the culture, analysed as a set of generative principles, and of practice itself? The principles must be embodied in some form, and if practice becomes a matter of habit, then they are embodied, most particularly, as classed and gendered mental, physical and linguistic habits.

Bourdieu's concept of structure, however, is by no means restricted to the underlying structures of the classical Lévi-Straussian variety. On the contrary, the reference in his work is extremely wide, and there is nothing to be gained by attempting to find a precise definition of 'social structure' in his work. Some awareness of the range the concept of structure has acquired in this sociology is, however, necessary to critical appreciation. Those most familiar with Bourdieu's approach to social theory are fully aware that such investigations are both fruitless and frustrating. The conflation of what may be called, for the sake of convenience, the classical structures of anthropology and the structures of phenomenology in Bourdieu's work often goes unremarked (Shilling, 2001). This may have something to do with the fact that phenomenological texts present difficulties of comprehension that surpass even those involved in the mastery of the classical concept. Nevertheless, the influence of phenomenology to the development of Bourdieu's position has been emphasised by all leading commentators (Crossby, 2001; Robbins, 1991, 1999; Lane, 2000) and cannot be ignored. Bell (1990: 229), commenting on Husserl (1970: 111–12), shows how the phenomenological structures of the life-world – known at the level of individual perception – were finally linked by that thinker to their social origin: 'The identity and integrity of a society or culture ... are functions of the possession by its members of a body of beliefs and practices "taken for granted" and "made use of as unquestioned and available".'

Bourdieu studied Husserl intensively at one point in his intellectual career, and the concept of habitus in his work owes to that thinker, it not its first origin, then certainly the deep theoretical frame of reference it always retained. The practical knowledge of the social world that is presupposed by 'reasonable' behaviour within it implements, as it were *automatically*, historical schemes of perception and appreciation that function below the level of consciousness and discourse. The instruments of perception that organise our life-world are, moreover, in class-divided societies, the product of the objective class structure. As the incorporated presence of the fundamental structures of society, these principles of division are common to all who live within it, and in this way a shared and meaningful world is constructed. Habitus is thus conceived as a generative schema in which social structures come, through the process of socialisation, to be embodied as schemes of perception that enable a practical mastery of the world, a knowledge of the 'rules of the game' within fields of practice, in such a way that individuals necessarily (or almost necessarily) reproduce the underlying structures.

In a further eclectic extension of the reference of 'social structure', Bourdieu includes all those properties of social systems Durkheim called 'social facts'. The structure–agency problem arises in an almost identical form when explanations of social events are given in terms of positions (established by social relations) and practices (as prescribed roles) necessary to organisational functioning, in as much that the only property of agents necessary to this scheme is an adequate knowledge of the implicit rules that enable successful role performance. It is not surprising that Parsons's theory requires a strongly socialised agent, so strongly socialised, in fact, that the break with structural-functionalism, all but total in the minds of the sociological generation that came of age at the end of the 1960s, was dictated by its effective denial of agency and consequently of social change (Dawe, 1970). The difficulty here is that any sociological theory that attempts to explain *reproduction*, rather than *transformation*, will tend to privilege structure over agency, and the force of collective habit over the energy of the individual will. The structure–agency problem is, in this sense, given by the question posed to the social world. For Bourdieu, the central issue is how societies reproduce their existing structures, which for him is always the radical question of how relations of class domination are reproduced through agencies of symbolic control (Bourdieu, 1986, 1991). In this respect, if not in too many others, Bourdieu's scheme can be compared with Parsons's more conservative interest in 'pattern maintenance'.

The concept thus unites phenomenological and 'objective' structures in an integrated generative scheme. In this eclectic manner, the term 'structure' in Bourdieu's usage includes, at least: (i) the 'pure' structural principles of the classical variety (raw/cooked, clarity/obscurity, restricted/elaborated and so on); (ii) taken-for-granted categories of everyday life (high/low, male/female, theoretical/practical and so on); (iii) principles of action, from those of traditional, folk culture ('neither a borrower nor a lender be', 'a stitch in time', 'too many cooks' and the like) through to the politicised slogans of contemporary life ('user pays', 'transparency', 'accountability' and so on); and (iv) the structures of the labour market, the distribution of educational credentials and such like, abstracted by sociological analysis (Porpora, 1989). All are supposed to be embedded in the dispositions of the habitus. In Bourdieu's theory the cognitive structures which social agents implement in their practical knowledge of the social world are internalised, 'embodied' social structures of almost any kind. Bourdieu is also prepared, moreover, simply to assume the existence of a generative habitus in order to construct global accounts of social practice. The dispositions that constitute the habitus may not include *everything* – they seem not to include, for example, specific cognitive abilities and talents (an interesting lacuna) – but the concept is certainly wide-ranging.

The need for a mediating process between structure and agency arises from a theoretical problem of some magnitude. It is widely accepted that there is a problem to be resolved, and the claim to have achieved that goal, is one to be taken seriously. The difficulty is essentially theoretical, of course, not practical. In this context, many sociologists have accepted that agents' dispositions provide sociological theory with a mediating link between social structures and social behaviour. There can be little doubt that this is the theoretical reason for the introduction of habitus to Bourdieu's conceptual scheme. According to Waquant (2000: 107, quoting Bourdieu et al., 1965: 22), who might be regarded as an authorised commentator in this field, Bourdieu wishes to accord:

> the practical categories and competencies of agents a critical mediating role between 'the system of objective regularities' and the space of 'observable behaviours' … without which sociology is doomed to run aground on the reefs of the realism of structure or to get stuck in mechanistic explanations unfit to grasp the practical logic that governs conduct.

The sharp horns of the structure–agency dilemma threaten to impale any sociologist unable to display a bit of smart footwork. Wacquant's account indicates where the dangers lie. The 'system of objective structures' is primarily a *structuralist* reference to the set of principles that supposedly constitute the formal cultural system that gives each functioning society its particular form and integrity (Lévi-Strauss, 1978). Wacquant further suggests that these deep structures should not be regarded as real. This is not everyone's view, and Robbins (2000b) presents sound reasons for thinking that Bourdieu does treat them as real. The point for this discussion, however, is that such structures contain in themselves the information necessary to construct an explanation of social practice, provided that agents are not required to be other than non-autonomous bearers of structural principles. That is one horn of the dilemma, and Bourdieu does not intend to stand in the same dangerous position as Lévi-Strauss, but nor does he intend to move to the equally dangerous position occupied by the intentionalist models of rational action theory. Bourdieu's (1977) declared purpose is to synthesise those theoretical accounts of the social world that, on the one hand, emphasise and, on the other, neglect structure or agency. Seeking to avoid the polarities of structuralist determinism and phenomenological individualism, Bourdieu attempts to construct a new theory of practice in which the sterile opposition of the old debate (conscious/unconscious; explanation by cause/explanation by reason; mechanical submission to social constraint/rational and strategic calculation, individual/society, and so on) can be transcended. With the concept of habitus, as an internalised mediating mechanism that more or less automatically – as a doxic relation to the world embodying the strategic mechanisms imposed by the structures of the field – produces practice, Bourdieu occupies, as he puts it, the space between structuralist and intentionalist accounts. It seems, therefore, as if Bourdieu's sociological theory requires an agent endowed with dispositions able to translate structural principles of the culture into lived practice, with sufficient autonomy to allow observed social transformations to take place, but sufficiently conditioned as to effect the actual reproduction of social institutions. Bourdieu's habitus, as the operative set of socialised dispositions that fulfils this function and generates practice in accordance with the regulating structure of cultural principles, has become widely accepted on these terms. The incorporation of the field as set of relations, 'as a structured ensemble of offers and appeals, bids and solicitations, and prohibitions' (Bourdieu et al., 1999: 512), into the explanatory scheme is essential, but it does not affect the status of habitus. Whether it succeeds in these respects is largely a matter of interest to those who work within the theory, but whether it captures the nature of social behaviour is of wider concern.

The Uses of Socialisation Theory

If habitus rests on socialisation theory, then what additional explanatory power, if any, is obtained by *naming* the effective set of internalised dispositions? This is the crux of the theoretical debate, and there are critiques, both naive and sophisticated, far from convinced that the answer amounts to very much. It is not surprising that a growing number of commentators have expressed reservations about the explanatory role of habitus. Margolis (1999) has questioned the very idea of a faculty-like disposition to follow a set of 'rules'. In the same vein, Bouveresse (1999: 60) expresses his suspicion that, 'the explanation in terms of "dispositions" or "habitus", when the terms are not characterised independently of the simple description of the sort of regular behaviour which they purport to give rise to, are purely linguistic.' The problem of the circular argument in faculty, or dispositional theories, will be discussed in greater detail, but it will first be useful to examine the explanatory potential of socialisation theory.

Socialisation theories explain how people come to be members of their culture, and explanations of their actions or 'practices' in terms of socialisation are basically observations that people do what they have been brought up to do. It is scarcely possible to find a sociologist who would not agree with this statement. Sorokin's (1962: 342) remark, for example, that 'a person, in contradistinction to a mere biological organism cannot help becoming a mirror of his sociocultural universe' has no claim to be original. Such accounts do provide an explanation of sorts, if the evidence suggests that small boys tend to play with toy guns because they have been permitted and encouraged to do so, then it is established, at least, that such behaviour is not innate, but the information has a somewhat limited value. If a young man from an American, middle-class, Baptist family graduates from college with a business degree, gets a job with H.R. Block and marries the girl-next-door, no one is particularly surprised, and it can all be explained, to the extent that anything in this trajectory is considered sufficiently problematic to need an explanation, by the working out of habitus. Let the young man develop an interest in Islam and end up fighting with the Taliban, however, and there is so much explanation called for that one scarcely knows where to begin. It will obviously not suffice to construct a narrative in terms of habitus, and the theoretical problems raised by these commonplace observations are actually rather troubling. First, if the explanation of unexpected trajectories does not provide any useful information, it is by no means clear that the explanation has much merit in the case of expected trajectories. Of course, the theory is designed to account for *reproduction*, which could not happen unless the former trajectory were a great deal more common than the latter, but that fact does not demonstrate that *reproductive practices* are generated by habit. The argument that the theory is concerned to explain collective, not individual, action is a non sequitur in this context. The entire theory rests on the assumption that unreflected habitual actions effect reproduction, and that cannot be grounded on the fact that reproduction is generally and broadly achieved. Nevertheless, the concept of habitual behaviour is extremely powerful. The entire animal kingdom runs on instincts that can be regarded as natural habits. If a learned action has become *second nature* then it has acquired something like the status of the *first nature* of unlearned instinct (Camic, 1986). The complex social life of great apes, extensively studied by field ecologists, is entirely regulated by practices that arise from instinctual dispositions. The cultural forms of human societies, however, are so variable that instinct has little if any relevance in sociological and anthropological accounts. Human societies possess a wide range of practices. In the area of family organisation, for example, the established forms may prescribe endogamy or exogamy, monogamy or polygamy, primogeniture or ultimogeniture, matrilocality or patrilocality, and so on. These practices are arbitrary in the sense that all can be adopted; they are functionally equivalent in so far as one is as 'workable' as another, and it is certain that at this level the routines of human societies, unlike those of the great apes, are not genetically determined. This concept of arbitrary, which is given a further elaborated meaning in linguistic theory by Saussere (1974), is also crucial to understanding Bourdieu's sociology.

Robbins (2000a: xiii) has pointed out that Bourdieu regarded society as a series of arbitrary cultures 'which were in competition with each other and in which dominance was secured, not as the result of any intrinsic merit or superiority, but one of *force majure*'. In the broad anthropological sense, all knowledge can be regarded as arbitrary within a given society. The practices that constitute and reproduce society are analysed in terms of their fundamental *principles* that are naturally acquired through the process of socialisation and thus maintained as learned habits. These core principles will – it is possible to say almost necessarily – be transmitted from generation to generation as embodied dispositions. Such knowledge, moreover, has the property of symbolic violence in as much as it is the cultural property of a particular group and mobilised in the struggle for dominance. What is widely taken as a Bourdieusian theory of social reproduction is based on the belief that, in capitalist (or perhaps industrialised) societies, the knowledge systems of the dominant and dominated classes are arbitrary cultural products. Grenfell and James (1998), for example, argue with Bourdieu that the dominated reject as alien classed knowledge readily assimilated by those for whom it is designed. There is no need to suppose that school knowledge is organised and taught with the conscious intention of excluding those with an inferior habitus; nevertheless, as Bourdieu (1974) argues, it effectively achieves that end. This concept of the arbitrary, drawing further support from the concept of symbolic violence, is the basis of the widely accepted argument that the cause of *inquality/ difference*, within the school, is the classed and culturally arbitrary curriculum. The theory appears to be derived impeccably from Bourdieu's conceptual framework and is a reasonable Bourdieusian position. It is not, however, Bourdieu's own position. Lane (2000) is the most recent commentator to have noted Bourdieu's insistence on the necessity of a universal curriculum and pedagogy. This may be inconsistent with elements of his general theory, but it locates him firmly in the Enlightenment tradition from which the theory arises.

Nevertheless, the theoretical celebration of the arbitrary, which is, of course, a commitment to epistemological relativism, has implications for realist sociology – particularly with respect to explanations of inequality/difference – that require some discussion. It is one thing to argue that specific social conditions give rise to specific dispositions, and quite another to maintain that the valuation of these habitus is other than arbitrary and determined by the structure of the field. The influence of Saussere is obvious in Wacquant's (2000: 115) assertion that:

> To uncover the social logic of consumption thus requires establishing, not a direct link between a given practice and a particular class category (e.g., horseback riding and the gentry), but the structural correspondences that obtain between two constellations of relations, the space of lifestyles and the space of social positions occupied by the different groups.

There is no *logical* inconsistency in, for example, Wacquant's insistence here that practices follow structuralist logic in being distinguished by the arbitrary relations between them, and his observation (Wacquant, 1999) that the experience of the American urban ghetto produces recognisable types marked by the stamp of deprivation. This position is, however, certainly incompatible with an ontological commitment to the nature of human being and flourishing as outlined, for example, in Bhaskar's (1993) realist ethics. It is interesting that Charlesworth (2000), who draws extensively on Bourdieu, has no doubt that to be working class – at least in the English northern town of Rotherham – is to suffer within a culture that denies access to the full possibilities of a decent life, and prevents people becoming what they are capable of being in more favourable circumstances. It may be Heidegger's (1974) rather than Bourdieu's influence that drives Charlesworth (2000: 160) to declaim that working-class people 'are, in a very real sense, only partly alive' who go through the motions of life as 'the zombies that British culture has created by condemning them to the living death of a stigmatised, abject, being' but this is certainly an extreme view. At least it is evident that Charlesworth does not suppose the social value of cultural practices to be conferred by a system of relations and consequently having an arbitrary valuation conferred by the structures of the field. Indeed, Wacquant (1999) himself speaks of the cultural form of *hustling*, and the recognisable type it creates, one with 'the ability to manipulate others, to inveigle and deceive them, if need be by joining violence to chicanery and charm, in the pursuit of immediate pecuniary gain' (ibid. 142), one that has emerged as 'an expressive lifestyle which alone can make life somewhat bearable by loosening the taut and oppressive grip of the daily round in the ghetto' (ibid. 151), in terms that indicate its limitations and final unacceptability. In other words, this way of life, this set of dispositions and cultural practices, is produced by the social conditions of the ghetto and is a form of symbolic capital functionally adapted to it, but whether it can be accepted as a way of *human flourishing* is doubtful even to Wacquant. The relativist epistemology prevalent in the sociology of education draws strength from the celebration of the arbitrary and, notwithstanding Bourdieu's own commitment to the necessity of the *universal*, the unresolved tension in his theoretical position continues to be a source of strain.

Dispositions and Powers

The reality of human dispositions is not problematic. As Bourdieu says, 'to deny the existence of acquired dispositions, in the case of living beings, is to deny the existence of learning' (Bourdieu, 2000: 136). It is self-evident that dispositions, considered as the product of the natural *conditionability* of human bodies, are a species capacity. What matters, therefore, is not the fact that people acquire knowledge and skills, but *what* they learn, *how* they learn and *what they do* as a result of their learning. There is a realist position – basically Aristotelian – that explanations of events can be given in terms of the natural powers of entities. Harré and Madden (1975) argue, in a path-breaking defence of this scheme, that it may be said that a window shatters because it is brittle – which property can be recognised as a power or tendency of the glass – provided that this explanation sketch is offered in the context of a search for nature of the material structure, in this case at the molecular level, of the entities involved. Bourdieu shows himself to be aware of the academic debates about the status of dispositional properties in scientific explanations (Ryle, 1984). He argues:

> just as we should not say that a window broke because a stone hit it, but that
> it broke *because* it was breakable ... one should not say that a historical event
> determined a behaviour but that it had this determining effect because a habitus
> capable of being affected by that event conferred that power upon it. (Bourdieu,
> 2000: 148–9)

This is unexceptional. In a realist scheme, the window, indeed, does not break because it is hit, but because it is hit *being brittle* and, therefore, by virtue of that state, is disposed to shatter when subjected to a sharp blow. Moreover, it is entirely proper to maintain, for example, that the defeat of Germany in 1918, the terms of the Treaty of Versailles, and the monetary inflation and economic slump that followed gave rise to Nazism. But *only* because of the resentment, weakened sense of collective identity and ontological insecurity – a habitus that has received extensive investigation from critical theorists who drew on Marxism and psychoanalysis – that consequently affected many Germans.

Social positions do create socialised dispositions. The term 'disposition' is used here to cover a wide range of acquired personal states, including those states of mind recognised as beliefs, which are conceived as habits embodied in a more or less durable manner. One of the most important tasks of social and cultural studies is to investigate what dispositions are learned within specific social contexts and to show how the practices of socialised actors generate collective social effects. If one knows what dispositions inform people's actions, then to that extent one has an explanation at that level for what they do.

Sociology insists on the need to recognise properties of social systems and include these in explanatory accounts of social reproduction and social transformation. Sociologists are thus to be found engaged with large and comprehensive social conditions: bureaucratisation, colonisation, globalisation, secularisation, urbanisation and with the effects of cultural ideas, or ideologies, expressed in a single concept (patriarchy, racism, *glasnost* and so on). Social explanations in these terms often seem to leave agents with little effective autonomy. This is why Harré, for example, finds such 'big word' theories highly problematic and insists that causal agency cannot reside in 'powers' at such a level of abstraction. The difficulty also arises with so-called 'causal sociology', which draws inferences about causal relations from regular statistical associations. Durkheim's (1982) approach to these problems, how the relationship of causality between social conditions and the suicide rate could exist without admitting psychological mediation, is so obscure that it has generated a small library of learned exegesis (Schmaus, 1994). The least one can say about all this is that, if the *conscience collective* is real, then it is an entity of a very curious sort. Whether Bourdieu's concept of habitus can resolve these difficulties is open to question. The answer may hinge on the acceptability of dispositional explanations.

The recognition of the 'powers', 'tendencies' and 'dispositions' of collective entities as legitimate within explanatory accounts is gaining ground (Bhaskar, 1993). It is thus possible, for example, in this way to speak of the tendency of a colonised people to resist oppression, of capitalist enterprises to expand, of the dominant classes to support low taxation policies, and so on. These references are to the tendencies or 'dispositions' of *collectives* and should not be confused with the *psychological* dispositions of people. Such 'powers', it is true, depend for their realisation on human action, and action is always a product of an effective disposition of mind, but it is crucial to distinguish between the powers and tendencies of social entities and those of individuals (Nash, 1999b). Habitus represents an attempt to unite these properties – but that is exactly why many critics find it so deeply problematic. The problem arises in an acute form when 'dispositions' are attributed without specification of their character and merely inferred from their effects. It does not help in this context to argue, as some critical realists do, that the properties of social entities can be detected by their effects. In a literal sense, this is necessarily so – a desk is only known to exist because its properties, particularly its mass, can be detected – but the argument has some dubious applications. To infer the existence of an entity from some event requires more than the observation of the event. Psychometrics uses exactly this argument to justify its belief in the demonstrated existence of the 'g' factor as the fundamental entity of general intelligence. Fowler's (1996: 9) support for Bourdieu's assumption 'that the ... low percentage of the children of workers and peasants who achieve educationally at the levels of the children of the *haute bourgeoisie*, is in itself proof of the operation of such generative relationships which often act against the will,' is an example of the genre. The argument is inescapably circular. Moreover, when Fowler (ibid. 10) argues that, '[t]he habitus is the consequence of people's material experience and early socialization: it provides the basic or meta-dispositions towards ways of perceiving, knowing and appreciating the world', and goes on to say that, '[h]umans internalize their "life-chances", so that a reading off of any situation permits a sense of whether or not "this is for the likes of us"', the situation is not improved. If the argument is that 'working-class children fail at school because of their working-class habitus which is evidenced by their collective failure', then it cannot possibly carry conviction.

When socialisation theories are used to explain why students engage in a particular practice, let us say remaining at school or dropping-out, the explanation is likely to be unsatisfactory unless a description of the social structures in which the effective actions are located, the techniques of socialisation, the dispositions generated, and the practices adopted as a result, are provided. It is unconvincing, for example, to argue that a student left school because of a disposition to leave that reflects the objective chances students in the group into which he/she was socialised (which is to construct an explanation by an assumed global habitus). If, however, there is a detailed ethnographic description articulated within a fully developed theory, the situation is somewhat different. If it can be shown that the experience of a certain social group produces a culture that disposes those brought up within that culture to develop characteristic preferences, then actions that follow those preferences are explained to the extent, and only to the extent, that those preferences can be demonstrated to be responsible for their engagement in a practice. It is the origin of established practices that interests Bourdieu. This is a perfectly traditional explanatory scheme, in this respect, and it does not depend on the concept of habitus: one might argue, in fact, that that the concept of habitus depends on the fact that social structures, socialised dispositions and generated practices are necessarily connected in the way they are.

The circularity in 'dispositional' theories has always been their weakness. Aristotle supposed that one who had acquired a brave disposition more readily performed brave acts, and there is a certain truth in that, but there must be a criterion by which bravery can be recognised independently of the particular act it explains. Dispositional theories of action are, however, indispensable to social science. The human capacity to act clearly does depend on social knowledge and skills embodied in the form; if one likes, of a habitus, and to the extent that such dispositions are *demonstrable* they have a place in the explanation of social events. As Harré (1997: 184) is aware, 'the whole of psychology, as a discipline, hinges on whether and to what degree we should assimilate habits to causes or to monitored actions.' This elliptical remark hints at another problematic aspect of the agency–structure relation. To base a theory on the general proposition that habituated action is capable of explaining the maintenance of practices (thus effecting reproduction), just to the extent that they are maintained, is circular and begs the question of whether actions within practices can be accounted for by ordinary processes of individual decision-making based on a more or less intelligent weighing-up of resources and opportunities. As Godelier (1986: 172) points out, 'in a matrilineal society where it is the norm for a man to transmit his goods to his sister's son, people are not unaware that one *could* do otherwise and transmit them to one's own son'; moreover, if it suits their purposes, that seems to be exactly what they do. These should all be matters for empirical enquiry: if there is an organising structure, revealed by relations of homology, then there is: if the adaptive practices that maintain these structures are followed as a matter of unreflective habits, then that is how they are maintained. What is much more dubious is the theoretical assertion that this is how life is lived, particularly by illiterate peoples, peasants and the working class, and that this is almost sufficient in itself as an explanation of their practices.

Realism and Structure–Disposition–Practice Accounts

It has been argued that the SDP scheme is the general form of explanation in the sociology of education, and perhaps in sociology more generally. Several otherwise distinct formal theories take this form and construct models that require the internalisation of social structure by socialised agents to effect the mediation between structure and agency. This assertion may be illustrated, for example, by reference to one of the most widely read texts in the sociology of education. Willis (1978) argues that capitalist forms of appropriation generate a culture of working-class resistance that provides the basis for opposition to schooling: in other words, specific structural conditions give rise to dispositions of resistance, and these lead to the production of confrontational practices. This explanatory scheme is so common, in fact, that methodologists have perhaps never thought it worth the trouble of formal discussion. The issues discussed in this chapter with reference to Bourdieu are not raised uniquely by his work and, in fact, are widely shared. The explanatory scheme, which links social structures to dispositions, and dispositions to practice, might be even more fruitful were it recognised for what it is. Many of the theoretical problems raised in this chapter are attributable to errors of conceptualisation that are capable of being resolved. It will be useful to provide a discussion of what is required.

In realist sociology the concept of structure is almost always seen to be a reference to the emergent properties of social or organisations (Archer, 1995; Bunge, 1998). A summary of the realist position will not be out of place. It will demonstrate that a structure–disposition–practice account cannot be developed mechanically and, perhaps, also illustrate why ambiguity and contradiction is all but inevitable when 'structure' can be given such multiple distinct references. Social organisations have their existence as real entities by virtue of the relations and interactions between the people who constitute them. All organisations are necessarily structured by the social relations that constitute them, and as a result these entities possess certain emergent properties. Social organisations – let us say, families, factories and the schools – all possess: (i) a definitive set of social relations (parent–child, employer–employee, teacher–pupil); (ii) a definitive set of practices (nurturance, production, education); and (iii) a set of resources, which includes all cognitive and non-cognitive dispositions, necessary to those practices (love, productive skills, specialist knowledge). All these properties are structured, in as much that they are composed of elements related together in some ordered way, and so may all be recognised as 'social structures' of one sort or another. This wide reference of the term 'structure' is responsible for considerable ambiguity in sociological theory. The connection between relationships (structured by position), practices (structured by hierarchy and distribution) and disposition (structured by type and distribution) is intrinsic to the emergence of social entities. A social organisation may be recognised as the kind it is by having regard to the nature of the social relations that constitute it, the practices appropriate to those relationships, and to the dispositions of the agents necessary for the maintenance of those relations and practices. In this sense, relations (social positions), dispositions and practices occupy the same level as distinct ontological properties of social organizations; there is no linear causal linkage between them and, although the idea that positions generate dispositions and dispositions generate practices has some merit as a framework for explanation and as a heuristic for the conduct of research, it should be understood that the structure–practice–disposition scheme is also a practice–disposition–structure scheme. This conceptual reordering does more than express a 'chicken and egg' problem, but the complex matters raised by this remark cannot be enlarged any further in the context of this discussion.

The structure–disposition–practice scheme is not truly a theory, but a model to be used whenever appropriate to construct a full explanation of social events and processes. It is necessary, therefore, in order to construct a realist narrative, first, to specify structural properties in an adequate concept and devise appropriate indicators and, second, to provide an adequate account of the relation of causality between them. This work is conceptual and therefore draws on philosophy;

historical, because practices have a history; and psychological, in as much that individual dispositions have that character. To acknowledge the dispositional properties of people necessarily brings the discipline of sociology into conversation with psychology, for the methods of observation, both clinical and cultural, become essential in this scheme to sociological enquiry. Dispositions, frames of mind, 'mentalities', all the cognitive and non-cognitive habits of mind and body that sociologists and psychologists recognise in their studies of social behaviour, may be accepted as real properties of individuals. This is not to say that all purported dispositions are real: there cannot be, for example, as the discussion has noted, an actual psychological disposition to have a one-in-ten probability of entering higher education, but dispositional properties of people undoubtedly exist and various more or less adequate methods to determine their character have been established. The demonstration of psychological dispositions, in fact, must be approached through the various methods of clinical psychology, not excluding the psychoanalytic tradition, in addition to those of anthropology and interactionist sociology. The frank recognition of the relevance of personal characteristics to sociology represents, of course, a break with structuralist theory, and a rejection of Durkheim's form of realism in which 'collective representations' are supposed to influence social members without any form of psychological mediation (Durkheim and Mauss, 1963; Schmaus, 1994). All of this is presented as an argument *with* Bourdieu, rather than *against* Bourdieu, and as a way of making explicit matters that are too often left implicit in research that seeks inspiration in his sociology.

Theoretical problems, interestingly enough, are not necessarily reflected in the substantive findings of empirical studies, and researchers with divergent theoretical positions often produce comparable accounts. A theory that fails to generate concrete research into social practices – the conditions of their generation, and their local and non-local effects – with a distinctive character would appear to be redundant. It must be acknowledged, however, that the products of social research can be surprisingly independent of the specific theoretical position that generated them. A comparison of the ethnographic studies of English working-class life by Skeggs (1997) and Charlesworth (2000), for example, is instructive in this respect. The former uses 'positioned' as often as the latter uses 'being', but their insights into working-class culture are, if not interchangeable, at least more than similar. Both writers, in fact, adopt a structure–disposition–practice scheme that actually does the real work of explanation – leaving their ostensible 'theories' better regarded as conceptual lexicons – with a rather limited function. What would it matter were Alexander's (1995: 130) throughgoing critique of Bourdieu's 'failed synthesis' as 'irredeemably flawed' demonstrated to be correct? It is entirely possible that it would make little difference to the conduct of empirical research. An increasing number of sociologists have looked to Bourdieu's writing (including this author) for guidance, but it is far from self-evident that much of the research that has been generated would have been in any substantive respect different without his influence, other than for the fact that it might not have been done at all, which is admittedly a large proviso to grant. This is the gist of

Tooley and Darby's (1998) complaint against Reay's (1995) ethnographic studies of primary school classrooms: habitus to them looks like a superfluous concept having little to do with the method adopted or the interpretation offered. Nash (1999F) has commented on the naivety of such critiques, but there is something to them. It is interesting to note that Robbins (2000b) has fully appreciated one of the implications of the 'relative autonomy' between theory and research practice. His somewhat polemical assertion that it would be entirely possible to make a Bourdieusian analysis without reference to any one of the concepts that are taken as the very essence of Bourdieu's theory is intended to thrust the point home. This conclusion is entirely consistent with Bourdieu's frequent reminders that his substantive work has always been concerned with studies of practice in specific fields and should be recognised as a methodological rather than purely theoretical contribution. His account of *Distinction* (Bourdieu, 1986) as 'a synthetic account of a set of empirical investigations geared to a well-defined objective' (Bourdieu, 1990: 108) will stand as an example. The polemics directed at 'theory' are often scathing: '[W]hat is called theory is generally verbiage fit for manuals' (Bourdieu, 1993: 29), and the contempt for 'pedantic' scholastic concerns with definitions and logical consistency, in favour of development and flexibility in the context of an ever-changing social reality, undisguised. The structure–disposition–practice scheme, and perhaps the broad insight that competition for status distinction is a fairly universal feature of social life, may become naturalised, thanks largely to Bourdieu (ibid. 30), as a realist methodology of choice in sociology: '[to] be scientifically intelligent is to place oneself in a situation that generates real problems and real difficulties.'

Conclusion

There is an impatient mood in the policymaking circles of education. It seems that there is no sound reason, given the resources and technology at our disposal, why inequality of educational opportunity – inequality/difference – should prove so difficult to eliminate. The sociology of education has evidently disappointed those who expected the discipline to accumulate a body of systematic evidence that might be used in the construction of applied models of the causes of social differences in education. If there has been progress in the sociology of education in the last, let us say, 30 years, it has certainly not been of that kind. The emerging recognition of Bourdieu as a realist thinker, even if his realism is closer to that of realpolitik than to Bhaskar's critical realism (still less Bunge's version of scientific realism), should be welcomed as a progressive movement. It would be a step further to bring this realism to bear on the ambiguities, contradictions and circularities in Bourdieusian forms of argument – the status of the arbitrary and the necessary would be one place to start – that may need to be resolved if we are to attain even that level of elaborated common sense about the causes of inequality/ difference that might be all the discipline has to offer. Many sociologists appear to have realised that it will always be necessary to live with a form of elaborated common sense. This position is entirely consistent with realism, although rejected by Bourdieu whose scientism in this respect insists on the need for an epistemological break, and should not be regarded as a methodological calamity. As Sayer (1979) points out, common sense is often right in many domains of practice, and it would be foolish indeed to suppose that an idea is wrong simply because it is generally held. The formal adoption of the structure–disposition–practice explanatory scheme – which should not be mistaken for a theory – may provide an effective way to realise that attainable quality in our research. It is a scheme that can accommodate 'numbers and narratives', which is imperative if the sterile methodological opposition between qualitative and quantitative approaches is ever to be overcome, and allow a productive engagement with developments in social theory that, notwithstanding their insular dismissal by 'practical' workers in education, should rightfully be a source of inspiration to sociologists in this field who take seriously their disciplinary allegiance. What we have in the sociology of education is a crisis, not so much of theory or methodology, but of *explanation* and thinking with Bourdieu may, after all, help us to resolve that crisis realistically.

References

Alexander, J. (1995). *Fin de Siècle: Social Theory Relativism, Reduction and the Problem of Reason* (London: Verso).

Archer, M. (1995). *Social Theory: The Morphogenetic Approach* (Cambridge: Cambridge University Press).

Barley, N. (1986). *The Innocent Anthropologist: Notes from a Mud Hut* (Harmondsworth: Penguin).

Bell, D. (1990). *Husserl* (London: Routledge).

Bernstein, B. (1996). *Pedagogy, Symbolic Control and Identity: Theory, Research, Critique* (London: Taylor and Francis).

Bhaskar, R. (1993). *Dialectic: The Pulse of Freedom* (London: Verso).

Bourdieu, P. (1974). The school as a conservative force: scholastic and cultural inequalities. In Eggleston J. (ed.). *Contemporary Research in the Sociology of Education*, trans. J.C. Whitehouse (London: Methuen): 32–46.

Bourdieu, P. (1977). *Outline of a Theory of Practice*, trans. R. Nice (Cambridge: Cambridge University Press).

Bourdieu, P. (1986). *Distinction: A Social Critique of the Judgement of Taste*, trans. R. Nice (London: Routledge).

Bourdieu, P. (1990). *In Other Words: Essays towards a Reflexive Sociology*, trans. M. Adamson (Cambridge: Polity Press).

Bourdieu, P. (1991). *Language and Symbolic Power*, ed. with an intro. J.B. Thompson, trans. G. Raymond and M. Adamson (Cambridge: Polity Press).

Bourdieu, P. (1993). *Sociology in Question*, trans. R. Nice (London: Sage).

Bourdieu, P. (2000). *Pascalian Meditations*, trans. R. Nice (Cambridge: Polity Press).

Bourdieu, P. Boltanski, L. Castel, R. and Chamboredon, J.-C. (1965). *Un art moyen: essai sur les usages sociaux de la photographie*, 10th edn (Paris: Les Éditions de Minuit).

Bourdieu, P. et al. (1999). *The Weight of the World: Social Suffering in Contemporary Society*, trans. P. Parkhurst Ferguson, S. Emanuel and S.T. Waryn (Stanford, Calif.: Stanford University Press).

Bouveresse, J. (1999). Rules, dispositions, and the habitus. In R. Shusterman (ed.), *Bourdieu: A Critical Reader* (Blackwell: Oxford): 45–63.

Branson, J. and Miller, D. (1991), Pierre Bourdieu, In P. Beilharz (ed.), *Social Theory: A Guide to Central Thinkers* (Sydney: Allen and Unwin): 37–45,

Bunge, M. (1998). *Social Science under Debate: A Philosophical Perspective* (Toronto: University of Toronto Press).

Camic, C. (1986). The matter of habit, *American Journal of Sociology*, 91(5): 1039–87.

Charlesworth, S.J. (2000). *A Phenomenology of Working-class Experience* (Cambridge: Cambridge University Press).

Coleman, J.S. (1991). What constitutes education opportunity? *Oxford Review of Education*, 17(2): 155–67.

Crossby, N. (2001). Embodiment and social structure: A response to Howson and Inglis, *Sociological Review*, 49(3): 318–26.

Davis, A. and Dollard, J. (1940). *Children of Bondage: The Personality Development of Negro Youth in the Urban South* (Washington, DC: American Council of Education).

Dawe, A. (1970). The two sociologies, *British Journal of Sociology*, 21(2): 207–18.

Dewey, C. (1983). *Human Nature and Conduct: The Middle Works, 1899–1924*. vol. 14 (1922) (Carbondale and Edwardsville, Ill.: Southern Illinois University Press).

Durkheim, E. (1982). *The Rules of Sociological Method, and Selected Texts on Sociology and its Method*, ed. with an intro. S. Lukes, trans. R. Halls (New York: Free Press).

Durkheim, E. and Mauss, M. (1963 [1903]). *Primitive Classification*, trans. with an intro. R. Needham, (London: Cohen and West).

Davies, B. (1994). Durkheim and the sociology of education in Britain, *British Journal of Sociology of Education*, 15(1): 3–25.

Elias, N. (1982). *State Formation and Civilization* (Oxford: Blackwell).

Fowler, B. (1996). An introduction to Bourdieu's 'understanding', *Theory, Culture and Society*, 3(2): 1–16.

Freud, S. (1922). *The Psychopathology of Everyday Life*, trans. A. Tyson and ed. J. Strachey (New York: Norton).

Grenfell, M. and James, D., with Hodkinson, P., Reay, D. and Robbins, D.M. (1998). *Bourdieu and Education: Acts of Practical Theory* (London: Falmer Press).

Godelier, M. (1986). *The Mental and the Material: Thought, Economy and Society* (London: Verso).

Harré, R. (1997). Forward to Aristotle, *Journal for the Theory of Social Behaviour*, 27(2/3): 173–91.

Harré, R. and Madden, E.H. (1975). *Causal Powers: A Theory of Natural Necessity* (Oxford: Blackwell).

Heidegger, M. (1996). *Being and Time*, trans. J. Stambaugh (Albany, NY: State University of New York Press).

Howson, A. and Inglis, D. (2001). The body in society: Tensions inside and outside sociological thought, *Sociological Review*, 49(3): 297–317.

Husserl, E. (1970). *The Crisis of European Sciences and Transcendental Phenomenology: An Introduction to Phenomenological Philosophy*, trans. with an intro. D. Carr (Evanston: Northwestern University Press.

Lane, J.F. (2000). *Pierre Bourdieu: A Critical Introduction* (London: Pluto).

Lévi-Strauss, C. (1978). *Structural Anthropology*, vols 1 and 2 (Harmondsworth: Penguin).

LiPuma, E. (1993). Culture and the concept of culture in a theory of practice. In C. Calhoun, C.E. LiPuma, E. and Postone, M. (eds), *Bourdieu: Critical Perspectives* (Cambridge: Polity Press): 14–34

Margolis, J. (1999). Bourdieu: habitus and the logic of practice. In R. Shusterman (ed.), *Bourdieu: A Critical Reader* (Blackwell: Oxford): 64–83.

Mauss, M. (1979). *Sociology and Psychology: Essays*, trans. B. Brewster (London: Routledge & Kegan Paul).

Mead, G.H. (1934). *Mind, Self and Society*, ed. C.W. Morris (Chicago: University of Chicago Press).

Merleau-Ponty, M. (1974). From Mauss to Claude Lévi-Strauss. In M. Merleau-Ponty and J. O'Neill (eds), *Phenomenology, Language and Sociology: Selected Essays of Maurice Merleau-Ponty* (London: Heinemann): 111–22.

Nash, R. (1997). *Inequality/Difference: A Sociology of Education* (Palmerston North: ERDC Press).

Nash, R. (1999). Bourdieu, 'habitus', and educational research: Is it all worth the candle?, *British Journal of Sociology of Education*, 20(2): 175–87.

Nash, R. (2002). A realist framework for the sociology of education: Thinking with Bourdieu, *Educational Philosophy and Theory*, 34(3): 273–88.

Parsons, T. (1954). *Essays in Sociological Theory* (New York: Free Press).

Porpora, D.V. (1989). Four concepts of social structure, *Journal for the Theory of Social Behaviour*, 19(2): 195–211.

Reay, D. (1995). "'They employ cleaners to do that": Habitus in the primary school', *British Journal of Sociology of Education*, 16(3): 353–71.

Robbins, D.M. (1991). *The Work of Pierre Bourdieu: Recognising Society* (Milton Keynes: Open University Press).

Robbins, D.M. (1999). Bourdieu on language and education: Conjunction or parallel development? In M. Grenfell M. Kelly (eds), *Pierre Bourdieu:*

Language, Culture and Education: Theory into Practice (Berne: Peter Lang): 313–33.

Robbins, D.M. (2000a). *Bourdieu and Culture* (London: Sage).

Robbins, D.M. (2000b). The English intellectual field in the 1790s and the creative project of Samuel Taylor Coleridge: an application of Bourdieu's cultural analysis. In B. Fowler (ed.), *Reading Bourdieu on Society and Culture* (Oxford: Blackwell/The Sociological Review): 186–98.

Ryle, A. (1984). *The Concept of Mind* (Chicago: University of Chicago Press).

Saussere, F. de (1974). *Course in General Linguistics*, ed. C. Bally and A. Sechehaye in collaboration with A. Reidlinger, intro. J. Culler, trans. W. Baskin (London: Owen).

Sayer, D. (1979). *Marx's Method: Ideology, Science and Critique in Capital* (Brighton: Harvester).

Schmaus, W. (1994). *Durkheim's Philosophy of Science and the Sociology of Knowledge: Creating an Intellectual Niche* (Chicago: Chicago University Press).

Schutz, A. (1972). *The Phenomenology of the Social World*, trans. G. Walsh and F. Lehnert (London: Heinemann Educational Press).

Shavit, Y. and Blossfield, H.P. (eds) (1993). *Persisting Inequality: Changing Educational Attainment in Thirteen Countries*, Boulder, Col.: Westview Press.

Shilling, C. (2001). Embodiment, experience and theory: In defence of the sociological tradition, *Sociological Review*, 49(3): 327–44.

Shusterman, R. (ed.) (1998). *Bourdieu: A Critical Reader* (Oxford: Blackwell).

Skeggs, B. (1997). *Foundations of Class and Gender: Becoming Respectable* (London: Sage).

Sorokin, P. (1998). *On the Practice of Sociology* (Chicago: University of Chicago Press).

Sorokin, P.A. (1962). *Society, Culture and Personality: Their Structure and Dynamics* (New York: Cooper Square Publishing).

Tooley, J. and Darby, D. (1998). *Educational Research, A Critique: A Survey of Published Results* (London: Office of Standards in Education).

Wacquant, L. (1999). Inside 'the zone'. In P. Bourdieu et al., *The Weight of the World: Social Suffering in Contemporary Society* (Stanford, Calif.: Stanford University Press): 140–67.

Wacquant, L. (2000). Durkheim and Bourdieu: The common plinth and some of its cracks. In B. Fowler, (ed.), *Reading Bourdieu on Society and Culture* (Oxford: Blackwell/Sociological Review): 105–19.

Willis, P. (1978). *Learning to Labour: How Working-class Kids Get Working-class Jobs* (Farnborough: Saxon House).

PART 2
Early Class Differentials
in Cognition

Chapter 4

Class, 'Ability' and Attainment: A Problem for the Sociology of Education

The difference in the levels of achievement reached by the highest and lowest 10 per cent of school leavers is very substantial. If the top 10 per cent can manage *Timon of Athens*, the lowest 10 per cent would have trouble with the *Tailor of Gloucester*. In mathematics, if the top 10 per cent have mastered calculus the bottom 10 per cent would struggle to work out the area of a room 7m x 9m. The difference between the mean attainment of the highest and lowest social classes, which is to compare approximately similar proportions, is not quite so great but it is substantial enough to ensure a tenfold difference, or thereabouts, in the rates of access to university education for these groups. The sociology of education once took intelligence theory seriously (Halsey, 1958) and often deferred to psychological opinion on intelligence and its social distribution. Many accepted the conclusion that variability in class access to education was largely a reflection of intellectual differences between social classes caused by environmental and genetic processes. The authors of *Inequality* (Jencks et al., 1972), one of the most influential texts in the sociology of education, thought it necessary to include a genetic component in its causal model of attainment differences between social classes. Other sociologists, of whom Boudon (1981) is the best known, have preferred to distinguish between 'primary effects' on attainment (those that might be attributed to intelligence) and 'secondary effects' (those that remain evident between social classes when prior attainment is controlled). Boudon argues that secondary effects contribute more to inequality of educational opportunity than primary effects – the critical moment happens when students from different social origins with the same level of qualification chose different destinations – and is thus not troubled by this decision to limit sociology to the residual variance granted by psychometry. This degree of respect for the psychometric paradigm is probably not shared by most sociologists of education. The majority view may be that adopted by Bourdieu (1978: 178), who rejects the entire approach: 'I think one should purely and simply refuse to accept the problem of the biological or social foundations of "intelligence", in which psychologists have allowed themselves to be trapped'. Bernstein (1996), whose work will be extensively discussed in this chapter, has a more complex position, but his sociolinguistic thesis was received so enthusiastically in the 1960s precisely because it proposed an alternative to the dominant psychometric tradition: it was not 'intelligence' (read genetics) but 'language' (read environment) that 'made the difference'. Bernstein's theory, however, is actually a theory of cognitive socialisation, and the failure to recognise that character and extend it through connections that beg to be made, with Vygotsky, for example, represents a wasted opportunity. It is not a retrograde step to discuss Bernstein's contribution in the context of IQ theory and its demise: the sociology of education has yet to settle its accounts with intelligence theory.

The importance of IQ or 'ability' tests in multivariate models of class differences in attainment is evident in every well-designed statistical study. The best 'predictor' of educational attainment in any subject is a test of attainment in that subject at an earlier time. Tests of cognitive ability, designed as a matter of 'validity' to provide the highest possible correlation with attainment in academic subjects, are also good predictors of school success. Scores from IQ-type tests often account for some 40 per cent of the variance in academic attainment, by far the largest proportion that can be allocated. This is why IQ theory is so powerful: it appears to explain the largest proportion of the variance in academic attainment. To ignore such work, as many sociologists prefer to do, is actually misguided. The interpretation of multivariate research findings depends not so much on 'theory', and certainly not on IQ theory, but on the fact that scores on attainment tests broadly related to performance at school at one time almost always correlate with scores on similar tests at a later time. There is an area where the sociology of education has, in fact, shown itself more than willing to accept arguments based on such procedures, and the reasons for this open-mindedness are worth noting.

The average difference between the assessed intellectual level of children brought up by professional and unskilled working-class parents amounts to more than a standard deviation as they enter school and is quite dramatic (Willerman, Broman and Fiedler, 1970; Shavit and Blossfield, 1993). It may be a specific kind of intelligence, and perhaps one that is somewhat overvalued, but it has been widely recognised for a long time. The broad set of acquired cognitive skills that psychologists recognise as indications of the operations of an intelligent brain – they are extremely difficult to define and differences in cognitive performance within the normal range cannot be identified reliably with any distinctive neural property – might be expected to be peculiarly sensitive to forms of education and training. Early childhood educators are convinced that intellectual stimulation of an appropriate kind in the first few years of life can lead to the development of lasting cognitive skills (Hoskins, 1989). There is little doubt that social deprivation of a rare and pathological kind will inflict permanent damage on the linguistic and cognitive abilities of children. Recent history has provided opportunities enough to serve as a reminder that children, like those adopted from Romanian orphanages, have an impressive capacity to recover from severe social and intellectual deprivation in their early years, but this adaptive resilience should not be overstated. The most recent longitudinal study (O'Connor et al., 2000) reports that, at the age of six years, children who spent between 6 and 24 months in deprived conditions had cognitive scores almost one standard deviation lower than a sample of UK adoptees. They were probably closer to two standard deviations behind the norm reached by middle-class children of that age (these orphans were adopted mostly by middle-class families) and their future course of development does not seem promising. The analysis shows that the effects of deprivation are more or less linear: the longer the period of institutionalization, the worse the prognosis for their recovery. Children who had spent between 24 and 42 months in institutions were distinctly retarded.

Capron and Duyme's (1989) adoption research is frequently cited by critics of IQ theory, including sociologists of education, because it indicates significant environmental effects (although the research is actually compatible with a considerable degree of genetic determination) and employed a particularly interesting cross-matched method. A sample of adopted children, placed in working-class and middle-class families, was divided into two categories by the IQ scores of their biological mothers (the means being approximately 114 and 98), and tested themselves in middle childhood. The results show an interesting hierarchy. Children born to mothers with low scores and raised in working-class families achieved the lowest scores; those born to mothers with high scores and raised in middle-class homes achieved the highest scores; and the intermediate categories followed the same pattern. In summary form: low/low, 92.4; low/high, 103.6; high/low, 107.5; and high/high, 119.6. The effect of class background on intellectual development, almost certainly generated by the processes of linguistic and cognitive socialisation interrogated by Bernstein and Vygotsky, is evident in these data. To be brought up in a middle-class family adds about half a standard deviation to one's score on a test that, notwithstanding all the criticism that can justly be directed at IQ theory, assesses, in large part, those linguistic and cognitive abilities that contribute to success at school.

Intelligence and IQ Theory

It is often supposed that teachers were 'sold' intelligence theory by psychometricans. There is no doubt that the testing industry is a huge and profitable business, particularly in the United States, but this history overlooks the fact that intelligence testing began with the search for a technique with a greater degree of scientific objectivity than the informal assessments of intelligence by teachers. It is likely that teachers have always held a theory of natural intelligence. References to 'intelligence', 'understanding', 'natural capacity' and so on are plentiful well before the construction of a formal psychological theory of intelligence in the late nineteenth and early twentieth centuries. A few random illustrations in evidence of this statement may be useful. From Dickens (1964 [1867]: 200): 'I find that the natural capacity of Dombey is extremely good and that his general disposition to study may be stated in an equal ratio.' From Gissing (1968 [1880]: 229): 'Is Miss Venning an apt pupil? Extremely so. Her intelligence is admirable.' And from Gough (1979: 73): 'He was very dull at learning, which caused Mr Sugar to say very often that he had no guts in his brains.' This is actually from a diary of about 1780 and describes the response of a schoolmaster to a slow pupil: the boy who had no 'guts' in his brains would later be said to lack intelligence, but the theory is the same. Schoolmasters of this time had their own informal test of intelligence: the fifth Euclidean theorem was known as the 'bridge of asses' and boys who failed to cross it were written off as unsuited for further academic study. All the subsequent work by psychometricians never took the theory of intelligence much beyond this point. The scale became more refined, the standardisation more representative, the ranking by standard deviation units more reliable, but the fundamental assumptions of a causal relationship between intelligence and scholastic attainment were reproduced in the theory of general intelligence.

There can be no theory so thoroughly and relentlessly criticised from every perspective as the standard theory of intelligence (Flynn, 1984, 1987; Devlin et al., 1997). The periodically recycled controversy flared up most recently, generating a burst of critical activity, with the publication of *The Bell Curve*. In this notorious work, Murray and Hernnstein (1995) presented the unrevised, and unrepentant, case for intelligence as the most important cognitive property of people and the cause, above all else, of their educational attainments and overall success in life. The theory of general intelligence, *g* theory (Jensen, 1981), maintains, at least, the following propositions: (i) intelligence is a property of people (in fact of brains); (ii) intelligence is an efficient cause of scholastic learning; (iii) intelligence can be constructed as an object of measurement; (iv) intelligence is normally distributed in the population (necessarily as the result of genetic organisation); and (v) IQ tests can be distinguished, conceptually and practically, from attainment tests. A realist theory of cognition can accept the first of these propositions, and probably the second (without endorsing the concept of intelligence defined by IQ theory), but on the evidence presented should reject the others. The propositions of *g* theory are not easily proved, but they are not easily disproved either, and to that extent its research programme has some plausibility.

In this context, the use of IQ-type tests by sociologists, in studies of school effects for example, is a potential source of embarrassment, and the presence of the term 'ability' in the texts of those who reject classical intelligence theory outright seems to demand an explanation. Some explanations, however, are more adequate than others. Thrupp (1999: 12), in the context of the Smithfield project, settles the account thus: '[f]ollowing Bourdieu and others, I regard "ability" as primarily socially constructed'. The term 'socially constructed' is problematic enough in itself, but how a concept can be 'primarily' (that is partially) socially constructed defies comprehension. Whatever the phrase 'primarily socially constructed' might mean with reference to 'ability', the very fact that this formulation is so thoroughly ambiguous testifies to a characteristic lack of sociological interest in the relationship between intelligence and school attainment. The quantitative problem is actually very substantial. Those who dismiss IQ theory as incoherent are right in as much that the standard theory *is* incoherent, but they are misguided to believe that individual differences in developed cognitive skills are irrelevant to the production of educational inequality. The problem is this: even if every proposition of standard IQ theory were false, it would not matter as far as the development of effective cognitive skills in socially variable early childhood environments is concerned. The Ptolemaic theory of heavenly crystal spheres proved to be absurdly wrong, but observations and methods of calculation within that framework did enable the apparent movement of the planets to be predicted to the practical satisfaction of mariners and others for many centuries. It similarly may not matter, for certain purposes and in certain respects, that IQ theory is wrong. If the neural structures that do our thinking at that level develop differentially, with more or less permanent effect, as a result of the environments in which children are raised, that will be 'theory' enough to give assessments of developed cognitive skill a role in the explanation of social variation in access to education. In other words, it is likely that some differences in test performance and schoolwork are due to differences in relevant brain properties. The significance of this is not lost on IQ theorists. We can expect before long to be confronted with two strands of evidence that will be interpreted by IQ theorists as support for their position. First, exploration of the human genome map will almost certainly identify a number of genes regulating the development of neural properties and, consequently, associated with variance in cognitive operations. Second, developments in brain-imaging technology will probably reveal patterns of variation within the living and working brain (research into dead brains has been singularly unrewarding) causally associated with specific forms of cognition. Any such property found to be associated with variance in thinking of the kind required by IQ tests, particularly if it is observed in early infancy and proves to be relatively stable, will be taken by IQ theorists as strong support for their position. That conclusion would be unsound, but the arguments necessary to oppose it will need to move beyond mere dismissal. The point is less to provide a rationale for the continued use of IQ-type tests in sociological research in education as to argue for greater clarity with respect to the specific relevance of psychometric theory. IQ theory, in particular, is thoroughly ambivalent, not least in its discourse of 'natural' and 'inherent' ability, and should not be employed in a context of indifference to its epistemology. As 'social facts', IQ-type tests do have social effects. The practices of selection within and between schools legitimated by such instruments are a proper concern of the sociology of education. It is precisely for these reasons that it is important to examine the emergence of post-IQ discourses that legitimate contemporary 'test and measurement' practice, including psychometric revisionism and the 'competence' movement.

Post-IQ Theories of 'Ability' and 'Competence'

Standard IQ theory has actually been out of favour with the test and measurement industry for at least a couple of decades. Indeed, the vacuum created by the near abandonment of IQ theory, once part of the taken for granted background knowledge of everyone working in education, is rapidly being filled by alternative discourses. The form of operationalism adopted by contemporary psychometry should be recognised as one of these. This position, given authoritative expression by Cleary et al. (1975), makes no claim to measure a property of people, denies that intelligence is a cause of learning, and asserts that IQ tests are attainment tests of a particular kind. In this minimalist thesis it is apparently sufficient to argue that a test is a test of 'scholastic abilities' because: (i) it contains items that test 'scholastic ability' (has 'content validity'); (ii) it correlates with school attainment (has 'predictive validity'); and (iii) because an individual's test scores are much the same on repeated attempts (has 'reliability'). This series of blatant non sequiturs masquerading as argument, evidently formulated to allow educational testing to continue in an increasingly litigious environment by denying in advance by fiat all necessary implications about the object of measurement embedded in the test-texts, is thoroughly tedious. As a result of this intervention, group intelligence testing under that concept is now rarely carried out routinely by schools, but that has probably had little effect on the discourse of teachers – 'exceptionally bright', 'gifted', 'able', 'got some brains', 'not the brightest' and so on – which is readily supported by tests of 'scholastic ability' with, in fact, a less coherent justification than that form of professional common sense legitimated as 'folk psychology'.

'Competence' and 'performance' are Chomsky's rationalist concepts that refer, respectively, to the level of the organic generative mechanism (the 'grammar') and to the level of practice (Chomsky, 1976). Bourdieu (1997) and Bernstein (1999) have criticised Chomsky's concepts: but 'competence' and 'performance' stand in the same relation to each other as those other couplets, 'habitus' and 'practice', and 'code' and 'speech act'. Although it is plainly an error to construct 'competence' as an object of measurement, a considerable body of work *does* attempt to test competence, and the implications of that aspect of the competency movement should be discussed. The term 'competence' asserts a degree of freedom from the unacceptable constraints of IQ theory. Tests of 'reading competence' are simply tests of reading, usually of reading comprehension, but the half-acknowledged allegiance to the tenets of the competency movement can often be detected in the presentation and interpretation of the results of such instruments. Tests of 'competence' are not necessarily constructed – which always requires the conscious application of psychometric technique – to generate a normal curve of distribution. It is a little easier, therefore, to nominate a particular level of attainment as high or low by some criterion deemed appropriate by their constructors. It is also possible to argue that, as what has been assessed is 'competency' (necessarily through a 'performance'), their scores have no predictive 'validity'. This has the consequence, for example, that a primary school with a high proportion of new entrants tested as 'novices' in 'reading competence' should experience no necessary difficulty, because of the children's existing state of knowledge, in teaching them to read by an appropriate pedagogy or, indeed, in enabling them to become quite as 'expert', within a reasonable period of time, as those who started school nearer that level. This must truly be the sharp edge of the competency movement as far as schools are concerned: nevertheless, the movement is fuelled by an ideology subscribed to by many in education (Wylie, Thomson and Lythe, 1999).

The competency movement is particularly strong in early childhood education and has begun to influence the reception of cognitive theories. Davies (1995), taking up some hints from Bernstein, has outlined five central elements of competency as a doctrine. There is, first, the assertion that all children are inherently competent, unless afflicted by some specific organic handicap, to become proficient members of the society in which they are raised. Second, in accomplishing this developmental task, in becoming competent, they are culturally engaged in the creative process of constructing with others a valid system of meaning and practice. In this way, third, the oral language of everyday meanings merits recognition and celebration as a fully viable mode of expression. Fourth, the importance of tacit learning deserves acknowledgement against the explicit pedagogy of official socialisation, and finally, there is recognition that the hierarchical relationships of institutionalised schooling need to be reconstructed within a concept of democracy and cooperation in education. Davies points out that this set of assumptions is unsympathetic to Bernstein's project in so far as it discourages systematic analysis of the principles of control that result in children socialised into different forms of cognition. This chapter may be seen as an attempt to develop that insight.

IQ theory, with its focus on individual 'differences', its apparent support for genetic determination, its obsession with intelligence as a general property expressed by an unchanging numerical value, and its tacit concept of limits to learning, is rejected by the discourse of competency. The new paradigm, however, does not provide an adequate critique of IQ theory and is not in itself a theory of cognitive development. In fact, it is more the expression of a 'mood' than the statement of a theory, as is made obvious by the fact that Chomsky's basic conceptual distinction is muddied, if not muddled, within its discourse. All the difficult questions, all the questions about what is real, are ignored by the competency movement. The tests produced within this discourse are 'texts', like all other tests, and how the forms of thinking they demand of children have been developed, how they should be described in an appropriate concept, and whether they are more or less durable in their efficacy, although ignored by the rhetoric of competency, remain as cogent as ever. Things, of course, are as they are, and if children are socialised into effective modes of cognitive operations of a more or less durable kind, then the effects of that fact, if such it is, on educational attainment will continue unchanged. The notion of competency, however, is even less likely than IQ theory to generate the systematic research programme that might produce secure and accurate knowledge of what is the case in this area. Simon (1978: 163) once argued for a 'genuine *educational* psychology concerned to elucidate the inner mental processes involved in learning, the social and emotional aspects of learning, and the practical problems of teaching' – for only then could schools profit from the advice of psychologists – and deplored the pernicious use of mental tests, an activity which, as he realised, actually 'operates to *obscure these problems*'. What Simon expected to supersede IQ theory has yet to be developed – and is most unlikely to be developed within the ideological parameters of psychometric 'conventionalism' or of the 'competency' movement. There is a real possibility that the discourses of psychometric revisionism and competency will simply be merged in an incomprehensible muddle. A realist theory of cognitive socialisation might be better advised to reassess Bernstein's contribution to this area, perhaps in relation to Vygotsky's developmental psychology with its emphasis on language and the function of social concepts, than engage with this movement.

Bernstein's 'Sociolinguistic' Theory: Making Connections

It may be impossible to discuss Bernstein's ideas without misrepresenting them in some more or less fundamental way – it has been done often enough – but the risk must be taken if they are not to be passed over in silence. Bernstein's earliest exposition of the thesis associated with his name appeared in 1958 and the most recent, as this is written, four decades later at the very end of the century. The terms still most strongly associated with Bernstein, the 'restricted' and 'elaborated' code used to analyse speech, will provide as good an entry as any to the complexities of the theory. These terms actually replaced the earlier concept of 'public' and 'private' speech, and they in turn have been superseded by the recently introduced reference to 'horizontal' and 'vertical' forms of discourse (Bernstein, 1999; Bernstein and Solomon, 1999). The dominant explanation of social class differences in educational attainment throughout the 1950s, when Bernstein began his career in a London further education college, was IQ theory. Bernstein recognised that the working-class boys he taught were no less intelligent than middle-class boys. The working-class boys appeared to differ not so much in intelligence, at least when non-verbal tests were used, but in the contrasting forms of English they spoke. It seemed that working-class boys spoke as if the context of their speech was understood by the listener – which it usually was as they talked to each other mostly about concrete things and situations – to such an extent that when transcribed it was often difficult to tell what the conversation was about. In that sense, it was a 'private' form of communication only intelligible to those who shared a taken-for-granted sense of its context. Middle-class boys, however, seemed to use a different form of language: they employed terms that made their communication accessible outside the immediate group, and in that sense their speech seemed 'public'. In educational settings these boys were accustomed to discussing subjects requiring a more abstract form of expression than those to which the working-class boys seemed limited. As Bernstein (1971a) reflected on this insight, the terms 'elaborated' and 'restricted' were introduced to express more precisely the nature of the principle that controlled these speech forms. That ordinary word 'principle' will need to be explained because the theoretical object of Bernstein's work – the word 'code' refers to it – is actually *the principle that governs the act.*

Bernstein is fundamentally a structuralist and, unless the implications of that are grasped, it is impossible to make sense of the term 'code' in his work. The interrelated set of distinctions that Bernstein has struggled to explicate in successive formulations, but always in the familiar dichotomised forms of structuralism, concern, at one pole, the common-sense knowledge of face-to-face groups, families, peer groups and so on (which is context specific, loaded with affect, and embedded in the concrete) and, at the other pole, the theoretically informed, systematically structured and explicit knowledge of specialised groups (which is independent of context, impersonal and abstract). Code as a principle refers to an abstract property of speech, at the level of semantics and meaning, which is further conceived as a mechanism of production. It seems that there must be some kind of operational linguistic mechanism and, as it is absurdly premature to talk in neural terms (and perhaps unnecessary), the hypothetical entity that controls the production of language and speech genres common to specific groups and social contexts may be referred to as a principle of speech or meaning. Thus, 'code' is a principle that regulates the selection and organisation of speech events and which can be detected, and can necessarily only be so detected, through an analysis of speech. In a strict sense, it is solecism to refer to 'restricted' and 'elaborated' language, for it is the *code* that has those properties, and the features of speech that serve to identify the principle that generated them are, equally, not to be regarded as instances of 'restricted' or 'elaborated' speech. At the same time, it is evidently necessary for the purposes of empirical research into speech and meaning to devise coding systems by which individual speech acts can be allocated to one category or another. This operationalisation, unavoidable if any empirical research is to be conducted, blurs the reference of code, and in many applications the concept plainly is used to designate properties of speech, as much as to the hypothetical code that generates it.

Bernstein argues that the 'elaborated' code generates a language of social power whereas the 'restricted' code generates a language of subordination. (This is one of those oversimplifications that invite refutation, but having started, we might as well finish.) The class that controls capital, labour and culture, the financial, human and symbolic resources that underpin industrial capitalism, must necessarily employ a discourse with the capacity to express generalised and abstract conceptions. The class without control of capital, which sells its labour power and is required to submit to the discourse of power, is more or less limited, by virtue of these relationships, and in contexts dominated by them, to more limited forms of expression. The discourse of the middle-class transcends the local context and is the effective means of symbolic control. The educational system, which effectively reproduces the structures of social power through pedagogic action, is implicated organically in that process by the production of students socialised into particular discursive forms. The relations that control access to areas of discourse, in curriculum, pedagogy and evaluation, have been discussed by Bernstein (1971b) in papers no less influential than his work on language. The school is, and must be, concerned with the transmission of a universal knowledge within forms of pedagogic discourse characterised by an elaborated code. A school that failed to teach its students the necessarily abstract concepts of language and mathematics would simply not be a school in the modern sense at all. As a result of this, however, the school confers an implicit, and very substantial, privilege on those students who enter school with a ready command of the forms of meaning it transmits. It is a potent and influential theory. By the age of five, at least, children have become sensitised by the differential linguistic and cognitive socialisation they have experienced, so that, whereas some are able recognise and respond to the discourse of school in ways that facilitate their learning, meet with institutional reward and promote the emergence of a positive self-concept, others are left in a rather different situation.

A number of theoretical objections have been directed at Bernstein's account of the origin of social differences in education. The structuralist epistemology on which the concept of code depends (which is nowhere adequately discussed in his work) is a constant source of difficulty. Many critics fail to understand that code is not a property of speech at all. The conceptual distinction Bernstein recognises in speech genres, the elements of the 'restricted' and 'elaborated' code, has frequently been rejected. It is argued that the distinction fails to capture anything of particular significance about speech, rests on a superficial analysis of relatively trivial surface-level features of language, and is merely another variant of deficit theory. This particular criticism, 'vociferously and tediously debated in education since the 1960s' (Bernstein, 1995: 402), not surprisingly, attracts a sharp response. These critics often argue, further, that working-class and middle-class speech do not differ so markedly as the theory implies, at least to any extent that is necessarily important to their capacity to succeed at school, and point out that any speech genre can be acquired, more or less readily, as the social context demands, by any one motivated to do so. There is, in this view, no reason to accept that working-class students, as result of socialisation into specific forms of thought, acquire a set of cognitive dispositions with a lasting causal effect on their capacity to succeed at school (Edwards, 1987). A further objection is directed at the argument that the school must necessarily be concerned with the transmission of knowledge within the 'elaborated' code. The power relations, ultimately those of capital and patriarchy, that control the educational system, determine what is taught in school in such a way that the entire curriculum is transparently constructed to reflect the theory/practice division of mental and manual labour, and thus serve the interests of the dominant classes. Many working-class school students, at least half-aware of this through their insertion into a specific culture of resistance, consequently reject schooling and the values it upholds, and are to that extent right to do so. There is a certain irony here in that, although this critique can actually be expressed in Bernstein's concepts, it is nevertheless often directed against his position (Walkerdine and Lucy, 1989). The core difference lies in the fact that Bernstein accepts that schools cannot do other than transmit knowledge within an elaborated code. This is rejected by many critics on what is basically an argument about the arbitrary and relativist nature of knowledge, which does not accept that the school curriculum should give any 'privilege' to concepts specialised for abstraction and systematic analysis. In this view, the massive failure experienced by working-class students as a group is created within and by the school system, with its finally arbitrary preference for 'middle-class' modes of thinking, and whatever differences might be observed in the language use of children with different social origins should be understood as relatively superficial attributes, themselves the result of economic and social disadvantage and privilege, with no necessary consequences for school learning provided only that appropriate forms of pedagogy, curriculum and pedagogy are set in place (Whitty and Young, 1976). This is a comprehensive set of criticisms, and whether Bernstein has responded to them in an entirely satisfactory manner is open to doubt, but the issues they raise need to be discussed.

The important questions, then, are these:

- Is the speech of working-class and middle-class children characterised by features included in Bernstein's concept of 'elaborated' and 'restricted' code?
- Does the school demonstrate a preference for 'elaborated' forms of discourse?
- Is that preference principled and necessary, being based on the forms of knowledge intrinsic to intellectual control, or does it merely reflect an arbitrary bias for 'middle-class' forms of knowledge?
- If the answers to the first three questions suggest that Bernstein's theory is broadly correct, how can it be shown that the relative failure of working-class school students has this cause and to what extent?

The evidence that the speech of working-class and middle-class children (and of their mothers) differs in ways caught by Bernstein's central concept is reasonably satisfactory. Studies of speech samples analysed by an appropriate technique reveal differences rather less emphatic than implied by the stark association middle-class/elaborated and working-class/restricted, but these are ideal type distinctions, and Bernstein accepts the point. These empirical questions continue to be the focus of a programme of research into linguistic and cognitive socialisation maintained across the world, predominantly by Bernstein's students, within his theoretical framework (Morais, Fontinhas and Neve, 1993). Studies of teachers' classroom speech often find it to have the characteristics of a 'restricted' rather than an 'elaborated' code, but that is not really the point; what matters is whether the school's curriculum, even more than its modes of pedagogy and evaluation, is structured in such a way that access to its meanings is more or less confined to those who have mastered the 'elaborated' code. Bernstein (1994) has demonstrated with one of his critic's own data that the elaborated character of pedagogic discourse in schools can generally be recognised. There is no real dispute that school knowledge is structured in this way, even if the concept used by Bernstein is rejected, and the issue is, therefore, whether the school's demonstrated preference for such forms of discourse is principled and necessary, being based on the forms of knowledge intrinsic to intellectual control, or merely the reflection of an arbitrary bias for 'middle-class' forms of knowledge. Hasan (1996: 409), whose well-conducted studies of language genres have broadly substantiated the thesis on class-associated speech forms, has commented directly on these deeply contested issues. In the first place, she found clear evidence that the practices of teachers do seem to be guided by the principles Bernstein has articulated:

> I believe that the sorts of perspectives typically needed for knowledge production are taught throughout schooling but they are taught invisibly. In analysing the language of the classroom in a picture-reading session in the first year of schooling in some suburban schools in Australia, I found … that as early as the very first year of schooling, teachers already insisted on objective evidence; they rejected answers that were not explicitly supported by some evidence in the picture. They also rejected conclusions that were not logical; to be received with approval, conclusions had to be implicated in their reasoning; and the responses that the teachers favoured highly were those presented as universal generalisations.

This empirical evidence should be accepted: teachers *do* behave like this and they do so because they hold a theory of education that is basically correct. School knowledge has that character virtue of the fact that only such forms of knowledge will give access to the structures of the real world.

Finally, is it their socialisation into differentiated forms of discourse, broadly conceptualised in these terms, that accounts for the relative underachievement of working-class students and the relative overachievement of middle-class students? It would really be something to know that children acquire specific and lasting cognitive schemes as a result of literate socialisation practices. There is a great deal of work to be done before the conclusion that the idea is entirely sound can be reached. Nevertheless, there is something basically right about Bernstein's account of social class and educational attainment. A realist should accept that there are class-associated socialisation practices of the kind he describes; they do produce children differentiated by cognitive and linguistic capabilities; and the school has necessarily to recognise those capabilities in its curriculum, pedagogy and forms of evaluation. The theory of cognitive socialisation developed by Bernstein could with advantage be discussed within the context of other theories and its potential to provide an explanation of class-differentiated educational attainment examined. One theory with clear similarities to Bernstein's should certainly be included in this comparative analysis: Vygotsky's account of cognitive development, in which the higher mental functions are acquired through a specifically social process based on language. The basic question is this: In what ways are children able to think as a result of the socialisation they receive?

Vygotsky and Bernstein approach that question in somewhat similar ways, even though contributing to different theoretical disciplines. Vygotsky's higher-order thinking, the abstract, logical, sequential thought recognised by the school, relies on specific cognitive tools with a social, and therefore historically and culturally variable, distribution. Bernstein is precisely concerned with the class distribution of forms of speech and thought generated by class-differentiated socialisation practices. The operations recognised by Vygotsky as belonging to the higher mental functions are, moreover, recognisably similar to those captured by Bernstein's principle 'elaborated' and 'restricted'. It may be because Bernstein's work is situated within the tradition of sociolinguistics that these connections have not been given the attention they merit. In fact, notwithstanding the recognition many leading sociolinguists, including Halliday (1976) and Hasan, have paid to Bernstein, the core interest of his work is not inherently linguistic at all. The original impetus of the theory, in effect, was to show that differences in verbal intelligence were generated by class-specific modes of socialisation and reflected in distinctive speech characteristics. Neither Bernstein nor Vygotsky (and still less Bourdieu) have any formal interest in what is known as the psychology of individual differences. If children differ in their intelligence, as the result of a process of genetic maturation within a social environment, then that will account in no small degree for variance in educational attainment. This, of course, is IQ theory and it has no attractions for those whose work is being considered here. Despite the risks, however, IQ theory forces the crucial issue to the forefront of attention. The hypothesis that children acquire durable modes of thinking as a result of their early childhood linguistic and cognitive socialisation is consistent with IQ theory and it may even be for that reason that the implications of the core theses of cognitive development implicit in work outside that tradition, and developed in opposition to it, have been discussed with so much circumspection. It is extremely important to place these questions at the centre of a theory of linguistic and cognitive development, which attempts to explain the origin of individual and social differences by reference to socialisation practices.

It is hardly surprising that Bernstein should decline to engage with IQ theory. There are, however, repeated hints in his writings that children who have experienced the literate socialisation practices characteristic of the middle-class family display forms of language and cognition recognised by teachers and IQ tests alike as signs of intelligence. In a collaborative work, Brandis and Bernstein (1974: 70), this link was made explicit in a comment with particular significance:

> Teachers' ratings and IQ tests are substitutable, not just as measures of whatever it is they are measuring, but as potential selective devices in the educational system. If there were a political controversy about modes of selection at infant-school level, then the classic 'tests versus teachers' argument would appear. The findings in this paper suggest that the winner of the great debate would have little or no substantive effect on the selection of children, since both 'alternatives' are overwhelmingly oriented to the same dimension, a widespread and consistent notion of intelligence which is inextricably part of the educational system at its earliest stages.

Again, to put the issue in the plainest terms, the argument is that children who experience literate forms of socialisation in early childhood are able to demonstrate, in Vygotsky's terms, 'higher mental functions', and in Bernstein's, an 'elaborated semiotic code', and as a result make better progress at school than those who do not. This is not necessarily inconsistent with the established fact that the mean IQ scores of middle-class children are higher than those of working-class children (Silva and Stanton, 1996). The association could hardly be otherwise, for the items included in the Stanford–Binet test require precisely the forms of thought recognised by Vygotsky and Bernstein as indicative of the higher mental processing and 'elaborated' thought necessary to the mastery of school knowledge.

Conclusion

There is in this respect an incoherent argument at the heart of the sociology of education. It seems to be acceptable to use tests of 'ability' and evidence generated by them whenever it is convenient to do so, including 'environmentalist' accounts of cognitive development in different social classes in so far as they refute 'genetic' interpretations. An argument scorned as 'deficit' theory in one context is immediately put to work in the service of another. It seems acceptable to regard the concept of 'ability' as (primarily!) socially constructed, while at the same time acknowledging that any number of material factors (oxygen deprivation at birth, foetal alcoholism, environmental pollution, etc.) will inhibit intellectual development with more or less permanent effects on school attainment. The obvious inadequacies of IQ theory are taken as sufficient ground to dismiss any mention of the concept without regard for the fact that IQ theory probably has no relevance to the substantive issue under investigation. The role sociologists have played in undermining IQ theory is not a matter of shame – on the contrary – but it is our responsibility, as much as that of anyone else, to encourage sound research into the sociology of cognitive development. Sociologists of education certainly have a responsibility to take the question of intelligence and ability seriously as a cause of social differences in educational attainment.

If the outline of cognitive development sketched in this account is broadly correct, then we have some idea of how relevant differences in cognitive ability are created, and how they might generate differences in school learning. As for Bernstein, the term 'code', which has caused so much misunderstanding, is not essential to the study of language and cognition. In constructing what is essentially a theory of cognitive socialisation as a theory of sociolinguistics Bernstein has not spared himself the sharp criticism of those who regard his work as a 'deficit' theory. If it is a theory of language then – the presumption is readily made – pedagogic intervention becomes largely a matter of effecting a linguistic shift in the arbitrary discourse of the school. After all, in principle, with sufficient motivation and instruction, any one can learn any language, and certainly a specific genre within a particular natural language, but one cannot, even in principle, teach calculus to a student whose higher mental functions – the operative mental schemes that permit abstraction and symbolic manipulation – have first not been developed to the necessary level, even though it is not easy to know what that level is or how to specify it in concrete terms. What is required is: (i) a concept that accurately defines the features of speech and thought in the dimension of interest; (ii) an account of how those features are transmitted by socialisation processes; and (iii) how they are implicated as a cause of specific forms of learning. Bernstein's structuralism has allowed him to link these components of his theory in the concept of 'code'. The task of conceptual development demands a particular form of intellectual rigour – it is a difficult theoretical and empirical labour and, in as much as the idea of the 'principle' has been useful to Bernstein, there is no reason why it should be discarded – but it may also be important to accept that dichotomised concepts do not necessarily describe the features of the world as they are. When as sociologists we find it expedient to use the concept of 'ability' in our explanatory accounts and 'ability' tests in our research, we would be wise to acknowledge the theoretical ontogeny of the concept and to challenge rather than contribute to its ambiguities and contradictions.

References

Bernstein, B. (1971a). *Class, Codes and Control, Vol. 1: Theoretical Studies towards a Sociology of Language and Socialization* (London: Routledge & Kegan Paul).

Bernstein, B. (1971b). On the classification and framing of educational knowledge. In M.F.D. Young, (ed.), *Knowledge and Control: New Directions for the Sociology of Education* (London: Collier–Macmillan): 47–69.

Bernstein, B. (1994). Edwards and his language codes: Response to A.D. Edwards, 'Language codes and classroom practice', *Oxford Review of Education*, 20(2): 173–82.

Bernstein, B. (1995). A response. In A.R. Sadovnik (ed.), *Knowledge and Pedagogy: The Sociology of Basil Bernstein* (Norwood, NJ: Ablex): 165–218

Bernstein, B. (1996). *Pedagogy, Symbolic Control and Identity: Theory, Research, Critique* (London: Taylor and Francis).

Bernstein, B. (1999). Vertical and horizontal discourse: An essay, *British Journal of Sociology of Education*, 20(2): 157–73.

Bernstein, B. and Solomon, J. (1999). Pedagogy, identity and the contribution of a theory of symbolic control: Basil Bernstein questioned by Joseph Solomon, *British Journal of Sociology of Education*, 20(2): 265–79.

Boudon, R. (1981). *The Logic of Social Action: An Introduction to Sociological Analysis* (London: Routledge & Kegan Paul).

Brandis, W. and Bernstein, B. (1974). *Selection and Control: Teachers' Ratings of Children in the Infant School* (London: Routledge & Kegan Paul).

Capron, C. and Duyme, M. (1989). Assessment of the effects of socio-economic status on IQ in a full cross-fostering study, *Nature*, 340: 552–4.

Chomsky, N. (1976). *Reflections on Language* (London: Temple Smith).

Cleary, T.A., Humphreys, L.G., Kendrick, S.A. and Wesman, A. (1975). Educational uses of tests with disadvantaged students, *American Psychologist*, 30(1): 15–41.

Davies, B. (1995). Acquiring the means of acquisition: Is pedagogic practice a crucial variable?, *International Studies in Sociology of Education*, 5(2), 189–202.

Devlin, B., Fienberg, S., Resnick, D.P. and Roeder, K. (eds) (1997). *Intelligence, Genes, and Success: Scientists Respond to 'The Bell Curve'* (New York: Springer).

Dickens, C. (1964). *Dombey and Son* (New York: Signet, New American Library).

Flynn, J.R. (1984). Banishing the spectre of meritocracy, *Bulletin of the British Psychological Society*, 37: 256–9.

Flynn, J.R. (1987). Massive gains in 14 nations: What IQ tests really measure, *Psychological Bulletin*, 101(2): 171–91.

Gissing, G. (1968). *Workers in the Dawn*, vol. 3 (New York: AMS Press).

Gough, R. (1979). *The History of Myddle* (Sussex: Caliban Books).

Halliday, M.A.K. (1976). *System and Function in Language: Selected Papers* (Oxford: Oxford University Press).

Halsey, A.H. (1958). Genetics, social structure and intelligence, *British Journal of Sociology*, 20: 15–28.

Hasan, R. (1996). Literacy, everyday talk, and society. In R. Hasan and G. Williams (eds), *Literacy in Society* (London: Longman): 377–424

Hoskins, R. (1989). Beyond metaphor: the efficacy of early childhood education, *American Psychologist*, 44: 274–82.

Jencks, C., Smith, M., Acland, H., Bane, M.J., Cohen, D., Gintis, H., Heyns, B. and Michelson, S. (1972). *Inequality: A Reassessment of the Effect of Family and Schooling in America* (Harmondsworth: Penguin).

Jensen, A.R. (1981). *Straight Talk about Mental Tests* (New York: Free Press).

Morais, A.M., Fontinhas, F. and Neve, I.P. (1993). Recognition and realization rules in acquiring school, *British Journal of Sociology of Education*, 64(1): 48–63.

Murray, C. and Hernnstein, R.J. (1994). *The Bell Curve: Intelligence and Class Structure in American Life* (New York: Free Press).

O'Connor, T.G., Rutter, M., Beckett, C., Keaveney, L., Kreppner, J.M. and the English and Romanian Adoptees Study Team (2000). The effects of global severe privation on cognitive competence: Extension and longitudinal follow-up, *Child Development*, 71(2): 376–90.

Shavit, Y. and Blossfield, H.P. (1993). *Persisting Inequality: Changing Educational Attainment in Thirteen Countries* (Boulder, Col.: Westview Press).

Silva, P. and Stanton, W.R. (eds) (1996). *From Child to Adult: The Dunedin Multidisciplinary Health and Development Study* (Oxford: Oxford University Press).

Simon, B. (1978). *Intelligence, Psychology and Education* (London: Lawrence and Wishart).

Thrupp, M. (1999). *Schools Making a Difference: Let's Be Realistic! School Mix, School Effectiveness and the Social Limits of Reform* (Buckingham: Open University Press).

Vygotsky, L. (1994). *The Vygotsky Reader*, ed. R. Van der Veer and J. Valsiner (Oxford: Blackwell).

Walkerdine, V. and Lucy, H. (1989). *Democracy in the Kitchen: Regulating Mothers and Socialising Daughters* (London: Virago).

Whitty, G. and Young, M.D.F. (eds). (1976). *Society, State and Schooling* (Lewes: Falmer).

Willerman, l., Broman, S.H. and Fielder, M. (1970). Infant development, pre-school IQ, and social class, *Child Development*, 41(1): 69–77.

Wylie, C., Thompson, J. and Lythe, C. (1999). *Competent Children at 8: Families, Early Childhood Education and Schools*, Report to the Ministry of Education (Wellington: New Zealand Ministry of Education).

Chapter 5

Cognitive Habitus and Collective Intelligence: Concepts for the Explanation of Inequality of Educational Opportunity

Introduction

Intelligence is a problem for educational policy. The classical IQ concept – Burt (1962) insisted that 'intelligence' referred to an innate, general, cognitive ability – may have given way to more cautious formulations, but the central ideas seem those educational practices that seem to ensure the classed distribution of attainment in schools are maintained with complete efficacy despite there now being no more solid a basis to support them than a taken-for-granted professional 'folk' theory of 'ability'. Test and measurement psychology officially abandoned the core tenets of IQ theory a generation ago in a response necessitated by often successful challenges to its bolder claims mounted in the US courts by representatives of disadvantaged ethnic minorities (Cleary et al., 1975). Contemporary scholastic tests are marketed to provide assessments of learned abilities, disavow any predictive utility and are darkly ambiguous about the causal relationship between tested abilities and subsequent educational attainment (Lidz, 2003). It is a curious fact that conventional 'scholastic ability' tests continue to bear a striking relationship to traditional IQ tests while the psychological theory that supports the official discourse of test marketing has been so thoroughly expurgated. It is as if test users in schools act without reference to this new-fangled theory, perhaps rightly conferring on it the status of a confession made under duress, while retaining under plain covers the original and true doctrine as a practical guide to action. The concept of an innate, general, intelligence may have been all but driven out of educational discourse, if not entirely from that of psychology where g theory has its unrepentant defenders (Murray and Hernnstein, 1994), but this expulsion has had, it seems, little if any effect on teachers who, in Gillborn and Youdell's view, yet adhere so strongly to the classical position that the patterns of class inequality once generated by IQ theory are replicated in exact degree by an informal theory of 'ability'. Whether this explanation of the generation of social disparities in educational attainment is convincing or not is, at this stage, beside the point, but it draws emphatic attention to the potency attributed to formal and informal theories of intelligence and ability in sociological accounts of the causes of inequality of educational opportunity.

Is there an answer to this fundamental question for the sociology of education? Is there any merit, for example, in attempting to reinstate, in an up-to-date and revised version, the concept of *intelligence* to the discourse of radical education policy? This is the expressed intention behind Brown and Lauder's (2000) appeal to replace the concept of *personal intelligence* with that of *collective intelligence*. These critics, influential in policy-directed sociology of education, advance a position that surely merits discussion. Let us replace the tired notion of individual ability, they reason, with the fresh idea of a collective capacity to solve joint social problems. What is important in the progressive movement for educational equality, they argue, is the creation of environmental conditions – political, economic and cultural – in which the collective intelligence of organised communities can emerge and flourish. However, can teachers who cling so illegitimately to their informal concept of 'ability' be expected to abandon it for the concept of collective intelligence? If teachers believe that individual variation in intellectual capacities is a major cause of individual and social differences in scholastic attainment, might that not be because this view more accurately describes the state of the world? This possibility, however, is difficult to theorise without the concepts of a declining and non-approved psychological paradigm. If there is anything in this view – and it will be advanced as a serious hypothesis – then the concept of collective intelligence may need to co-exist with the concept of cognitive habitus (Nash, 2003a). We should pay attention to collective intelligence, certainly in Dewey's sense, and understand that the investigation of cognitive habitus will actually require close attention to the environment of practices in which the structures of cognitive habitus are developed: there is no necessary contradiction in a discourse characterised by the successful reference of both concepts.

Those involved in educational policy analysis understand that the modes of enquiry necessary to solve practical problems do not present themselves within the confines of disciplinary boundaries. One problem demands economic and political research, another historical and cultural study, and yet another calls for philosophical and conceptual enquiry. The problem of intelligence falls into the latter category. The concepts of potential, skill and ability must be distinguished; what can be measured must be specified; and what constitutes an explanation must be agreed. Then we must be clear about whether the concepts of collective intelligence and cognitive habitus make successful reference to actual entities, and decide what are the most appropriate methods for their study. All this sounds more like a philosophical investigation than anything else, and so it is, but it is an investigation carried out for the purposes of educational policy analysis. Brown and Lauder reintroduce the concept of collective intelligence, it should be noted, in support of their demand for a caregivers' wage, which they regard as a crucial policy instrument in the struggle for equality of educational opportunity. There will be no successful policy decision-making in this area until the concepts of the debate are clarified.

Collective Intelligence

Brown and Lauder suggest that Dewey's (1937) concept of collective intelligence offers a solution to the substantial problems at stake in the explanation of social disparities in education. Their aim is to situate the concept of collective intelligence in the discourse of progressive education as a bid to reclaim 'intelligence', a term deeply embedded in common sense, for the language of critical pedagogy. In the discourse of teachers, 'intelligence' will no longer refer to the 'golden egg' of individual IQ, but to a capacity created by a community able to apply its organised cognitive resources to the solution of shared problems. Is it the case that, as a consequence of differences in cognitive habitus formed in environments with a different emphasis on literacy, children are equipped, by virtue of their developed problem-solving skills, with durable dispositions to acquire the necessary literate knowledge of the school? If this is the real situation, then it will be necessary to possess a theoretical and conceptual framework that will allow it to be studied by the established methods of scientific research (Bhaskar, 1993).

'Intelligence' has a central place in Dewey's philosophy. To act intelligently is to select means appropriate to one's chosen ends, to reflect on the consequences of one's projected actions, and to conduct oneself in accordance with the standards of reason. In Dewey's political philosophy, the conditions of intelligent action, and, thus, those in which native powers are developed, are constituted by an environment of positive freedom in a democratic society where opportunities for economic and cultural advancement are open to all: 'the basic freedom is that of freedom of mind and of whatever degree of action and experience is necessary to produce freedom of intelligence' (Ratner, 1939: 404). Dewey's 'social intelligence' was a way of talking about what a community is capable of achieving given its state of economic and political development. The 'method of intelligence' is simply the scientific method, and the growth and application of these critical techniques within a society exemplifies 'collective intelligence'. When Brown and Lauder reject the conventional definition of intelligence as one 'dominated by the precepts of scientific reason' (Brown and Lauder, 2000: 1765), and offer this as a reason for adopting collective intelligence in its place, they break with Dewey in this respect, for his own concept of collective intelligence is tied to a more or less conventional notion of modern science. Dewey actually regards the growth of collective intelligence as synonymous with the success of the project of civilisation, reason and rationality: 'organized intelligence', he writes, 'has made an advance that is truly surprising when we consider the short time in which it has functioned' (Ratner, 1939: 358). In this vein, Dewey recognises that a society based on an advanced technology owes its existence to those few pioneers endowed with the extraordinary capacities required to design the new science-based machines – steam engines, dynamos, telephones and so on – but insists that, as such devices become the everyday tools of modern life, they greatly increase capability for intelligent action by everyone in the community. In this transformed environment, moreover, a higher level of cooperative intelligence, in which new opportunities for initiative and enterprise and the effective release of intelligence are possible, is thereby constituted.

Dewey is one of the most influential of all philosophers of education. The implications of his thought were, moreover, supported by a personal engagement with school education with few modern parallels. Dewey never doubted that children came into the world with different innate potential to develop their intellectual capacities. He firmly insisted, in direct contradiction to the biological determinism propounded by many IQ theorists, that these capacities were not so different as to require any modification to his bold vision of a United States governed by the informed participation of a thoroughgoing democratic polity, but, at the same time, he accepted as a given fact that individual capacities for the exercise of intelligence were shaped by widely variable social and cultural environments. Even when Dewey adopted a behaviourist usage, defining intelligence as a property of action rather than the actor, he did not thereby deny the presence of an effective disposition for cognitive thought. This behaviourist definition of intelligence was, in fact, standard in psychometric theory for many decades (Anastasi, 1968) and had no discernable effect on the practical interpretation given to IQ scores.

It is possible to argue, with considerable justification, that Dewey accepted many of the core propositions of classical IQ theory. He certainly accepted that people were not cloned with respect to their native endowments: '[n]obody can take the principle of consideration of native powers into account without being struck by the fact that these powers differ in different individuals' (Dewey, 1937: 135). And he endorsed, moreover, the recognition given by psychologists and teachers to the importance of the initial years of development: 'the ways in which the tendencies of early childhood are treated fix fundamental dispositions and condition the turn taken by powers that show themselves later' (ibid. 136). From all this, Dewey drew a tough-minded conclusion that seemed to follow: educators, he thought, 'must take the being as he is; that a particular individual has just such and such an equipment of native activities is a basic fact' (ibid. 86), and conceded that, native powers 'furnish the initiating and limiting forces in all education' (ibid. 133). A teacher who failed to recognise this and who fell into the 'too prevalent habit of trying to make by instruction something out of an individual which he is not naturally fitted to become' (ibid. 87) would simply waste energy and generate irritation. It was, thus, clear to Dewey, always of course concerned to emphasise the importance of development in optimal pedagogic environments, that, 'while a careful study of the native aptitudes and deficiencies of an individual is always a preliminary necessity, the subsequent and important step is to furnish an environment which will adequately function whatever activities are present' (ibid. 87). In short, Dewey held that our non-identical native endowments set limits to what each of us as individuals can achieve, and that teachers must take their students as they are and not feel obliged to dissipate their energies in attempting to bring them to a level they cannot reach. That Dewey also argued that knowledge of intelligence for the purposes of comparison is irrelevant to the teacher – '[h]ow one person's abilities compare in quantity with those of another is none of the teacher's business' (ibid. 203) – should be noted as no more than an apparent inconsistency in his position. To form a sound professional assessment of a student's capabilities does not logically require comparison with others.

Dewey's seemingly uncomplicated style often conceals deeply calculated philosophical positions. It would be an error to suggest that his construction of 'intelligence' was without its subtleties. As Dewey coins one term after another, apparently introducing synonyms for the sake of stylistic variation, 'collective intelligence', 'corporate intelligence', 'experimental intelligence', 'organized intelligence', 'social intelligence' and 'scientific intelligence', as sentence follows sentence, they might readily be taken to have the same reference, and this allows the senses in which 'intelligence' denotes both a human capacity and a body of knowledge to shift and blur in such a way that it is sometimes impossible to determine what precise meaning should be taken from a passage. The cumulative effect of this characteristic textual practice is, in fact, to construct a neo-Durkheimian concept (are we meant to hear an echo of *conscience collective*?) with a meaning that, never being made explicit, invites and tends to receive only minimal critical resistance. But this unstable duality cannot be maintained and when forced to the point Dewey must acknowledge that it is with 'the control of collective intelligence, operating through the release of individual powers and capabilities' (Dewey, 1968: 109), that social and educational policy is necessarily concerned. Dewey's concept of social or collective intelligence cannot be used, notwithstanding Brown and Lauder, in order to displace the fundamental idea that the capacity for intelligent action is developed differentially in classed environments.

Dewey is a sophisticated philosopher: his theory of habit has many similarities to Bourdieu's theory of practice, and he may be included among those who have thought most deeply about the nature of cognitive habitus. The social environment produces in individuals, he argued, 'a certain system of behaviour, a certain disposition of action' (Dewey, 1937: 13). This is a disposition, needless to say, to behave with intelligence, and it is not impossible to behave intelligently without having the capacity to do so.

Potential, Skill and Ability: Three Essential Concepts

What is the point of attempting to assert that people can act intelligently without being intelligent? This awkward manoeuvre is actually over-motivated in the IQ debate. Behaviourists dislike references to mental entities, particularly those superfluous 'ghosts in the machine' that haunt the explanatory accounts of human conduct; sociologists believe they can do without the individualist concepts of a rival discipline; and critics of the standard concept of intelligence are understandably attracted to the possibility of eliminating the term as a reference to a measured personal quality and limiting it to the description of certain kinds of behaviour. The term 'disposition', which is used in the definition of habitus, was favoured by neo-behaviourist analytical philosophy (Ryle, 1963) because it seemed to support an argument that intelligence was a description of behaviour rather than a property of the individual. But the attempt to assert that people are disposed to act intelligently, in given circumstances, without it being necessary to state that they possess a faculty of 'intelligence', was not intended to refute the observation that people are intelligent beings. In a realist theory of science a concept has no place in a causal explanation unless it has an actual reference: and the most successful reference of 'intelligence' is, in fact, to a property of the brain. There is, however, no useful pedagogy to be conducted at the level of neural mechanisms, and the discussion of modes of thought and speech developed by Bernstein (1996) and Vygotsky (1994) may still offer the most productive model for the conceptualisation of educability and social differences.

The discussion of human capabilities requires three distinct concepts. First, there is the concept of potential to develop and learn. An infant has the potential to learn to talk: it just needs to be exposed to speakers of a natural language. Second, there is the concept of skill as a state of being that enables one to perform, as an efficient property of the body or one of its constituent organs, whatever action demonstrates its exercise. And, third, there is the concept of ability as the capacity to carry out certain skilled actions. Reading is a skill that confers the ability to read, to learn from books, and so on. A *potential* is an inherent condition of a thing to develop in accordance with its nature; a *skill* is an actual state of a living organism; and *abilities* are conferred by skills exercised in appropriate contexts. It is very difficult to find a discussion that formally acknowledges these concepts. There is no consistency in psychology, or in common usage, about the concepts employed in the 'ability' debate. The three concepts outlined are not always distinguished, and when they are the terms used to refer to them are not necessarily those adopted here. 'Potential', 'skill' and 'ability' can all be used interchangeably, sometimes even in a single text, with no precise meaning. 'Capacity' sometimes means same as 'potential'; 'skill' has gained a bewildering number of synonyms ('faculty', 'factor', 'function', 'module', 'operator', 'processes', 'scheme' and 'tool' are just a few); and 'ability' attaches itself promiscuously to whatever concept is paying the bill. These terms sometimes refer to *organs* that perform the function of thought and are, therefore, the effective cause of those forms of thought, and sometimes to a *skill*, and as the distinction between properties of an implied generative organ and properties of a skilled performance is unclear the object of measurement is to that extent left unspecified.

This analysis drives a wedge between 'skill' and 'ability' that may need to be justified. When typists exercise their skill they demonstrate their ability to type, but, if 'skill' is to refer to a durable state of the body that confers some ability, the reference of 'skill' and 'ability' are not the same. There are not, however, two entities – a 'skill' and an 'ability' – but simply the state of the body that confers the ability to behave in a certain way. This is not, incidentally, the distinction between competence and performance. In Chomsky's usage, 'competence' refers to an entity with the properties of an organ (language acquisition device) and 'performance' refers to an activity (speaking in a grammatically formed language) generated as a result of learning made possible by such a device. A skill is not an organ, and the abilities conferred by skills are not performances. It may be worth noting in this context, moreover, that a skill is not to be confused with whatever tool or instrument might be necessary to its exercise. All skills require some instruments and the body is always one of them: typists use their fingers as well as a keyboard as tools, and it is entirely meaningful, indeed, to say that it is in their fingers that their skill resides. 'Skill' and 'ability' are intimately linked and yet cannot be synonyms because it is necessary to recognise how durable states of the body confer the ability to exercise such skills. It is improper to suppose that a skill confers a skill to exercise a skill, but it is not improper to say that to possess an ability is to be able to exercise a skill.

The Measurement of Potential, Skills and Abilities

'Potential' is not an actual property of a thing and cannot be an object of measurement. The most plausible sense given to the 'measurement of potential' might be exemplified by the forecast of adult height from an examination of the length of an infant's limbs. This is not, of course, a measurement operation performed on a property called 'potential' and is simply an estimate of a future condition. Skills are states of an organism that enable it to perform actions of the type instantiated by their performance. If a skill is an object of measurement, then it is necessarily quantified through its performances. It is almost always possible to standardise performances, assess them against established criteria, rate them in order of merit, and so on. The major theoretical problem with the measurement of skills arises when it is not clear what skill a performance is held to reveal. The very fact that such a doubt can arise is an indication, of course, that something has gone badly wrong with the process of conceptualisation. If a typist can achieve 60 words a minute, and if the object of measurement is 'typing skill, then this can be compared with a standard (most office managers would find it acceptable) or with a relevant population norm (about average for general office work), and nothing in this is problematic. Suppose, however, that a student can solve 30 verbal analogies in 10 minutes. This can be compared with an arbitrary standard and, if population data are available, it can be located at some point on the normal curve. But what is this skill called? Obviously, it is a 'verbal analogy solving skill', but what if these performances, and others like them, are held to be instantiations of a skill called *intelligence*? This is exactly where the central problem that psychometrics has, variously, ignored, asserted its right to settle by fiat, or attempted to resolve by the concept of 'validity', is encountered. To discuss whether the measurement of 'ability' is possible would merely be to duplicate this analysis.

Most of these problems arise as a direct consequence of the positivist theory that makes no distinction between the object of measurement and the measured object, supposes that any operation of counting achieves the measurement of some 'concept', and remains indifferent to the relationship between models and the real world they simulate. There is no objection in the conventional scheme to the measurement of what are referred to as the concepts of 'potential', 'skill' or 'ability', but it is necessary for a realist science to ask whether these terms refer to properties that are, in fact, quantitative in nature and are, therefore, suitable objects for the operations of measurement. The answer to the question of what a mental test 'measures' (which is better formulated as an enquiry into the nature of the psychological skills exercised in the performance of a test) is usually given in terms of the practices of measurement. Psychological testing is first and foremost a practical business (actually a large and profitable industry) and must justify its approach to measurement. But there are profound difficulties with the standard theory of measurement when applied to non-physical entities. The operations of measurement performed on mental properties are best concerned as scaling, and as natural units of measurement are rarely available there is no alternative but to use standard deviation units (Berka, 1983). This means, however, that the observed scale differences in levels of performance are essentially arbitrary. If Jane earns £240 a week and Jack earns £200, then Jane earns 20 per cent more than Jack: but if Jane's IQ is 120 and Jack's is 100, Jane is not 20 per cent more intelligent than Jack. Moreover, if Jane's typing speed is 60 words per minute and Jack's is 10, then we know that Jane has the ability to type a 6,000-word paper in less than a couple of hours, whereas Jack will take all night. But although there may be psychologists who think otherwise, it cannot be said on the basis of their IQ scores that Jane has the ability to complete an advanced degree course and Jack does not. There is, indeed, no way of knowing what an individual with a given IQ can achieve in the educational system other than by a sort of actuarial calculation based on information about the level of attainment reached by others with known scores (and whose access to education may have been controlled by them). Jane's IQ of 120 indicates the relative rank of her score on a given test, and the assertion that this constitutes a more or less discrete set of cognitive skills that can be called 'intelligence' and is instantiated in the performance of scholastic labour, cannot be supported convincingly by the standard arguments of psychometrics.

The attempt to 'validate' a test as an instrument that has successfully measured the 'concept' stated by its designers to be the object of measurement is, in the terms of realist science, recognised as an attempt to demonstrate that the putative reference is successful. The only satisfactory demonstration in this field, however, will be one based on some neural property shown to be causally associated with information processing skills of an appropriate kind. The psychologists who developed IQ theory, certainly in the case of Spearman (1927) and Burt (1962), were entirely aware of all this. They often, thus taking advantage of positivism as a non-realist theory of science, presented their theories as (merely) models and invited educators to consider what might be so were their assumptions correct. This is a common practice in science. Geographers, for example, who affect to believe that their discipline operates with a 'model' of the earth as a globe, behave in exactly the same fashion. When IQ theorists are able to report that their predictions, in the form of correlations between IQ test scores and educational attainment, for example, have been more or less confirmed, they can adopt the unassuming diffidence of geoscientists, fully aware that as everyone knows that the earth *is* round, so are they also likely to accept that IQ *is* an innately regulated, relatively stable, normally distributed, set of general cognitive processing skills instantiated in the performance of schoolwork.

The Explanatory Status of Potential, Skill and Ability

The explanation of educational attainment by the exercise of intelligence asserts that individuals possess the necessary mental skills involved – such skills are the material basis of a disposition but not its reference – in the form of a cognitive habitus. But a disposition is just a tendency to act, and the scope of what can be explained by dispositions is limited. If a child is having difficulty in learning to read because he cannot distinguish *b* and *d*, and if that is due to some organically based disorder, then the effective mechanism at that level has been identified. One real problem with IQ theory is that it purports to offer a mechanism in terms of the efficiency of an assumed neural operator when nothing more specific than the brain itself can be identified. Any dispositional explanation of behaviour should be regarded as incomplete, or undeveloped, unless the specific nature of the generative mechanism, which requires a reference to the level of efficient skills, is described.

What status can be given to data generated by a scientific model that does not accurately represent the actual nature of the world? It would be easy to conclude that such data must necessarily be worthless, but this would be too hasty a judgement. In fact, it is often only as a result of data collected within the framework of an inadequate theory that better theories are able to emerge. This is, indeed, almost necessarily so. Let us suppose that IQ theory is wrong: the concept of a set of general cognitive skills does not successfully refer to an actual property of human beings and that, consequently, all assumptions about the origins, stability and conditions of exercise of 'general' intelligence are unfounded. How, in this case, are relatively strong correlations between tests of educational attainment at different ages, at seven and fifteen, for example, to be explained? It is no trouble to show that IQ theory suffers from internal contradictions and is quite incapable of demonstrating that its models accord with reality, but it is much more difficult to account for data reported by IQ testing by means of a superior model. Moreover, if early childhood socialisation generates a cognitive habitus, in the sense of a disposition to make use of information processing skills (always in the process of development) effective in the performance of schoolwork, and if that habitus is a classed product, then the consequences of this social variability in educational attainment must, given that IQ tests are designed as a matter of 'validity' to correlate with scholastic attainment, be associated with IQ test scores. Habitus is not a term that should be introduced casually into this discussion: at the very least, some account should be offered of its status in explanatory theories of social action.

Dispositions to Act and Explanation

Ryle (1963) argued that to possess a dispositional property, such as to have a skill, was not to be in a particular state, but to be liable to be in that state, that is to express a belief or to exercise a skill, when particular conditions obtain. Wittgenstein (1974), however, specifically notes that believing is a state of mind, with some duration, and is to be regarded as a kind of disposition of the believing person, and his argument suggests that skills should also be regarded as durable states of the body instantiated as dispositions. On this matter, Wittgenstein (1974: 58) writes: 'If one says that knowing the ABC is a state of the mind, one is thinking of a state of a mental apparatus (perhaps of the brain) by means of which we explain the *manifestations* of that knowledge. Such a state is called a disposition.'

To be able to recite the ABC is, in fact, a skill, which can be exercised only by one who has acquired the necessary knowledge and is thus in such a state that the skill can be exercised. When glass breaks it does so because being brittle it shatters. Ryle asserts that brittleness is not a permanent state or condition of glass but just its tendency to behave in a certain way. The fact that glass has a tendency to break as a result of its molecular structure does not, in Ryle's view, make the disposition of being brittle a reference to a durable property. Yet it seems more useful to accept that 'brittleness' may be regarded as a property of a substance that resides in some characteristic of its constitution, and to allow that a reference to its brittleness indicates some property of that kind. In the current discussion, the reference of 'skill' should be taken to refer to a durable state of the person by means of which the ability to exercise a skill is conferred. To say that someone is able to speak French is not just to list all the skills they are likely to exhibit (order a meal in a Parisian restaurant, read *Le Monde* and so on), as Ryle seems to argue, but refers to the fact that he/she has learned French, possesses that embodied skill and is consequently able to exercise it. The evidence that someone has a skill is not identical with what it means to say that someone has a skill.

Habitus is primarily defined by Bourdieu as a collection of dispositions. The word is derived from the Latin *habere*, 'to have', and denotes the fact that capacities (which can embrace potentials, skills and abilities) are all possessed by individuals and revealed by their exercise as dispositions to act. A disposition, then, is a tendency to act. What sort of explanation is offered by the concept of 'disposition'? A child who starts readily at the least sound may be said to have a nervous disposition; a man who lashes out at the slightest provocation has a violent disposition; and a student who is readily able to find solutions to abstract problems has a quick, clever or intelligent disposition. All dispositions are behavioural by definition, but emotional, physical and mental dispositions, as specific states of being that generate acts, can all be distinguished. Dispositions to act, as tendencies, necessarily rest on capacities of an appropriate kind. To say that a man has a violent disposition, which is likely to be invoked by certain stimuli, is necessarily to say that the man has a capacity for violence.

There is something not entirely satisfactory, however, about explanations of performances, and variations in performance, in terms of dispositions as capacities or powers. It seems uninformative, for example, to argue that a man struck his wife because he has a violent disposition. This is akin to Molière's doctor who accounts for the effects of opium in causing sleep by appeal to its dormative powers. However, explanations of behaviour in terms of dispositions may have some worth, much depends on what one wants to explain, and need not be supported by a circular argument. It can be very useful to know an individual's dispositions. A school would be negligent, for example, to employ a paedophile with multiple convictions. And if such a man were to reoffend there is an explanation of sorts to be had in pointing to his disposition to behave in this way. There is no need, at least, to ask what made him act out of character. Moreover, we can investigate the conditions in which such a disposition is usually formed, the contexts in which it is activated, and so on, and in this manner accumulate a body of systematic information from which certain laws or tendencies of a probabilistic kind can be derived. This is all far from useless.

However, what sort of explanation is it to argue that social disparities in educational attainment can be explained, to the extent that this is the case, by differences in the social distribution of intelligence? Is there anything to be gained, for example, from an explanation of a student's high attainments by reference to his or her intelligence? Consider the form of the argument: Why is Jane top of the class? Because she is intelligent. How do we know she is intelligent? Because she is top of the class. This is obviously both empty and circular. But is the argument substantially improved if the final statement reads: Because she has a high IQ? This seems only to mean that she can perform at the same relative level those cognitive operations – in whatever terms they might be specified – required in order to gain a high score on IQ tests and on tests of mathematics (Harré, 2002; Howe, 1989). Yet this argument *is* different and it is, in fact, one of the principal grounds on which psychometric theory attempts to validate its claims to practical utility in providing assessment instruments. All dispositions are revealed by indicative performances, and if these can be standardised the information has some value. An indicative performance on such a test, particularly at a young age might, moreover, provide evidence of a skill at an initial stage of development and offer a means to determine its stability. Furthermore, although it may be vacuous to explain the effects of opium on an organism in terms of its 'dormative powers', it is not improper to investigate what doses of the drug are effective, nor to conduct a programme of research designed to isolate the specific compound responsible for its operation. Much the same arguments can be advanced in the case of cognitive powers and the search for genetic markers and neural properties associated with the development of cognitive dispositions and their functioning are sooner or later likely to be located.

An explanation of attainment, and variation in attainment, in terms of specific mental operators is different in kind from an explanation in terms of dispositions. A disposition is a tendency to act, but a skill is a state of the body – to be able to type is necessarily to have a skill – which is acquired by practice. Speech is a skill, reading is a skill and so on. Intelligence is not a skill, but the exercise of intelligence necessarily depends on skills. This leads to the conclusion that it is the task of psychology to describe the skills that constitute cognitive habitus. To say that Jane is good at mathematics because she has a high IQ is a dispositional explanation: to say that she is good at mathematics because of the state of her developed skills to process abstract, symbolic expressions, the psychological parameters of which can be described, is an explanation in terms of effective skills that confer abilities to do mathematics.

The Content of Cognitive Habitus

The study of cognitive development relies on psychological operations as the effective tools of thought. Many items still found in IQ tests – verbal analogies, logical syllogisms, number sequences and so on – were designed as tests of psychological operations, Spearman's (1926) 'eduction of relations and correlates' is an early example, and in this way an attempt was made to ground IQ tests in psychological theory. The content of cognitive habitus, that is to say the distinct skills that confer the ability to think in specific ways, must be described if the status of an explanation of attainment is to move from the level of disposition as a tendency to the level of disposition as a demonstrable skill. To know that someone has a disposition to act in a certain way does not necessarily disclose the mechanism by which the performance is enabled. To say that Jane's mental disposition is such that she is able to embark on the study of higher mathematics is not to specify the nature of the cognitive and non-cognitive skills by which that disposition is formed. This use of cognitive habitus, incidentally, should be distinguished from that proposed by Tomasello (1999) who makes it a reference to the environment of practices within which cognitive development occurs. In fact, Tomasello's cognitive habitus is quite similar to Dewey's collective intelligence, in as much that it refers to the social milieu that provides the context for the development of the capacity to become an intelligent actor. An environment of practices and a disposition to act are clearly not identical, but, as the explanatory force of Bourdieu's theory of practice rather depends on their being conflated, it is not surprising that scholarly opinion differs on whether the principal reference of habitus in Bourdieu is actually to practices or to dispositions (Pizanias, 1999). It is certainly possible, given this structured ambiguity, to recognise Tomasello's approach as consistent with the emerging Bourdieusian tradition. In any event, Tomasello's materialist psychology of development may be valuable in the realist project to identify the skills involved in abstract thought and the conditions of their development and exercise.

If habitus is defined as a collection of embodied dispositions, and if a disposition is a tendency to act, then what is actually embodied? A tendency is not the kind of thing that can be embodied. Skills, on the other hand, are always embodied (as habits), and tendencies to follow habituated modes of conduct are essential to Bourdieu's explanation of social reproduction. If dispositions are regarded as embodied habits, then the actual reference is to *skills*, which are states of the body that confer the capacity to perform the actions by which their performance is known. The only way the skill to read can be detected is by observation of the act of reading. There is no sense in attempting to locate a skill, as if it were a discrete module, in any organ of the body, but it does not follow that a skill is not identical with, or supervenient on, a material state of the organic body. There is, as yet, no technology that will enable science to examine a brain and show that it is the brain of one who has learned to read, but that this state does exist, for example, in the form of neural assemblies with a specific organisation, is certain.

Tomasello argues convincingly that knowledge of the relation of causality is crucial to the emergence of specifically human intellectual skills. 'Faculty', 'scheme', 'module' and so on all refer to effective mental operations that perform some function of thought. In some theories these are stated to be localised (the phrenologists looked for bumps) and in other theories they have the status of hypothetical (in the sense of imaginary) entities employed in models for the purposes of conducting psychological investigations. The concept of cognitive habitus as a set of mental dispositions to process symbolic information – that is to acquire the tools of communication, and specifically those of literate communication – and to be able to use these mental operators effectively in appropriate conditions, is entirely defensible. As with all explanatory accounts that rest on dispositions, what features of the world can be explained by such entities is limited by the status of dispositions as mechanisms, and the improvement of such explanations depends on the extent to which the nature of these has been revealed by scientific enquiry.

The Study of Cognitive Habitus

How should cognitive habitus be studied? Bourdieu provides the answer to this question: habitus is studied through the practices by which it is revealed. And if habitus is revealed by its practices the most useful way to describe it is, in fact, in the language of practice, and this is no doubt why many followers of Bourdieu actually define habitus as the environment of practices, rather than as dispositions to act in accordance with taken-for-granted social codes. Bourdieu thus shifts the attention of research from the actual psychological states with which tendencies to act are associated – that is with properties of temperament and character – to those imputed by practice as a socially regulated system. When Bourdieu studies the life of working-class youths in the impoverished outer suburbs of a French city he shows how their practices emerge in a field structured by the inadequate provision of educational and occupational opportunities (Bourdieu et al., 1999). If the young men see nothing for them, it is not so much their boredom and restlessness that interests Bourdieu, but their taken-for-granted knowledge of how, being in that state of mind, a common way of life can be created. What patterns of thought order the routine conduct of their day-to-day existence, in the sense of what generative codes make, in one familiar setting after another, one response thinkable and another unthinkable? That there is boredom and restlessness goes without saying, but the effective dispositions Bourdieu's analysis reveals are those that generate conduct by providing a sense of what is possible, which is always mediated by language, and specifically by the language of the community, in the form of common sayings and accepted forms of expression, and it is for this reason that the investigation of the social habitus involves a characteristic study of cultural practice.

There is a deeply important sense in which habitus is always cognitive. The framework of concepts available for symbolic mediation constitutes a cognitive framework, and to study this structure is to study habitus (Bourdieu, 1971). However, there are also specific areas of thought, acknowledged by Bourdieu, that may be the province of a more narrowly specified cognitive habitus. And the study of this cognitive habitus, or this aspect of habitus if the formulation is preferred, must proceed on similar lines. The classic example of work in this mode is, of course, that carried out by Bernstein (1996). Classed 'codes' of speech are defined in structuralist terms and the code manages a dual reference to a disposition (based on skills specified in epistemological terms) and to the modes of speech it generates. Bernstein's research is precisely concerned with cognitive habitus. (That Bourdieu and Bernstein kept each other at arm's length throughout their working lives is not germane in this context.) An investigation of cognitive habitus, perhaps more so than the study of social habitus, which is Bourdieu's more common concern, must engage with psychological studies of cognition. This should not be an unduly provocative remark. Lizardo (2004) has pointed out, in a most interesting analysis, that Bourdieu's concept of habitus, as a generative structure of practical action, is expressly concerned with cognition, in a broad sense, and has more in common with Piaget's structuralist psychology that many commentators have recognised.

The effective skills that confer dispositions to act, the schemata, modules and so on, are important in as much that the operations of cognition must be carefully specified, and that requires attention to psychological investigations. An influential school of cognitive psychology actually defines its mental operators in epistemological terms (Sternberg, 1979). This comes close to Bourdieu's approach to the study of habitus in its more general modes of operation, but it is not the only available approach, and not necessarily likely to be the most productive. Tomasello's materialist psychology, for example, analyses cognition as skills conferring abilities to process information within parameters set by their forms of operation. At a certain age, for example, infants recognise a gesture as an indication that the other intends them to share attention, which means that the child must imagine what that sharing would be like, and this in turn implies the emergence of a mode of self-awareness. The object of studying cognitive habitus is always, of course, to describe the relations of causality between social structures, dispositions and practices. The emergent properties of social organisations establish a context or field within which dispositions to act (which necessarily requires the skilled use of resources), analysed in terms of the psychological and cultural skills that constitute their basis, can be seen as effective schemes leading to the adoption of social practices. Structures, dispositions and practices are linked together, and a complete explanation of the causes of social events, the origin and maintenance of social states of affairs, and the modes of operation of social processes, all require an explanatory narrative that incorporates a reference to the relationships between them (Nash, 2003b).

The Politics of 'Deficit Theory'

What political risks are likely to be incurred by adopting the concept of cognitive habitus? Many sociologists of education maintain an implacable resistance to explanations of social disparities in education that refer to individual abilities, especially when these are supposed to have a substantially genetic origin, holding them self-condemned as 'deficit' theories that support policies of division and exclusion in education that must be opposed. This is an understandable reaction. The history of educational selection by intellectual ability, legitimated by the scientific authority of educational psychology and in particular by the theory of general intelligence, is one of the systematic exclusion of large numbers of working-class students from access to high-status schooling. The uncompromising struggle against IQ theory has been necessary, but at one level, as Gillborn and Youdell (2000) may have perceived more clearly than Brown and Lauder, it has been at the same time successful and yet ineffectual.

Educational psychology has now maintained as dogma for several decades that the distinction between ability/aptitude tests and attainment/achievement tests is one of convention; that standardisation to a normal curve is a technical device from which no theoretical assumptions can be derived; and that test scores have no explanatory or predictive value (Kozulin, 1998). In this academic environment, students of education are no longer taught the general theory of intelligence as a dominant paradigm; teachers may cling to their folk theory of 'ability', as they always have, but without the legitimacy granted by a once powerful scientific theory; and policymakers are more likely to insist that schools should achieve standards of 'excellence' than accept 'excuses' based on a theory that entire classes of students are relatively ineducable. The problems of intelligence and ability may lie elsewhere.

The psychological revisionism that has formally abandoned IQ theory, unprincipled and incoherent as it may be, testifies by its constant reiteration to the concern of educational psychology to distance itself from the classical concepts of intelligence. The retreat from IQ theory has been made, moreover, onto a terrain where intelligence flourishes in an increasing multitude of new states. Gardener's full model generates no less than 120 'intelligences', while other writers have extended the boundaries so far as to include the concepts of social and emotional intelligence (Gardener, 1993; Goleman, 1995). There might seem no reason why Brown and Lauder's reintroduction of Dewey's 'collective intelligence' should not be welcome in such broad-minded company. The concept of cognitive habitus, however, is not a candidate for admission. One of the problematic consequences of IQ theory, perhaps likely to be its most enduring, is the close association between intelligence and measurement. Whenever the term intelligence is extended it carries with it the promise of measurement. If technocrats ever adopt the concept of collective intelligence, it will surely be developed as a quantitative indicator of non-formal systems for the transmission of local knowledge. Bourdieu's (1990) concept of social capital, reworked by Coleman (1988), was appropriated in exactly this manner.

The term cognitive habitus, in contrast, is not compromised by a long association with assessment and cannot be constructed as an object of measurement. Habitus is primarily defined in terms of dispositions, that is, as tendencies to act, and scientific attention is therefore concentrated on the analysis of social practice, in order that the effective cognitive skills of information processing are described in contexts that give them their form. Specific cognitive skills may sometimes be assessed with instruments standardised to an assumed normal distribution – when there are no natural units there may be no practical alternative – but this implies nothing for the concept of cognitive habitus. There is no sense in attempting to measure cognitive habitus: this would simply be to commit a category error.

Sociological research into the structure and origin of cognitive habitus can have nothing in common with that driven by IQ theory. The concept is not tied to measurement, does not refer, implicitly or explicitly, to theories of normal distribution, and its explanatory contribution invites clarity rather than confusion. The ease with which the ambiguities of 'ability' are exploited generates discussions worth reading only for the (no doubt suspect) pleasure to be gained from seeing muddle raised to the level of an art form. Reference to cognitive habitus cannot provide a ready-made explanation of individual and social disparities in educational attainment. Such an explanation has been gained only when specific cognitive skills have been described in the context of their social origin and with respect to the cultural modes of their transmission and acquisition. This will necessarily involve the construction of complex explanatory narratives linking together social structures, socialised dispositions and cultural practices (Bourdieu, 1974).

Research concerned with cognitive habitus is more likely to be located within the sociolinguistic tradition left by Bernstein, or within the reinvigorated Vygotskyian tradition, than associated with a concept of intelligence inextricably linked to test and measurement technology. And should it be the case that empirical research provides sound evidence that structural relations, including those that control the distribution and application of organised knowledge – what Dewey called collective intelligence – are implicated in the development of cognitive habitus in such a way that certain identifiable intellectual skills are developed differentially in social classes, then the theoretical and practical implications of that for education must be confronted. In this context, it might be useful to note that a *causal* narrative is not necessarily a narrative of *blame*. The concepts of causality and responsibility are not identical: the former belongs to a discourse of science and the latter to a discourse of ethics. When Marx (1975), in the 1844 *Economic and Philosophical Manuscripts*, pointed to the effects of capitalist oppression on the physical and mental development of workers he was not contributing a chapter to the history of so-called deficit theory. When Bourdieu (1998: 136) insisted that human potentialities, including the 'the ability to produce a complex chain of logical reasoning', cannot be expected to develop to the full under the 'inhuman social conditions imposed upon proletarians', he did no more than endorse the Marxian position (Geras, 1993). Bourdieu, of course, while fully aware of the dangers of confusing his political supporters and cheering his opponents, knew that nothing of lasting good could come of reforms based on unreal analyses. He was occasionally, indeed, so provoked by the censorship radical thought can impose on itself in its attempt to avoid all taint of deficit theory that he protested vigorously against the 'simplistic rhetoric of resistance', postmodernist relativism and 'populist illusions' that weaken and discredit so much contemporary radical advocacy (Bourdieu, 2000: 233). The concept of cognitive habitus might offer the sociology of education a way to approach the study of cognitive socialisation, particularly in early childhood, with greater confidence than it has so far been willing to show. The relationships between social class, the possession of literate resources, the generation of effective cognitive ability through specialised socialisation practices, and the achievement of literacy by children, being real states of affairs and processes, continue to have their effects whether they are acknowledged or not, and the investigation of cognitive habitus, by methods true to the radical tradition, could allow sociological research into inequality/difference to move forward. Thinking with cognitive habitus as a materialist reference to the capacities of our species being may provide a principled basis for radical educational policy and so constitute a passable route to the enhancement of our collective intelligence.

References

Anastasi, A. (1968). *Psychological Testing*, 3rd edn (London: Macmillan).

Berka, K. (1983). *Measurement: Its Concepts, Theories and Problems* (Dordrecht, The Netherlands: Reidel).

Bernstein, B. (1996). *Pedagogy, Symbolic Control and Identity: Theory, Research, Critique* (London: Taylor and Francis).

Bhaskar, R. (1993). *Dialectic: The Pulse of Freedom* (London: Verso).

Bourdieu, P. (1971). Systems of education and systems of thought. In M.F.D. Young (ed.), *Knowledge and Control: New Directions for the Sociology of Education* (London: Collier–Macmillan): 189–207.

Bourdieu, P. (1974). The school as a conservative force: Scholastic and cultural inequalities. In J. Eggleston (ed.), *Contemporary Research in the Sociology of Education* (London: Methuen): 32–46.

Bourdieu, P. (1990). *The Logic of Practice* (Cambridge: Polity Press).

Bourdieu, P. (1998). *Practical Reason* (Cambridge: Polity Press).

Bourdieu, P., (2000). *Pascalian Meditations* (Polity Press: Cambridge).

Bourdieu, P., Accardo, A., Balazs, G., Beaud, S., Bonvin, F., Bourdieu, E., Bourgois, P., Broccolichi, S., Champagne, P., Christin, R., Faguer, J.-P., Garcia, S., Lenoir, R., Œuvrard, F., Pialoux, M., Pinto, L., Podalydès, D., Sayad, A., Soulié, C. and Wacquant, L.J.D. (1999). *The Weight of the World: Social Suffering in Contemporary Society* (Stanford, Calif.: Stanford University Press).

Brown, P. and Lauder, H. (2000). Education, child poverty and the politics of collective intelligence. In S.J. Ball (ed.), *Sociology of Education: Major Themes, Vol. IV: Politics and Policies* (London: Routledge/Falmer): 1753–79.

Burt, C. (1962). *Mental and Scholastic Tests*, 4th edn (London: Staples Press).

Cleary, T.A., Humphreys, L.G., Kendrick, S.A. and Wesman, A. (1975). Educational uses of tests with disadvantaged students, *American Psychologist*, 30(1): 15–41.

Coleman, J. (1988). Social capital in the creation of human capital, *American Journal of Sociology*, 94: 95–120.

Dewey, J. (1937). *Democracy and Education: An Introduction to the Philosophy of Education* (New York: Macmillan).

Dewey, J. (1968). *Problems of Men* (New York: Greenwood Press).

Gardener, H. (1993). *Frames of Mind: The Theory of Multiple Intelligence* (Fontana: London).

Geras, N. (1983). *Marx and Human Nature: Refutation of a Legend* (London: Verso).

Gillborn, D. and Youdell, D. (2000). *Rationing Education: Policy, Reform and Equity* (Buckingham: Open University Press).

Goleman, D. (1995). *Emotional Intelligence* (New York: Bantam).

Harré, R. (2002). *Cognitive Science: A Philosophical Introduction* (London: Sage).

Howe, M.J.A. (1989). Separate skills or general intelligence: The autonomy of human abilities, *British Journal of Educational Psychology*, 59 (3): 351–60.

Kozulin, A. (1998). *Pyschological Tools: A Sociocultural Approach to Education* (Cambridge, Mass.: Harvard University Press).

Lizardo, O. (2004). The cognitive origins of Bourdieu's *habitus*. Unpublished manuscript (University of Arizona): http://www.member.cox.net/bourdieu. pdf, retrieved August 25.

Marx, K. (1975). *Early Writings* (Harmondsworth: Penguin Books).

Murray, C. and Hernnstein, R.J. (1994). *The Bell Curve: Intelligence and Class Structure in American Life* (New York: Fress Press).

Nash, R. (2003a). Inequality/difference in New Zealand education: Social reproduction and the cognitive *habitus. International Studies in Sociology of Education*, 13(2): 171–91.

Nash, R. (2003b). Social explanation and socialization: On Bourdieu and the structure, disposition, practice scheme, *Sociological Review*, 51(1): 43–62.

Pizanias, C. (1999). *Habitus* revisited: Notes and queries from the field. In M. Grenfell and M. Kelly (eds), *Pierre Bourdieu: Language, Culture and Education: Theory into Practice* (Bern: Peter Lang): 144–64.

Ratner, J. (1939). *Intelligence in the Modern World: John Dewey's Philosophy* (New York: The Modern Library).

Ryle, G. (1963). *The Concept of Mind* (London: Hutchinson).

Spearman, C. (1926). Some issues in the theory of 'G' (including the law of diminishing returns). Paper presented at the British Association Section J – Psychology, Southampton.

Spearman, C. (1927). *The Nature of Intelligence and the Principles of Cognition* (London: Macmillan).

Sternberg, R.J. (1979). The Nature of Mental Abilities, *American Psychologist*, 34(3): 214–30.

Tomasello, M. (1999). *The Cultural Origins of Human Cognition* (Cambridge, Mass.: Harvard University Press).

Vygotsky, L. (1994). *The Vygotsky Reader*, ed. R. Van der Veer and J. Valsiner (Oxford: Blackwell).

Wittgenstein, L. (1974). *Philosophical Investigations* (Oxford: Blackwell).

Chapter 6

Bernstein and the Explanation of Social Disparities in Education: A Realist Critique of the Sociolinguistic Thesis

Introduction

Anyone interested in the sources of social disparities in educational achievement and who studies the literature in search of theories with some explanatory content will soon encounter an introduction to the sociology of Basil Bernstein. Moore (2004) devotes the best part of a chapter to Bernstein's thought, first locating it in the Durhkheimian tradition; Erben and Dickinson (2004) review Bernstein's entire work for a new generation of students; and collections dedicated to Bernstein such as Morais et al. (2001) and Muller, Davies and Morais (2004) continue to appear. It is not at all unreasonable, therefore, to ask how Bernstein's sociology might contribute to the explanation of social disparities in education. We should not expect to construct a simple model. Bernstein (1990: 114) understood that 'Educational failure (official pedagogic failure) is a complex function of the official transmission system of the school and the local acquisition process of the family/peer/group/community.' This is not, of course, an explanation, but it does suggest that an account of the causes of inequality/difference in education must refer to the school, the home and the peer group as social organisations, and to the processes of teaching and learning considered as systems of practice. A satisfactory model of the causes of social disparities in achievement – that is to say a more or less integrated explanatory narrative – will certainly be complex. Contemporary accounts of Bernstein's sociology do not, however, offer a model that even begins to approximate that description. In fact, little if any attention is usually given to this problem, which was the central concern of Bernstein's initial research and stimulated the development of his most important concepts. Moore, for example, at the conclusion of a dense synopsis of Bernstein's later concepts, barely mentions the problem and suggests only that the familiarity of middle-class students with an 'invisible pedagogy' might advantage them in comparison with working-class students who, presumably, are more suited to a 'visible pedagogy'. The achievement of a complex model of generative mechanisms, outlined in Bernstein's sketch, is an aspiration we could all share. This chapter, then, is concerned with the nature of Bernstein's theories as a source of explanations for social disparities in educational achievement.

The general aim is to construct a secure framework for the production of theoretically coherent explanatory narratives of the generation of social inequality in education, which will be open, in principle, to empirical test and quantified expression. The discussion will take Bernstein seriously, which means critically, and examine closely what his sociology has to offer to this specific project. As many sympathetic commentators have noted, Bernstein's concerns extended far beyond the subject of 'educability', as it was once known, and there is a noticeable tendency to de-emphasise his attention to this 'limited' problem, the better perhaps to demonstrate the overall ambition of his sociology. This is no doubt all to the good, but the origins of social inequality in education, and its lasting consequences, are not a matter of secondary concern to sociologists of education, as might be so for linguists, for example, and there is no apology for the sharp focus of the present enquiry.

The best way to honour Bernstein's memory is to press forward with his major undertaking to investigate the processes governing the social distribution of knowledge. This must be a critical project. It will be necessary to revisit the ideas that ensured his early reputation, inspired the empirical research carried out by the Sociological Research Unit (SRU), and which, although the sociolinguistic thesis was put to one side, were never formally abandoned. In what respect does Bernstein's structuralism influence the explanations provided? How are Bernstein's sociological explanations to be distinguished from psychological explanations? What implications for pedagogical reform might be drawn from Bernstein's accounts? These are the central questions to be addressed.

The Sociolinguistic Theory

The status of the sociolinguistic theory has been uncertain for at least 30 years. The first paper was published in 1958 and, although it would be unwise to give a date for the last, it is clear that by the early 1970s Bernstein's interests had shifted to other matters. Lee (1973) noted in the context of an Open University introduction to the sociolinguistic theory – to which Bernstein added what amounts to an endorsement – its author's view that the argument had reached the limits of its development. Davies (1976) presented an account of Bernstein's emerging ideas that barely mentioned the sociolinguistic thesis at just the same time that Stubbs (1976), in a parallel text, subjected it to a dismissive critique. Atkinson's (1985: 10) influential introduction to Bernstein declined to discuss the sociolinguistic theory so as not to 'recapitulate major misunderstandings' and this view seems to have been widely shared. The commemorative edition of this journal contained only one article that gave more than passing mention to the sociolinguistic theory and its potential for development (Hasan, 2002). Yet Bernstein never conceded that his critics, certainly not Stubbs and certainly not Gordon (1990), had weakened the theory in any respect (Bernstein, 1990) and for decades the sociolinguistic explanation of differential achievement was left in a discursive limbo, as a matter no longer central to Bernstein's interests, and thus meriting nothing more than due notice in commentaries on his thought. Accounts have yet to be settled with this central and once highly influential aspect of Bernstein's theoretical and empirical work.

Not least of the difficulties resulting from all this is the absence of any definitive statement of the sociolinguistic theory, or its central hypotheses, thus making it necessary to reconstruct – always a risky business – an adequate summary. It should be safe to say, at least, that the sociolinguistic theory holds that speech is generated by *principles*, shaped by class relations, in such a way that middle-class speech *tends* to be elaborated (explicit, universal and abstract), whereas working-class speech *tends* to be restricted (implicit, particular and concrete), with the consequence that working-class children *tend* to underachieve at school, in comparison with middle-class children, because these restrictions on their speech inhibit their ability to realise their innate intellectual potential, in as much as these forms of language use are linked to the comprehension and expression of necessary school meanings. The principles that generate speech, however, are not to be understood as conferring a *competence* but as enabling *performances* realised in certain contexts, and the essential task of the school in this respect is thus to discover and provide appropriate pedagogical contexts in which working-class children will respond and produce meanings with the features of an elaborated code. The concept of code is central to Bernstein's sociology, but it may help first to clarify the competence/performance distinction.

In Chomsky's theory of language, 'competence' refers to a generative universal grammar and 'performance' to the speech generated by this entity. 'Competence', Bernstein (1971: 173) remarks, 'refers to the Ideal, performance, refers to the Fall'. This enigmatic comment calls for clarification. Bernstein must resist the view that his investigations are concerned with competence in the Chomskian sense. If codes are identified with such a competence, then their origin might be seen as innate, their modes of realisation less regulated by context, and their products as less open to transformation. Codes, however, are generative principles with much the same theoretical status as a grammar and language use is explained in quite the same way that a grammar explains the pattern of words spoken in the language it describes. It is impossible to restrict Bernstein's accounts solely to language use, or to eliminate reference to the level of a generative property, because this is exactly the function of 'code'. Bernstein's insistence that his theory is concerned with performance, not competence, may be understandable, but these considerations lack force within a Vygotskian approach. There need be no reference to what is innate, non-sociological or unalterable, for the higher mental functions, conceptualised for the purposes of explanatory accounts as if they were physical organs, are understood to be in a continuous state of development. The discussion may now tackle the fundamental concept of code.

Speech is not part of the definition of code. Bernstein (1990: 3) says that codes regulate 'cognitive orientation … dispositions, identities, and practices', and it will be noted that there is no mention of speech. Code is formally defined as:

a regulative principle, tacitly acquired, which reflects and integrates:

(a) relevant meanings	meanings
(b) forms of their realization	realizations
(c) evoking contexts	contexts

(Bernstein, 1990: 14)

Code is thus a regulator of the relations between contexts and as such generates principles for distinguishing between contexts (recognition rules) and principles for the 'creation and production of the specialized relationships within a context' (ibid. 15) (realisation rules). We might suppose, for example, that if a politician stopped in the street replies 'no comment' to a journalist's question, it is the recognition and realisation rules generated by distinctive codes that regulate the expression of *this* meaning (rather than, say, 'let me tell you about that'), in *this* form (rather than, say, 'you're not getting a word out of me'), and in *this* context (rather than, say, in the context of a press conference). It may be taken for granted that the politician is competent to produce these alternative responses as to the context makes appropriate. This assumption is less safe, however, as the discussion will note, with respect to cognitive functioning.

Bernstein's use of *code* is derived from structuralism. This is a mode of anthropological and sociological analysis perhaps developed to its fullest extent by Lévi-Strauss (1978), and it may be unfamiliarity with this tradition that perpetuates certain misunderstandings. Even some of Bernstein's warmest admirers give 'code' a reference that seems at odds with the authorised definition. Halliday (1995: 131), for example, states that 'codes are different patterns or habits of speech', although this is clearly inconsistent with Bernstein's own practice. That code is a structuralist concept, however, does not mean that Bernstein provides structuralist *explanations*, and this point is so important that it requires a section to itself.

Structuralism and Bernstein's Sociological Explanations

Bernstein's principles are faithful to the structuralist project. His analyses always specify the nature of the regulator with respect to a given axis, as elaborated/ restricted, visible/invisible, horizontal/vertical and so on, with an impressive intellectual consistency. In this respect, the judgement of those who, like Atkinson, place *code* at the centre of his work is sound, for the entire oeuvre would be nothing without the power of such analyses to illuminate the discursive structures of the social world. What needs to be pressed, however, is the status of such *principles* in Bernstein's explanatory accounts. Their remarkable descriptive authority is not in doubt, and the narratives in which they are embedded always have some explanatory content, but this is not exactly to the point: *what* they explain and *how* the explanation works must be clarified. Structural anthropology accounts for the regulation of conduct by rules typically unknown – at least in their full meaning disclosed by structuralist analysis – to those who follow them, integrates these rules according to a model of their 'inner logic' and reveals how such conduct performs specific functions necessary to the maintenance of the society.

Atkinson (1985: 84), who more than anyone has sought to expose Bernstein's structuralist roots, points out that Bernstein 'seeks constantly to uncover underlying principles governing the formal relationships between them, the structuring mechanisms which regulate their reproduction, transmission, and the transformative rules whereby their relationship may be expressed', and shows that an explanation in terms of codes as deep principles – structuring mechanisms – depends on discovering the implicit rules of social discourse.

As the account of the sociolinguistic thesis has stated, Bernstein's theory of social disparities in educational attainment supposes that the codes (structuralist principles) regulating language use, which have their origin in class relations, influence the expression of intelligence in specific educational contexts, in such a way that working-class students tend to achieve less than middle-class students. Although this argument has recognisable structural elements, it is not exclusively, and perhaps not predominantly, structuralist in form. It might be argued, in fact, that the structuralist elements are not even necessary, in as much as the explanation could be restated with no real loss of power were they entirely removed. Bernstein's explanatory models are arguably more properly assimilated to the structure–disposition–practice scheme generally found in substantive sociology. Bernstein's explanations of social events, processes and states of affairs should be recognised as a variant of a standard model that begins with social relations (as emergent structural properties), shows how these give rise to embodied dispositions to act and relates how such actions are structured by collective practices. If there is information about the structure of social relations, about the nature of effective dispositions (such as beliefs and skills), including the processes of their acquisition, social distribution and contexts of realisation, and about the recognised social practices of the community, then all the elements necessary for the construction of an explanatory narrative are present. An explanation of this scope seems to make a structuralist explanation redundant.

Although structuralist explanations are often illuminating, they can raise as many questions as they answer and subjecting them to stringent evidential test is next to impossible. Atkinson illustrates the nature of such structural explanations in a discussion of how elements of clothing may be combined according to certain rules. Guardsmen, he says, do not wear red tunics with khaki fatigues as this combination is not permitted in terms of the non-homologous relations existing between these items. The answer to the question 'Why do guardsmen wear red tunics *or* khaki fatigues' (but not both in combination) is thus: 'There is an underlying code that makes such a combination "unthinkable" for guardsmen.' But what is this explanation worth? In the case of guardsmen, for example, the 'dress code' is almost certainly explicit (there is bound to be something in Queen's Regulations), what makes it more 'homologous' to wear black trousers rather than khaki fatigues with a red tunic, is unstated, and the account is solely concerned with explaining the rules of combination rather than the consequent social effects of following those rules. As to that, if someone is content to say that guardsmen do not wear khaki fatigues with red tunics because it is not fitting for them to do so, and that such a combination cannot arise as a practical possibility, they might well be asked what kind of test could determine whether the hypothesis is correct or false. There is, moreover, a different explanation to be given in terms of the utility of camouflage as combat dress, the adoption of khaki (Urdu: 'dust-coloured') for that reason, and the senseless contradiction of wearing a red tunic with clothing designed to be much less conspicuous. That explanation is not necessarily incompatible with a structuralist account, but neither is it subsumed within such an account and might well be found more informative. It is also somewhat more open to evidential test in as much that the narrative can be checked against the historical record and the probability of soldiers wearing red or khaki in typical combat environments – above all dusty ones – becoming causalities may be calculated. Bernstein's substantive explanations of events, processes and states of affairs are not structuralist in this manner, and should be recognised as having a structure–disposition–practice form and examined for internal coherence, particularly the strength of the argument concerned with linkages between elements, and for their truth to reality.

Sociology and Psychology

Sociological theories that refer to internalised social properties and include such dispositions in their explanatory accounts thereby establish a relationship with psychology that calls for careful management. Sociological and psychological explanations more often compete than complement each other. Durkheim all but eliminated psychology by making socially acquired 'representations' (ideas, knowledge, beliefs) and the learned capacities (skills, abilities, proficiencies) dependent on their acquisition, the most basic 'social facts'. This theoretical declaration enabled Durkheim to incorporate what would ordinarily be regarded as individual and psychological properties – with the exception only of those residual emotions and volitions unmodified by culture – into sociological explanations (Steadman Jones, 2001). This is the basis of Durkheim's argument that sociological accounts explain social facts in terms of other social facts. There is nothing to be gained, as far as this view of sociology is concerned, from the psychological investigation of collective representations. In these respects, the influence of Durkheim on Bernstein's sociology is worth some comment.

When Bernstein identifies psychological properties, such as 'personality', 'intelligence' and 'verbal planning', it is implied that these are individual characteristics and, in as much as they follow an entirely genetic developmental trajectory, may be excluded from the category 'social facts'. The concepts of 'innate' and 'psychological' are thus contrasted with 'learned' and 'sociological'. If intelligence is defined as innate there is little incentive to direct sociological research into cognitive socialisation. The significance of this distinction between the sociological and the psychological is fundamental to Bernstein's sociolinguistic theory, and established a foundation for later thought that merits appreciation.

Bernstein supported the sociolinguistic thesis with the observation that working-class boys attending continuing education classes, although a close match for middle-class boys on non-verbal IQ tests, were markedly inferior on verbal tests. It seemed plausible to argue that the non-verbal scores indicated a level of native potential inadequately expressed as a result of the working-class boys' inability to manipulate the linguistic symbolisation of verbal IQ tests. The idea was not new, and Davis (1962), whose studies clearly influenced Bernstein's early work, carried out a major investigation of class differences in IQ item response in order to discover characteristic patterns. Davis's group also attempted to develop 'cultural-fair' tests, but the results were eventually shown to be less than promising, and the problems were revealed to be rather more complex than the initial hypothesis had proposed (Ells et al., 1951). Although Bernstein cites a number of studies with similar findings, there is no mention of those that report no significant differences in this respect, and this omission should not go unnoticed: Bernstein habitually looked for confirmation rather than disconfirmation (as the principle of *falsification* might suggest he should) and commentators have been known to accept Bernstein's interpretations at face value. Douglas (1964), however, reported no significant differences in the verbal and non-verbal IQ scores of children in the large and representative 1948 birth cohort. This dataset, and the following 1970 birth cohort, are now available for secondary analysis and it can easily be ascertained that social class means for verbal and non-verbal IQ tests are much the same. This evidence is quite contrary to Bernstein's and it seems most likely that his sample of 309 GPO telegraph messenger boys was not representative of working-class young people, perhaps in some respects biased, and the finding should by no means be accepted as an established fact. Bernstein maintained his position, notwithstanding this and other evidence to the contrary, and thus ruled out the very possibility of an investigation into the social origins of durable cognitive abilities. The working-class boys were deemed to be comparable in intelligence with middle-class boys and the expression of that capacity, in a form mediated by language, was supposed to limit their performance on verbal tests and to constrain their attainment in educational environments where such linguistic forms are considered essential.

The model of innate intelligence, or 'competence', mediated in its expression by acquired habits of language use, is arguably untenable. It is certainly unconvincing to argue that non-verbal cognitive performances are regulated by innate (hence psychological) dispositions and that verbal cognitive performances, being mediated by language, are regulated by acquired (hence sociological) dispositions. Vygotsky (1995) maintains that the higher mental functions are created by a developmental fusion of our pre-verbal capacities for thought – which are not inconsiderable – with speech thus forming a new plane of thinking under the control of conscious planning. There is no distinction between verbal and non-verbal intelligence in Vygotsky's approach. The higher mental functions, for all that they are intrinsically based on verbal concepts, are not in any sense to be identified with the expression of verbal intelligence, a concept that emerged from factor analytic studies within the psychometric tradition (Flynn, 2004). A principled engagement with Vygotsky's psychology is scarcely possible unless the inadequacies of Bernstein's sociolinguistic thesis in this respect are admitted. It is obvious that the concept of ability, or potential, in Bernstein's texts, in the sense of a durable and active faculty, largely or entirely innate, is retained as an explanation of cognitive performances, but not with respect to linguistic performances. Both cognitive and linguistic performances, however, have the same status in explanatory accounts as being the exercise of dispositions, and what matters, as Bernstein's contributions have emphasised, is the nature of those dispositions and the contexts of their acquisition and realisation.

On Cognitive Socialisation

The need to integrate Bernstein's theory with psychology has been noted by several commentators. Indeed, that writers separated by more than a generation can make the same point – 'the psychological aspect has been relatively neglected' (Lee, 1970: 35) and 'a psychological perspective needs to be brought to Bernstein's theory' (Ivinson and Duveen, 2005: 638) – suggests that there has been no rush to remedy this perceived deficiency. This is not to overlook, of course, attempts by Daniels (1995; 2005) and Hasan (1995) to forge links with Vygotskian psychology, but progress has undoubtedly been slow. If there is a need to take psychology more seriously it may not be without costs. Some of the support taken from cognitive and developmental psychology is at least open to alternative interpretations. These comments will be defended with reference to the researches of Luria and Hasan.

Luria's (1976) well-known investigations, undertaken 1930–31, into the intellectual capacities of peasants in Soviet Uzbekistan markedly influenced Bernstein's initial approach to language and thought and remained a significant source of inspiration. The findings seem to suggest that cultural contexts, especially as mediated by linguistic forms, are deeply implicated in cognitive functioning, and that intelligence tests are appropriate only for those who have acquired the forms of thought characteristic of the dominant classes. This interpretation of Luria's research may, however, be not quite so relevant to the development of the effective higher mental functions exercised in symbolic processing definitive of the school. The analysis must be worked through. Luria presented his subjects with classification problems such as 'Find the odd one out in the collection: hammer, saw, log, hatchet', and the peasants might answer, typically, 'If we're getting firewood for the stove, we could get rid of the hammer, but if it's planks we're fixing, we can do it without the hatchet' (ibid. 62). Luria expects the answer 'log', but the peasants' order of relevance is tied to their immediate, day-to-day interests. In Bernstein's terms, their responses reveal a *particularistic* rather than a *universalistic* orientation to meaning.

Holland's (1981) study, often cited by those sympathetic to Bernstein, is basically a replication of Luria's work. Holland asked young primary school children to classify common foods, and found a greater tendency among those from working-class families to group them by personal, idiosyncratic, criteria such as, 'it's what we have for breakfast', 'it's what Mum makes' and so on, rather than by general, material, criteria such as, 'these come from the sea', 'these all have butter in them' and so on. The implications drawn from these experiments are often treated as if they were self-evident: the results are predicted by Bernstein's theory and it is thus implied that the account of linguistically mediated cognitive performances is to that extent sound. Cognitive thinking is mediated by language, proves to be highly sensitive to context and, it seems, is more or less readily open to change by pedagogic action. One can understand the attraction of such a position. But if Luria is read more closely it is apparent that something else is going on. Luria posed typical schoolwork problems, such as: 'It takes thirty minutes to walk to village X, and it is five times faster by a bicycle. How long will it take on a bicycle?' Uneducated peasants were apt to respond: 'My brother in Dzhizak has a bicycle, and he goes much faster than a horse or a person' (Luria, 1976: 121). It is vital to understand that if such psycho-cultural barriers are removed, which Luria found required as little as a year's schooling, another more profound difficulty may be uncovered. For when a problem has been understood and accepted as a task to be undertaken, it must be solved, and that may require modes of symbolic processing very different from those that block its recognition. It is one thing to learn to attend to this question and find an appropriate motive to solve it – matters calling for relatively small cultural shifts – and quite another to recognise it, first, as a problem in division (30/5) and, second, be able to calculate the answer, six minutes. This crucial point has been overlooked by those commentators who, with all goodwill, have accepted Luria's research (and Holland's) as if it gave rather more support for Bernstein's position than is actually the case.

Hasan worked with Bernstein in the mid-1960s and since that time has made a significant contribution to sociolinguistic theory. She has remained faithful to his fundamental insights and brings impressive scholarship to bear on the relationship between language and cognition. Hasan's study of spoken exchanges between Australian mothers and their three-year-old children is particularly valuable in this context. Bernstein (1996: 133) observes that Hasan's findings are 'wholly derivable from the model of control' presented in his theoretical studies. The problem, however, is that being consistent with a theory it is not the same as a demonstration that *this* theory, rather than another, is more useful or correct. It is also vital to know what it is right about. Bernstein's engagement with Vygotsky was somewhat rhetorical, but Hasan's familiarity with Vygostkian developmental psychology is extensive and, if her findings are consistent with Bernstein, they may be yet more consistent with Vygotsky. The matter may be illustrated with two brief extracts, taken from different sources, but representative of the data:

M: (1) put it (= torch) up on the stove (2) and leave it there
K: (3) why?
M: (4) 'cause
K: (5) that's where it goes?
M: (6) yeah

(Hasan and Cloran, 1990: 83)

Hasan points out that the mother's (4) '*cause* as an answer to the child's (3) *why* is inadequate, since all it manages to say is something like, because is because. The child – Karen – is even driven to providing a possible adequate answer for herself. The next mother generates a different form of communication:

Mother:	(1) … you were certainly very brave
Cameron:	(2) (? I wasn't) very brave
Mother:	(3) yeah you were brave (4) you mightn't think you were brave (5) but I think you were
Cameron:	(6) what for?
Mother:	because you acted in a very brave way
Cameron:	(8) **no
Mother:	(9) **you hurt yourself (10) and you cried (11) and that's good to cry (12) when you hurt yourself (13) but you only cried for a little while (14) and then you climbed on your bike

(Hasan, 2002: 541)

Here the mother tells her son what it means to be described as 'brave' in certain contexts. And as Hasan comments: 'The information is an explicit mode of attempting to inculcate some concepts, irrespective of the domain within which the concept is located' (Hasan, 2002: 542; original emphasis). This is mentioned as being consistent with Bernstein's category of elaborated code, specifically the explicit/implicit axis of differentiation, and thus as support for the relevance of the concept.

So it amounts to this: there *are* systematic differences in the speech of professional and lower working-class mothers (Hasan calls them Higher Autonomy Professionals and Lower Autonomy Professionals) and these differences *are*, more or less, as Bernstein's theory predicts, but this is no evidence against the hypothesis that these contrasting modes of code-regulated verbal interaction give rise to systematic and durable class-associated variation in higher mental functions. This is a delicate area – Hasan is fully aware of what is at stake – but the scholarly circumspection of her text cannot suppress the hint that at this stage of development such may be the consequences of classed speech. Where Adlam (1977: 52), in the SRU monograph *Code in Context*, asserts that 'a sociolinguistic thesis focuses on how a child's measured ability acts, *through his socialization*, to affect his speech', Hasan's research might suggest exactly the opposite, that a child's demonstrated cognitive performance is evidence of effective higher mental functions acquired through verbally mediated semiotic processes. For if a child, like Karen, hears her mother speaking day after day in *that* mode, rather than another, she may well develop effective higher mental functions that will prove just a little *less* effective in the necessary contexts of the school than those of a child differently socialised. What children develop are, in fact, skills at processing symbolic information, most typically those forms of 'verbal analogic competence' that Bernstein himself observed (Brandis and Bernstein, 1974: 128) to be characteristic of middle-class teachers and which might be said to constitute a specific cognitive habitus. That such durable skills are developed differentially through linguistic forms of semiotic mediation is more than plausible.

The Possibility of Pedagogical Reform

According to Moore (2004: 139), Bernstein's 'concern was to identify the conditions under which members of different groups ... tend to realize restricting or elaborating variants and potentials' and in discovering 'the orienting conditions whereby particular groups come to recognize the specialized features of *contexts* that call for elaborating discourses *and* how effectively they can meet the criteria.' This interpretation invites a critical response. The sociolinguistic theory gave increasing recognition to the relevance of context as a condition for the realisation of code-regulated language use, but Bernstein's implicit programme of pedagogical reform rests on the assumption that schools and teachers have a latent power to provide contexts that evoke from working-class students language use regulated by an elaborated code. That being so, Bernstein, and those aligned with his position, might have been expected to direct their efforts to discovering and creating pedagogical contexts with such effects. Very little research of this kind has actually been undertaken. The emphasis on context to the realisation of code, although emphasised here, came rather late in the development of the sociolinguistic thesis.

If the answer to the question 'What are the contexts in which working-class children tend to recognise and meet the criteria of elaborating discourse' had always been central to Bernstein's concerns, then one might ask why *Talk Reform* (Gahagan and Gahagan, 1970), an entirely representative monograph from SRU, describes an action-research programme designed to provide working-class five-year-olds with school experiences intended to replicate the linguistic and cognitive effects of the informal pedagogy of the middle-class home. As Gahagan and Gahagan (ibid. 109) remark, '[i]t is the more rigorous cognitive demands made on the middle-class child at home which are responsible for his more flexible and varied use of language – and it was these demands that we tried to "stage-manage" in the classroom.' Twenty minutes of each school day were spent on language activities, games, puzzles and so on, of a kind instantly recognisable to any one familiar with conventional psychological approaches to compensatory education. Many of the sessions exposed children to problems entirely characteristic of standard IQ tests, with the clear purpose of enhancing intellectual skills in that domain. When the teacher engages in an activity devised so that she uses 'perhaps', 'might', 'if' and so on, in a highly didactic context (because '[r]estricted code is not amenable to expressing the hypothetical and the tentative' (ibid. 41)); when she points to the board with chalked squares of different sizes and colours and says, 'If a square is white, what else is it?', and so on; and when she is O'Grady and says, 'Put your hands over your ears if you have blue eyes', and so on, then what she is doing is training children in exactly those modes of thought intelligence tests are designed to assess. In a Postscript to *Talk Reform* Bernstein (ibid. 117) observed:

> if there is a discrepancy in the meanings and their linguistic realizations in the regulative, instructional, imaginative, inter-personal contexts, between the home and the school, then for such children there will be initial difficulties. These difficulties will be intensified if the school does not start with the commonsense every-day world of the child, family and community. The Gahagans in their book have focused on these four contexts and their programme attempted to encourage the children to explore these contexts in a number of ways.

This disingenuous comment at least admits the sociological imperative that the contexts of learning should be relevant to working-class conditions of life, but it is a misleading account of *Talk Reform*. Within a few years, Bernstein had unequivocally committed himself to the proposition that: '*If the culture of the teacher is to become part of the consciousness of the child, then the culture of the child must first be in the consciousness of the teacher*' (Bernstein, 1971: 199; original emphasis), but his Postscript certainly indicates that pedagogy is central to the reproduction, and potential interruption, of social inequalities in educational attainment.

Bernstein's clearest statement to this effect, which he repeated at least once in response to critics, may be given (Brandis and Henderson, 1970: 121):

> Even more can be done to ensure that the teacher's core responsibility, the transfer of skills and sensitivities, can be effectively carried out. For in the final count it is *what* goes on and *how* it goes on in the *school* that matters. Educational visitors, teacher/social workers, although highly relevant, are no substitute for constant appraisal of both the methods we are using and the culture and organization of the school.

This statement, although consistent with the emphasis on code realisation as controlled by context, remains unarticulated with a programme of pedagogical reform. Bernstein's general theory of symbolic control, which Atkinson sees as his major contribution to sociology, is now positioned somewhat uneasily as a theory of a process that occurs seemingly by virtue of the stubborn incapacity of teachers to change their practices and of school organisational structures to allow such change. Bernstein argues that reform is possible – his structuralism is not determinist – but the persistence of the conventional pedagogy that ensures class reproduction is unexplained. It seems to be taken for granted, in fact, that the account of normal pedagogy is correct. The matter might be open to doubt. Enormous numbers of teachers have dedicated their professional lives to reflexive practice without, it seems, managing to interrupt to any significant degree the 'inner logic' of the system. Was it really the case in 1970 that the consciousness of the teacher was not the consciousness of the child, when this was the basic thrust of post-Plowden primary school practice, and is it, indeed, still the case a whole generation later? These must stand as rhetorical questions for readers to answer as they may. In any event, Bernstein wrote nothing for teachers who took *this* message to heart, rather than the 'misunderstood' sociolinguistic theory that they were likely to have encountered – and to which it actually was offered as a corrective – and the question they might well have asked, 'What then?' was left for them to work out. But the translation of a modified teacher consciousness into a 'universal pedagogy' should not be regarded as automatic.

Conclusion

That Bernstein's thought has been fruitful in stimulating research is commonly asserted in defence not only of its overall significance as a 'general and systematic sociology or anthropology' (Atkinson, Davies and Delamont, 1995: xii), but, at least by implication, of the basic soundness of its central theses. We should distinguish, however, between work that employs Bernsteinian concepts, as 'vertical and horizontal discourse' are increasingly being used; work sympathetic to Bernstein's ideas that may confirm certain relationships, such as Hasan's discovery of code-regulated language used by Australian mothers; and work that attempts to test substantive hypotheses derived from his theories using an appropriate methodology. There are numerous studies in the first category, fewer in the second, and, even when the entire set of SRU monographs is included, no more than a handful in the third. The characteristic tone of Bernstein's contemporary 'recontextualisers', with a duty to introduce a lifetime's work everyone acknowledges to be touched by genius, anxious to expunge the 'Apocryphal' Bernstein and the 'Bernstein' of the best-forgotten textbooks, and more than disposed to concentrate on his strengths than his weaknesses, has here provoked a minor act of resistance. In this frame of mind, then, one or two self-evident points may be indulged. Citation rates are not theoretical tests: no conclusion can be drawn about the veracity of the sociolinguistic hypothesis, in particular, from the degree of recognition given to Bernstein's insightful analytical concepts. It is time to shift attention from the principled defence of Bernstein's theories, and the celebration of his undoubted authority as a sociologist, to a critical examination of the accuracy of his concrete explanations of specific social facts, not least that of the origins of inequality of educational opportunity.

References

Adlam, D. (1977). *Code in Context*, with the assistance of G. Turner and L. Lineker, foreword by B. Bernstein (London: Routledge).

Atkinson, P. (1985). *Language, Structure and Reproduction: An Introduction to the Sociology of Basil Bernstein* (London: Methuen).

Atkinson, P., Davies, B. and Delamont, S. (eds) (1995). Introduction. In *Discourse and Reproduction: Essays in Honour of Basil Bernstein* (Cresskill, NJ: Hampton Press): vii–xiv.

Bernstein, B. (1971). *Class, Codes and Control 1: Theoretical Studies towards a Sociology of Language* (London: Routledge & Kegan Paul).

Bernstein, B. (1990). *Class, Codes and Control 4: The Structuring of Pedagogic Discourse* (London: Routledge).

Brandis, W. and Bernstein, B. (1974). *Selection and Control: Teachers' Ratings of Children in the Infant School* (London: Routledge & Kegan Paul).

Brandis, W. and Henderson, D. (1970). *Social Class, Language and Communication* (London: Routledge & Kegan Paul).

Daniels, H. (1995) Pedagogic practices, tacit knowledge and discursive discrimination: Bernstein and post-Vygotskian research, *British Journal of Sociology of Education*, 16(4): 517–32.

Daniels, H.R.J. (ed.) (2005). *An Introduction to Lev Vygotsky*, 2nd edn (London: Routledge).

Davies, B. (1976). *Social control and education* (London: Methuen).

Davis, A. (1962). *Social-class Influences upon Learning (Inglis Lecture, 1948)* (Cambridge, Mass.: Harvard University Press).

Douglas, J.W.B. (1964). *The Home and the School: A Study of Ability and Attainment in the Primary School* (London: McGibbbon and Kee).

Ells, K., Davis, A., Havinghurst, R.J., Herrick, V.E. and Tyler, R.W. (1951). *Intelligence and Cultural Difference* (Chicago: University of Chicago Press).

Erben, M. and Dickinson, H. (2004). Basil Bernstein: Social divisions and cultural transformations. In M. Olssen (ed.), *Culture and Learning: Access and Opportunity in the Classroom* (Greenwich, CT: Information Age Publishing): 117–36.

Flynn, J.R. (2004). The sociology of IQ: enhancing cognitive skills. In M. Olssen (ed.), *Culture and Learning: Access and Opportunity in the Classroom* (Greenwich, CT: Information Age Publishing): 257–78.

Gahagan, D.M. and Gahagan, G.A. (1970). *Talk Reform: Explorations in Language for Infant School Children* (London: Routledge).

Gordon, J.C.B. (1981). *Verbal Deficit: A Critique* (London: Croom Helm).

Halliday. M.A.K. (1995). Language and the theory of codes. In A.R. Sadovnik (ed.), *Knowledge and Pedagogy: The Sociology of Basil Bernstein* (Norwood, NJ: Ablex): 127–43.

Hasan, R. (1995). On social conditions for semiotic mediation: The genesis of mind in society. In A.R. Sadovnik (ed.). *Knowledge and Pedagogy: The Sociology of Basil Bernstein* (Norword, NJ: Ablex): 171–96.

Hasan, R. (2002). Ways of meaning, ways of learning: Code as an explanatory concept, *British Journal of Sociology of Education*, 23(4): 537–48.

Hasan, R. and Cloran, C. (1990). A sociolinguistic interpretation of everyday talk between mothers and children. In M.A.K.,Halliday, J. Gibbons and H. Nicholas (eds), *Learning, Keeping and Using Language 1: Papers from the 8th World Congress of Applied Linguistics, Sydney, 16–21 August, 1987* (Amsterdam: John Benjamins): 67–99.

Holland, J. (1981). Social class and changes in orientation to meaning, *Sociology*, 15(1): 1–18.

Iverson, G. and Duveen, G. (2005). Clasroom structuration and the development of social representations of the curriculum, *British Journal of Sociology of Education*, 26(3): 627–42.

Lee, V. (1973). *Social Relationships and Language: Some Aspects of the Work of Basil Bernstein* (Milton Keynes: Open University Press).

Lévi-Strauss, C., (1978), *Structural Anthropology 1 and 2* (Harmondsworth: Penguin).

Luria, A.R. (1976). *Cognitive Development: Its Cultural and Social Foundations*, ed. M. Cole, trans, M. Lopez-Morillas and L. Solotaroff (Cambridge, Mass.: Harvard University Press).

Moore, R. (2004). *Education and Society: Issues and Explanations in the Sociology of Education* (Cambridge: Polity Press).

Morais, A., Neve, I., Davies, B. and Daniels, H. (eds) (2001). *Towards a Sociology of Pedagogy: The Contribution of Basil Bernstein's Research* (New York: Peter Lang).

Muller, J., Davies, B. and Morais, A. (eds) (2004). *Reading Bernstein, Researching Bernstein.*(London: Routledge/Falmer).

Steadman Jones, S. (2001). *Durkheim Reconsidered* (Cambridge: Polity Press).

Stubbs, M. (1976). *Language, Schools and Classrooms* (London: Methuen).

Vygotsky, L. (1994). *The Vygotsky Reader*, ed. R. Van der Veer and J. Valsiner (Oxford: Blackwell).

PART 3
Classed Identities in Formation

Can the Arbitrary and the Necessary be Reconciled? Scientific Realism and the School Curriculum

Questions about what counts as knowledge, and who should have access to knowledge, have been correctly placed at the centre of contemporary studies in the sociology of the curriculum. McEneaney and Meyer (2000), noting the tension that exists between theories that emphasise the allocational function of the educational system and those that focus on its construction of citizens able to participate in society, are conscious of the mechanism by which the 'allocational' (reproductive) agency of the school is achieved. The reproductive thesis maintains, McEneaney and Meyer remark, 'that the implicit knowledge carried in the system is consistent only with the arbitrary culture of higher status groups, so that lower status students are disadvantaged' (ibid. 190). This theme, that of the once-'new' sociology of education (Young, 1971), has been worked through with some thoroughness in the last 30 years.

There may, nevertheless, be work that remains to be done. In fact, there may be the rather troublesome task of *undoing* some of the things that have been done. This rather provocative remark demands an explanation. That knowledge is 'socially constructed' (and in some usually ill-defined sense, not therefore to be accepted as a true account of reality); that knowledge is necessarily an arbitrary social product; and that school knowledge has the symbolic power to maintain relations of social domination has become the conventional wisdom of an entire movement. When Bourdieu and Passeron (1977: 5) declared that, '[a]ll *pedagogic action* (PA) is, objectively, symbolic violence insofar as it is the imposition of a cultural arbitrary by an arbitrary power', they issued what quickly became the manifesto of a generation. This thesis has placed the sociology of the curriculum at the heart of the sociology of education: if social and cultural reproduction is effected through such mechanisms, then questions about the nature of knowledge and the world become ones of more general concern. The enquiries of curriculum specialists assume a broader dimension of relevance and become exposed to critique from outside the established confines of their field.

This chapter may be regarded as such a critique: for what may have to be undone is the assumption that the school curriculum is, necessarily and inevitably, adequately characterised as an expression of the cultural arbitrary. This is not to dispute the generally acknowledged claim, indeed, that the school is engaged in forms of symbolic violence, that it has a reproductive effect and so on; but it is to assert the realist case that accurate knowledge of the world can be obtained and should constitute a non-arbitrary element of the of the school curriculum. The status of realism as a philosophy of science will be outlined in its place and it will suffice at this point to note that the discussion will be based on the premises of realism.

The chapter will engage in this way with the theories of two sociologists who have powerfully influenced the curriculum debate. Some of Bourdieu's key concepts – symbolic violence, the cultural arbitrary, the conservative function of the school – have already made their appearance in this text. Bernstein's own life work might be summed up as a related investigation into the problems of knowledge and control (Edwards, 2002). And if Bernstein's analyses led him to refine our accepted concepts rather than introduce new ones, his achievements are none the less noteworthy for that. It is significant to note in the context of thesis to be developed that these thinkers, moreover, advanced arguments that have lent support to positions they themselves were reluctant to endorse. Both men, in fact, maintained a traditional Enlightenment concept of education while propounding theses that emphasised its social origins and, hence, its relative character. Whether Bourdieu and Bernstein might be recognised as scientific realists can be left an open question (Nash, 1999, 2002a). The argument with them, however, will be held on realist grounds: if realism is right then some knowledge, at least, is not arbitrary but necessary. In short, if the world is as it is, then that is what we should teach in schools. The argument, therefore, is that we should seek to reconcile the arbitrary with the necessary, or at least seek to distinguish the one from the other, and so attempt to place the school curriculum on realist foundations. It is mainly for the purposes of simplification that the focus of the discussion here is centred on the science curriculum and nothing that will be said should be taken to suggest that the principles are not equally applicable to other areas of school knowledge. The analysis will begin with a presentation of a powerful critique, deeply influenced by Bourdieu and Bernstein, which is so clearly non-realist in its epistemological foundations.

The 'New' Sociology's Critique of Knowledge and Control

A major tradition of 'critical pedagogy' asserts that the school actively excludes the majority of students who bring to the school modes of thought and practices that it 'systematically denies, dilutes, downvalues, or distorts' (Corrigan, 1990: 160). In this thesis, the school's curriculum, pedagogy and forms of evaluation of the school, in their grounded practices, are recognised as arbitrary social forms '[i]t has been well-argued that there is nothing universal or natural about the bodies of knowledge that come to be taught as school subjects – they are all social constructions with specific histories' (ibid. 167). Students from class-cultural communities socialised into codes of communication incompatible with those that regulate the transmission of school knowledge, and not recognised by the school as legitimate, are confronted with formidable barriers of incomprehension they are unable to surmount. In such a way does the school act as a conservative force effectively excluding students from the dominated classes by a non-benign form of neglect.

Young's (1976) critical investigation of the development of school science in England, for example, describes how science was introduced to the school curriculum, late in the nineteenth century, in order to increase the supply of trained scientists by preparing students with the necessary qualifications for entry to a university science course. Consequently, the subjects of school science, physics, chemistry and biology developed under university control as bodies of 'pure' knowledge consisting of abstract laws, methodological principles and lists of facts having little relation to each other or to areas of practical application. In this way, the academic distinction between the high-status 'pure' knowledge of theory and the low-status 'impure' knowledge of practice in those subjects was imposed on the schools. Stengel (1998) provides an interesting discussion of the relationship between school subjects and academic disciplines.

The substance of this critique would be accepted by many of those who have passed through modern school systems. It is a history shared, for example, in New Zealand where my empirical research happens to be carried out. A woman then in her mid-forties, speaking to an interviewer in 1990, made the following statement when she was asked if the girls' school she had attended made any special provision for 'non-academic' girls:

> No, for those of us who went through what – it was rigidly streamed – I went in what was called 3 'O' and we were the only third formers who did French and Latin. Then in the fourth form I dropped Latin and became in 3 'F' – for French not Latin. The assumption was that you would go teaching. A couple of brave girls got librarian studentships. That was a new thing. Then there were the girls who went through commercial, and all the dummies took home economics. There's still a bit of carry over from that. But you got that hierarchy. There was only a certain proportion they allowed to pass School Certificate. No, it was pretty much charted – OK, apart from dropping things like French – and once you went into that form you were in the technical stream. If you went in as an academic 99 times out of a 100 you stayed an academic, and if you went in the home economic or commercial that's what you'd do.

This heartfelt commentary on the organisation of school knowledge is a salutary reminder of the real suffering inflicted by such institutionalised symbolic violence (Bourdieu et al., 1999). It required a 'brave' act to reject the pedagogic identity offered by the school, and it is significant that the speaker, even within a critical attitude, continues to accept its fundamental distinction between 'academics' and 'dummies'. The core of the 'critical' argument, motivated by a genuine concern for those who suffer from symbolic violence, is that middle-class and working-class concepts of knowledge are different, basically as a consequence of their antagonistic positions in the division of labour, and that the school has an *arbitrary* preference for the former at the expense of the latter.

The critique, informed by concepts drawn from Bernstein and Bourdieu, is influential. However, to what extent – supposing it to be valid – does it continue to describe the reality of contemporary science in the upper school? And, if it remains substantially true, then how can this mechanism, among all the others that might be included in an analysis of social differences in education, be assessed? It is certainly true that the sciences taught at secondary school – biology, chemistry and physics – were developed in the nineteenth century to prepare students for university study and that they continue to have that function among others. The 'trick' in the construction of any school subject where the interests of the students taking it through to university entrance level cannot be compromised is to embed the knowledge those students require in the content of a universal curriculum for the majority, following a different trajectory, in such a way that the interests and needs of all are satisfied. It is a 'trick' more difficult to manage than might be thought. Although the content of the curriculum and modes of pedagogy have been transformed by wave after wave of reform, it continues to be possible to trace in current pedagogical practice vestiges of the tradition that created them.

The construction of knowledge by the school as theoretical/practical, pure/applied and so on blatantly endorses the mental (directive) and manual (directed) division of labour – perhaps even the ideal/material basis of philosophy – and continues to characterise elements of the upper-school curriculum. In New Zealand, for example, all students thus recognise that Year 13 Mathematics with Calculus is more highly esteemed than Alternative Mathematics, but the reasons for such relative valuations are neither self-evident nor invariably understood by students or their parents (Dowling, 1998). The examined courses certainly have a greater exchange value because they provide recognised qualifications, and the alternative, non-examined (so-called 'cabbage') courses, do not. However, that only throws the question back: Why, particularly when alternative courses make much of their 'practical' relevance (completing tax forms and so on), is it *these* courses that are left unexamined at the highest level of schooling and thus stigmatised with an inferior status? Many students never fully grasp the reason for this – including some that succeed in mastering the more abstract subjects – and develop a purely instrumentalist concept of knowledge that that seems to respect both the school's continual emphasis on the all-important matter of passing examinations and its ambivalent concession to 'relevance'.

The economic division of labour, driven by the imperative of efficiency (which is always a technical efficiency within a moral economy), divorces at every level conception from execution, theoretical knowledge from practical application, mental from manual work, and directive command from directed labour. In this context, working-class students are more likely than middle-class students to value more highly the exchange value than the use value of their studies. All this is so, and yet schools may fail in their educational task not because they give too little emphasis to credentials, but because they give too much. For there may, after all, be good reasons why Mathematics with Calculus is worth more on the market than Alternative Mathematics: it might actually be the case that mathematics in the strict sense provides knowledge about the real structures of the physical universe and in that sense is, for the most practical of reasons, the intellectual birthright of all. To signify that a course in mathematics is worth studying mainly because it is credentialed is actually to devalue it as a practical and universal accomplishment. Once again, these remarks may be seen as unduly provocative: it will be necessary to go more deeply into Bourdieu's account of symbolic power.

Bourdieu and Symbolic Power

In his most influential statements, Bourdieu (1984) sees differences in socially conditioned intellectual aptitudes as arbitrary forms of mentality treated by the school as unequal 'gifts of nature' and transformed by its institutional power into actual differences in objective educational qualifications. As a thoroughgoing phenomenologist, Robbins (1991, 1999), one of the most informed commentators in this area, has also recognised, Bourdieu is anti-essentialist in respect of objects and selves and so rejects not only *positivist* science but also an ontological commitment to scientific realism. Within this institutional framework, Bourdieu (1977, 1990, 1991) admits no realities behind appearances, and his theory of the relationship between scientific knowledge and the structures of the natural world must be considered one of philosophical scepticism. As far as Bourdieu is concerned, the relationships to be observed between social class, knowledge and the world itself must be regarded as finally *arbitrary*. The anthropological narrative of human society is one of difference. Cultures are even defined by the complex patterns of practice adopted by a collective as a solution to the problems of life specific to each community. Whether family social relations in a traditional society are organised by matrilocality or patrilocality, by endogamy or exogamy, by filial or non-filial inheritance, is arbitrary in the sense that one will function as well as another, and the selection is emphatically grounded in a cultural rather than a genetic code. This central concept of anthropological theory plays so large a part in Bourdieu's discourse that LiPuma (1993) has identified three distinct references: (i) any practice is arbitrary from a class-cultural standpoint in the sense that things could be otherwise; (ii) the social valuation afforded any practice within a given culture is arbitrary; and (iii) any practice will serve as a thus arbitrary symbolic marker of distinction. These several usages, not fully acknowledged as such by Bourdieu, contribute to the renowned complexity, if not obscurity, of his conceptual framework, pose a series of problems that require particular resolutions. Bourdieu's concept of cultural capital, for example, is at once relative and normalised: it is relative in the sense that what counts as cultural capital is *arbitrary*, that is specific to a type of society, and *normalised* in the sense that in modern class-based societies people with the habits of a literate culture possess a symbolic capital that is recognised and legitimated in certain fields of practice.

Bourdieu's concept of symbolic violence is a signal reminder that knowledge and its forms are not *given*, but the products of human beings who, indeed, have never done much without engaging in struggle and competition – in the intellectual fields of science and philosophy as in any other – although the capacity to construct science is not in any sense incompatible with scientific realism. Bourdieu's concept is essential to the analysis of the school curriculum in as much as it directs attention to the history of the curriculum, the concepts that structure its organisation, and the social relations that maintain it (Olneck, 2000).

The importance of Bourdieu's thought would be difficult to overestimate, and yet scientific realism requires a curriculum in which knowledge of the world is taught as necessary. And the suggestion that working-class students are effectively denied access to knowledge because of its structuring as abstract and universal, properties necessarily reflected in the discourse of educational transmission, is extremely difficult to demonstrate. Thus, it would be possible to write the contemporary history of curriculum reform as an attempt to eliminate the arbitrariness embedded in its forms. The tension in these struggles is always created by the desire to cleanse the curriculum of its *class arbitrary* (particularly of its tainted and elitist concepts that define the hierarchy of knowledge), and the need to retain the *real necessary* (the abstract and the universal) without which there can be no education worth calling by that name.

In a now-classic paper Bourdieu (1974) proposed the development of a 'universal pedagogy' that would make no assumptions about the forms of knowledge students bring to school, but the suggestion, which was seen as hinting at conventional deficit theory interventions (Baudelot and Establet, 1981), remained undeveloped. Lane (2000: 200) is among those who have noted the nature and source of Bourdieu's educational politics:

> His continued faith in the power of a scientific sociology to emancipate agents from the mystified vision of art and culture which keep them in their place, his qualified belief in the ability of suitably 'rationalized' forms of teaching to mitigate social inequalities, his determined defence of the universal values of scientific knowledge against postmodernist 'irrationalism' and 'nihilism' all point to the extent of Bourdieu's affinities with the Durkheimian tradition and the republican ideals and values that implies.

Robbins (1999: 330), perhaps more willing than most commentators to see Bourdieu's formal epistemology through to its relativist conclusion, actually scorns a popular error of interpretation, as he sees it, that has distorted the reception of Bourdieu's work:

> the appropriation of Bourdieu's social anthropological analyses of the experiences of students by an institutionalized discipline calling itself the 'sociology of education' rested on the false assumption that Bourdieu's work offered a blueprint

for the ways in which the existing structure of 'real' knowledge might be more efficiently and democratically communicated. It was a 'realist' appropriation.

This is an interesting argument, and counter to that developed here, which is that Bourdieu's analyses have more often supported a non-realist critique than otherwise, but it does reveal Robbins's clear perception that this work provides no blueprint for a rational pedagogy designed to transmit real knowledge. As Holton (2000: 93) has also pointed out that, while Bourdieu 'has not been unwilling to condemn what he sees as the nihilistic relativism of postmodern theory', his epistemological framework contains no principle, other than the 'realism' of realpolitik, to refute such 'excesses'. Bourdieu's recognition of the *arbitrary* may indeed need to be reconciled with his realist acknowledgement of the *necessary*. Related problems are to be found in Bernstein's work and these will now be discussed.

Bernstein's Sociolinguistic Theory

Bernstein's earliest paper on sociolinguistics appeared in the 1950s; the most recent, and sadly the last, more than four decades later. Throughout this long period Bernstein continually reworked his central ideas in academic journals, and there is still no definitive work of exposition – at least no popular or 'accessible' text – from his hand that presents an authoritative statement of the core argument. An introduction in a few paragraphs to so intricate a body of work cannot do other than misrepresent, to a greater or lesser degree, its multiple subtleties. The concept most strongly associated with Bernstein – 'restricted' and 'elaborated' speech codes (these terms actually replaced the earlier concept of 'public' and 'private' speech and have themselves been superseded by the recently introduced reference to 'horizontal' and 'vertical' forms of discourse) – will provide a convenient entry to the complexities of the theory.

Bernstein is fundamentally a structuralist and the term 'code' cannot be understood outside that theoretical framework. The related set of distinctions that Bernstein has struggled to explicate in successive formulations, but always in the familiar dichotomised forms of structuralism, has to do with, at one pole, the common-sense knowledge – context specific, loaded with affect and embedded in the concrete – of face-to-face groups, families, peer groups and so on, and, at the other pole, the theoretically informed, systematically structured and explicit knowledge – independent of context, impersonal and abstract – of economically specialised social groups. Code understood as a *principle* refers to an abstract property of speech, at the level of semantics and meaning, which is further conceived as a mechanism of linguistic production. It can be accepted that speech *is* structured, not only by grammar, but also by whatever underlying or overarching 'grammar' that generates speech in its 'restricted' or 'elaborated' forms. It seems that there must be some kind of operational linguistic mechanism and this 'theoretical' entity that controls the production of language, in the form of speech genres common to specific groups and social contexts, can be referred to as a principle of speech or meaning. Thus, 'code' is a *principle* that regulates the selection and organisation of language and which can be detected, and can necessarily only be so detected, through an analysis of language (Hasan, 2002).

Bernstein argues that the 'elaborated' code generates a language or discourse of social power whereas the 'restricted' code generates a discourse of subordination. The dominant class that controls capital, labour and culture – the financial, human and symbolic resources that underpin industrial capitalism – must necessarily employ a discourse with the capacity to express generalised and abstract conceptions. And the dominated class, dispossessed of capital, forced to sell its labour power and, thus, required to submit to the discourse of power, is more or less limited by these contexts and relationships to certain forms of expression. Middle-class discourse transcends the local context and constitutes an effective means of symbolic control: working-class discourse is locked into the particular context and constitutes a mechanism of domination. The educational system, which effectively reproduces the structures of social power through pedagogic action, is implicated organically in this process by the production of students socialised into these particular discursive forms.

This has been found an attractive theory but it is not immune to objection. There is a possibility, for example, that the cognitive formation developed by intense forms of literate socialisation is not at all arbitrary, in as much as it provides durable intellectual capacities entirely necessary to the competent mastery of the analytical and scientific knowledge that the modern school must teach. The relations that control access to areas of discourse in curriculum, pedagogy and evaluation have been discussed in papers no less influential than his work on language (Bernstein, 1971).

Bernstein's work is compatible with a realist ontology of the physical world (this was undoubtedly his personal view), and, as his support for empirical research into language and socialisation demonstrates, his structuralist approach does rule out scientific research based on that foundation. This level of commitment to realism, however, is not actually grounded in his conceptual apparatus. The implications of this fact are sympathetically analysed by Maton (2000) who has shown the inherent difficulty of moving outside the framework of a discourse that treats educational knowledge as a function of power relations. Moore and Muller (1999: 190) have also argued that a critique that 'privileges and specializes the subject in terms of its membership category as a subordinated voice' is likely to be at once misleading in its depiction of modern science; mistaken in its sociological account of this 'hegemonic' epistemology; mistaken in its understanding of the status of knowledge in the educational system; and mistaken in its conclusions about the consequences of knowledge transmission processes for social exclusion. The school is, and must be, concerned with the transmission of a universal knowledge within forms of pedagogic discourse characterised by an elaborated code. A school that failed to teach its students the necessarily abstract concepts of language and mathematics would simply not be a school in the modern sense at all. As a result of this, however, the school confers an implicit, and very substantial, privilege on those students who enter school with a ready command of the forms of meaning it transmits. This is the core thesis of Bernstein's theory of speech and meaning.

Scientific Realism and Truth

This discussion is concerned with *scientific* realism. There is more than one variety of realism: Platonists thought that the ideal forms of their philosophy were real entities, and in that respect their philosophy was realist; in politics, theorists with a tendency to realpolitik are called 'realists' in a different sense; in criminology, 'realism' is used similarly to describe the view that 'crime will always be with us', and so on. However, the basis of scientific realism is simply the view that the physical and social entities of the world exist. Scientific realists are convinced that a material world exists, that human beings have developed the capacity to gain an accurate knowledge of its nature, and have succeeded in doing so across a broadening range of natural phenomena. Bhaskar's (1993) increasingly influential 'critical realism' is a form of scientific realism that derives its ontology from the 'transcendental' fact that the explanatory models of modern science are so powerful that they must be accepted as effective demonstrations of the nature of the world (Collier, 1994; Danermark et al., 2000).

As an ontological doctrine, realism has a series of implications for the conduct and interpretation of science. The test of reality is *demonstration*. The existence of physical objects in the series 'stars, planets, mountains, houses, tables, grains of wood, microscopic crystals, microbes' (Smart, 1963: 36) can be demonstrated by acts of ostension, such as pointing, and this is so even in the case of entities too small, or too far away, to detect without instruments. To be demonstrated means to be *pointed out* in such a way that the evidence before one's senses can only be accepted or rejected. In the realist conception, the purpose of science is to explain what the world is like, and that requirement implies a realist ontology: there is no point in trying to explain an *unreal* world, and if theoretical statements do not refer to things that exist they might as well be about anything. It is for such reasons that Bunge (1996: 137), one of the most trenchant materialist philosophers, makes explanation dependent on ontology: '[t]o explain a thing ... is to show how it works, and to explain a fact is to show how it came to be.' To the extent that an explanation shows how the world is, it is also to that extent true. Most realist philosophers – although Bhaskar's position may be an exception – accept on these grounds that scientific realism requires a correspondence theory of truth in some form (Nimiluoto, 1999).

Many non-realist philosophers, however, understand a scientific theory as a set of theoretical statements, obviously constructions of the human brain and social practice ('culture'), and these statements are regarded as meaningful in as much as they constitute a *discourse*. It is not necessary, in this view, for scientific theories to 'refer' to 'things' outside the boundaries of a particular discursive field and, indeed, some philosophers consider the realist attempt to link 'discourse' and 'non-discourse' as a somewhat elementary mistake. The attempt to talk about things outside discourse, it is argued, must always fail: the attempt to introduce such objects into theory itself constitutes another object in discourse – simply introduces another element into the network of meaning – and thus frustrates the move to transcend discourse by an attempt at reference to something outside it. This view of the scientific enterprise is expressed in a characteristic idealist statement by Doyle and Harris (1986: 37): 'a statement apparently as innocently observational as "This balloon is full of helium" is already very far from a completely untheorized perception. No one has ever *seen* helium. It is an essentially theoretical concept which derives its meaning from an atomistic view of the world.' To a scientific realist, the term 'helium atom' refers to a material entity with certain properties: to an idealist 'helium' is a 'theoretical concept'. The specific error here is identified by Bunge (1974: 172): 'it is not that the "meaning of a scientific construct is theory-laden", as the fashionable trend has it, but the other way around: theories (even logical theories) are meaning-laden.' Sound or not, however, this philosophy has strongly influenced the teaching of science throughout the world (Forsnot, 1996). The movement has not gone unchallenged: Matthews's (1995) critique of the anti-realist theories that are seen to dominate New Zealand science education, for example, has yet to receive a response at the same thorough level of analysis.

The concept of knowledge is crucial to this debate. Bunge is particularly clear about the nature of knowledge and reality: knowledge, in his view, is that which is known by particular people (by living brains), and what people know may be compared, to a greater or a lesser degree, with the way things are. Thus, to adopt an example from a contemporary news report, one secondary school student might understand the function of the Fallopian tubes in the female reproductive system and be able to identify them on a diagram, another might know that they are part of the female body but be unable to recognise them in any form, while another might vaguely think that they are part of the city of Rome's underground railway system. The first student has more knowledge than the second (but probably less than a medical practitioner does), the second knows something that is right, and the third is completely in error. The concept of *truth* actually has little to offer a practical theory of knowledge. Realism almost certainly does require a correspondence theory of truth, but its value is semantic: the proposition that 'the Fallopian tubes are part of female reproductive system is true if and only if the Fallopian tubes are part of the female reproductive system' offers little to the programme of science. The *practical* difficulty is to determine whether, and to what extent, what we know is in accordance with the way things actually are. The task of science is to investigate the structures of the world and thus establish factual truth, not to 'search for the truth', which is a question for semantic enquiry.

This highly condensed account must suffice in this context as a statement of the realist position. The central tenets of realism are quite easy to understand and, indeed, almost everyone who has not encountered academic philosophy is a realist about the nature of the physical world, and while 'naive' realism is often castigated it is arguably less misleading than naive idealism as a foundation for a more considered philosophical position (Kirk, 1999). There is an influential view in the theory of science, however, a view that has deeply influenced the school curriculum, which rejects scientific realism in favour of idealist doctrines.

However, as realists we can say this: the world exists; we are beings so constituted by the capacities of our senses and our intelligence to know that it exists and to form theories about what it is like; we are able to check some, at least, of these theories against what the world is actually like and so gain accurate knowledge of it; and, therefore, the demonstrated knowledge of science and the social tools of its production must be given a central place in the school curriculum. The continual interrogation of the curriculum in these terms does not entail commitment to non-realist concepts of knowledge and truth. That French schools teach a literature of Molière and Stendhal and English schools a literature of Shakespeare and Dickens is an anthropological arbitrary at the level of their nationhood (Readings, 1996); that they both teach differential calculus is an anthropological arbitrary at the level of their existence as modern states dependent for their survival upon a sophisticated technology; that they teach literature *and* mathematics, however, is *also* a matter of universal necessity given that the purpose of education is to enable students to learn how the physical and social world is constituted and how it operates.

A Discussion for Practice

In the debate on social class and access to knowledge there are issues of such fundamental importance, issues so loaded with practical and ideological significance, that few writers in this field venture more than to hint at their existence. The problem concerns the status of knowledge as a means of understanding the world and the valuation consequently given to specific forms of knowledge. There are, in fact, two related problems. First, what principles and practices confer and sustain knowledge hierarchies? And, second, what principles and practices control social access to knowledge? These questions, although analytically distinct, are intimately connected precisely because the status accorded to knowledge is an important criterion influencing its social allocation. Both questions, therefore, give rise to a set of related questions that, could they be answered, might provide useful insights into these matters. What is the relationship between knowledge and reality? To what extent are social class differences in perception and cognition derived from class socialisation practices with a necessary structural relationship to economic and cultural production? On what grounds is the social distribution of knowledge structured by an illegitimate mapping of epistemological and social hierarchies?

The standard response of critical sociology of education of inequality of educational opportunity may be flawed in several respects. If scientific realism is right, the fundamental error may be that the character of the school curriculum, particularly in science, is less arbitrary and more universal than is assumed. And, if that is so, then the conventional ideology controlling class access to knowledge is deeply undermined. If the regulating principle for the provision of access to knowledge is actually one of right to real knowledge, for example, then certain divisions ('pure' vs. 'applied' 'theoretical' vs. 'practical' and so on) are more clearly recognised as the givens of a class arbitrary. It is in relation to Bernstein's theories that these themes of class, knowledge and social control have been most closely examined, and for that reason the discussion will pay particular regard to his concepts. The themes of the debate are, however, directly relevant to the 'reproductive' theses legitimated by Bourdieu.

Bernstein does not, as the discussion has recognised, share a view of the relationship between class, knowledge and cognition as *merely* arbitrary. It is more than understandable, given these tensions between his actual realism and the limitations of his critical scheme, therefore, that Bernstein (1995: 402) should prefer to approach the 'tedious' and 'vociferous' deficit theory debate with caution, and with dark hints at the implications of 'the semiotic time-bomb ticking away in all mass educational systems', but his final declaration, that it must be possible to distinguish a discourse that necessarily goes beyond the local context and is invariably the language of symbolic control with respect to the material or the symbolic universe, is an unequivocal statement of fact and principle. Middle-class people are more likely, he maintains, in contrast to working-class people, to recognise and respond to contexts of interaction and learning that require semiotic elaboration, explicit description and conceptual abstraction. And the contexts in which the control of capital and the direction of labour are exercised – *decision-making contexts* – necessarily have this character. This point is accepted by many of those considered by Bernstein to understand his work, by Halliday (1995), for example, and even more openly by Hasan. A linguist as familiar with Bernstein's work as anyone, and with the advantage of having carried out some of the most important empirical linguistic research within his conceptual framework, Hasan (1995: 193) goes so far as to expresses the fundamental insights, and their problematic implications, in these terms:

> Are there no *logical* reasons for better valuing such higher mental functions as those of abstraction, generalisation, deductive reasoning, disembodied thinking and so on? Are these functions valued highly *only* because they are associated with the dominant codes? Or are they valued because they are the ultimate point in the programs of the development of the human mind, necessary for subjugating the environment? These questions throw long shadows, and it is my conviction that neither the science of cognitive development nor of physics, have pursued these questions. This may be because no matter how we answer these questions, the answers are immensely disquieting and they certainly mock the facile pseudo-revolutionary postures of many academics today.

Hasan writes of 'subjugating the environment', and perhaps even to control the spread of disease and ensure a just and fair system of production and distribution of goods might be so described, but the case for scientific knowledge can certainly be stated in less aggressive terms. The desire to understand the nature of the world through a realist theory of science is not necessarily linked to the desire for domination over nature. The connection with class is not a matter of *logic*, but it is emphatically a matter for social practice, and of society as it is rather than as it must necessarily be. Not all Bernstein's commentators accept this conclusion. Danzig (1995), for example, prefers to see in 'codes, and in teachers' expectations towards those whose speech is structured by non-valued forms, a model of practice apparently sufficient in itself to explain social difference in educational attainment. There are also a multitude of commentators, some of whose work, like that of Walkerdine and Lucey (1989), actually supports the fundamental insights of Bernstein's thesis, but who nevertheless maintain the kind of stance that Hasan might well have in mind as 'facile pseudo-revolutionary posture[s]'. The economic division of labour in all actually existing industrial societies does, of course, ensure in practice that the positions of executive direction and technical control require comprehensive, universal, spheres of interest, and the consequences of this for education have been cogently explored by Bernstein.

The ensuing discussion will explore some implications of Bernstein's (1995) suggestion that these linkages *are* necessary. The nature of the world, and the problem that needs to be solved by knowing its nature, or the mechanism of its production, must influence the methods of enquiry adopted. Physical scientists are, in one sense, more fortunate than those whose interests lie in the social sciences, for their world is the actual universe of material entities that can be isolated, described and their several properties measured in various dimensions. Only at the very limits of theoretical physics does the nature of reality become elusive: the nature of quarks might be problematic, but the nature of chairs is not. This has enabled physical scientists to develop methodologies so robust that for all practical purposes it makes no difference whether an individual scientist affects a position of common-sense realism or outright Berkeleyian idealism. It is partly for this reason, that several contributors to the discussion about the place of the philosophy of science in the school curriculum, including perhaps Jenkins (1996) and Rudolph (2000), have decided that such instruction may have few practical implications.

The social sciences are differently placed. It *is* necessary to break with a reliance on theoretical models and methodological routines that constrain rather than enable our attempts to gain a more adequate knowledge of the structures of society and their effects on social practice. The most satisfactory way to accomplish that end, contrary to the disciplinary eclecticism proposed by Margison (1997), for example, is an integrated naturalism appropriate to scientific and critical realism. It is one thing to state, for example, that problems should be given an historical dimension: but it can hardly be said that there is *one* historical method and certainly not that there is but one mode of historical interpretation. The disastrous notion that 'the truth' can never be found in social enquiry has been interpreted as a reason for the adoption of an eclectic variety of disciplinary perspectives, theoretical models and methodological practices, in the hope of reaching an acceptable version of the truth. Thus, the prospect of 'legislated truth' (as, for example, in matters relating to 'Holocaust denial') is a predictable response to the rhetorical abandonment of truth in certain influential contemporary philosophies. The scientific realism of Bunge and the critical realism of Bhaskar offer social science – in which one must identify the levels of structure (system), individual disposition and practice – a more powerful basis for methodological studies than idealist relativism (Nash, 2003a).

The concepts of the popular debate on the curriculum, practical relevance *versus* abstract theory, a distinction reflected even in the university – where the most directly vocationally courses (teaching, social work, and nursing, for example) invariably have a 'practice' and a 'theory' division – is apparently inevitable. However, it is an unproductive debate. To be educated means, among other things, to possess the concepts and methods competent to reveal the structures of the physical and social world. Students do not commonly ask why they need to learn that the earth is a sphere in orbit about the sun, nor do they ask what 'use' this knowledge is to them, and yet they often do ask why they need to learn the fundamental laws that would enable them to observe for themselves, should they wish, that these facts are, indeed, capable of demonstration. The school should be able to provide an answer to that question. The measure of 'relevance' and 'practicality' is not to be determined solely by its exchange value. Democratic and effective teaching (Page, 1998), able to engage students' interest in a curriculum that continually makes reference to a wide range of practical applications, may also provide students with that sense of actual knowledge vital to their self-realisation as educated people (Witz, 1996). Knowledge is what is known – and what is known is known to people. It *is* people who know – not books or computers. This sense of actually *knowing*, the sense of satisfaction that comes from being able to demonstrate the properties of the world, should be inculcated systematically by the forms of a realist-based scientific education. Schools can assert more systematically the value of mathematics and science as knowledge and as qualities that define the educated person.

There is no one-to-one correspondence between membership of a social class and the willed capacity to find in learning and being learned both an intrinsic and an extrinsic value. The association between a social group and any practice is always tenuous. Such an association may, in fact, have three bases: (i) statistical frequency; (ii) 'objective' intrinsic interest; and (iii) custom and habit. These elements are not necessarily compatible and perhaps none should be accepted as essential. The relationship of class and forms of knowledge in this intellectual tradition is usually constructed as one of 'objective' interest and, that being so, there is no particular reason to expect a strong correspondence in other respects.

The concern in this area would, on the other hand, be very different if there were no parallel association with the common practice of class communities. Many students, particularly those from working-class families, have only the sketchiest outline of the great range of technical and scientific occupations available in the contemporary economy. School students might think of medicine or pharmacy, but rarely of biochemistry, food technology, meteorology, metallurgy, or any of the huge range of available scientific occupations. Bringing together the sciences in terms of their value, giving some attention to their history, and demonstrating to students the critical value of such knowledge would provide a contextualisation of great benefit. Through video production, debates, scientific clubs, magazines and other activities designed to demonstrate the fundamental unity of science, as argued by Bunge (1996) and Bhaskar (1993), among others, and the practical integration of its fields of application, students might gain a fuller appreciation of the value of their scientific education. It may be important that teachers and others who work in schools should give students an elaborated sense of the career opportunities open to them as people who have mastered a body of scientific knowledge. The reason, after all, why Mathematics with Calculus is valued more highly than Alternative Mathematics, is precisely because it is more useful to any one of the myriad technologies that sustain industrial civilisation. Students may need to gain a well-grounded sense, moreover, that mathematical and scientific knowledge is valuable, that it is applicable in the most direct sense to fields other than the strictly vocational. An informed participation in many areas of organised life, as a citizen and as a member of different communities, can only be enhanced by a scientific education. Debates about environmental and planning issues, often hotly contested, are effectively closed at the highest level to those with an uncertain grasp of the concepts and methods of modern science.

To know the world as it is should be recognised as being in itself a form of power: not a power over nature but over oneself in relation to nature. Where such knowledge and this sense of its worth is not part of the taken-for-granted cultural framework within students' families, then the school may need to assume the responsibility to provide such contextualisation. However, it may be accepted that working-class families generally *do* recognise the practical value of knowledge, in craft expertise, for example, and the foundations of working-class thought in a realist and practical conception of knowledge are secure. It is in this area that the constructivist influence on education might bear some reconsideration. Rudolph (2000: 412) notes that 'students often possess naïve realist perceptions of the nature of science' and 'privilege demonstration and experimentation over other forms of reasoning', and, if this is so then far from being 'a bad thing', it might provide a sound basis for a scientific education. Is it self-evident that the sort of idealism students might pick up from some constructivist teaching, which is unlikely to be a highly sophisticated understanding, is superior to 'naïve realism'? The realism considered so naive may more likely be grounded in a robust materialism, which is a philosophy with a long history in working-class radicalism. Because the demand of parents and students for credentials is so manifest, the school may find it all too easy to respond to that imperative as a source of motivation, but in so doing it may actually deny itself the opportunity to restructure the common-sense view many students have of the curriculum as abstract, theoretical and intrinsically useless for anyone not intending to be a 'rocket scientist'.

Above all, teachers should want students to learn what the world is actually like. Scientists do that by observation, developing theories, formulating hypotheses, carrying out experiments and so on. This is how scientists construct knowledge. It seems reasonable, therefore, to design a science curriculum in which students at school can do much the same. They will learn science by doing science as scientists do. Of course, they will not be smashing atoms, but they can weigh things in and out of water, roll marbles down inclined planes and so on, and with some unobtrusive guidance from the teacher they might get as far as the science of Archimedes and Galileo. The idea has certain attractions. It means, at the very least, that the curriculum will be full of purposeful activity directed at discovering something about the properties of material objects, and in practice this is probably how such a curriculum operates (Osborne, 1997). Nevertheless, the project is rhetorically embedded in a discourse that Matthews is not alone in finding objectionable. If students are to act as scientists, the argument goes, then the theories they construct as result of their observations and experiments should be taken seriously as *their* science. In principle, *their* scientific theories of specific gravity or momentum, for example, are as meaningful, considered as systems of discourse, as those of any other scientists. If students are to act as scientists, then their activities should be guided only in the most general methodological sense by the teacher who should certainly not impose her own theories. Indeed, it is even possible to argue that an individual completely ignorant of 'standard' scientific theories might be the ideal teacher for a constructivist classroom.

This discourse is grievously in error. It is wrong in suggesting, if not actually stating, that one theory is as good as other; wrong in thinking that school children can, in fact, rediscover Galilean science (which is highly sophisticated and actually contrary to common sense); and wrong about the appropriate role of the science teacher. Anti-realist conceptions of science, moreover, undermine the scientific project itself by downgrading the significance of demonstration and the possibility of more or less accurate knowledge.

Conclusion

The most influential theories in the sociology of education maintain that educational inequality is generated by institutional practices effected through the transmission of curriculum and thus embedded in the principles of knowledge itself. It is in this sense that *the* problem for the sociology of education is also at least *a* problem for curriculum studies. These theories are, moreover, not only influential, but rightly so in as much that they are to some extent correct. At the same time, however, it is necessary to press this explanation, developed at a very high level of abstraction, for a more detailed account of the mechanisms of social exclusion, and to *worry* at the limitations of a form of critique that has an inherent difficulty in asking questions about what is culturally and socially *arbitrary* in the construction of curriculum knowledge and what is *necessary* to human development within the universal elements of contemporary culture. The aims of education for a critical pedagogy are often defined – if in terms somewhat grandiose for all tastes – as being those of 'emancipation', 'liberation' and 'empowerment'. If a curriculum is a selection from all the knowledge that could be taught – and that must be so, for any viable curriculum is finite and what is known is in any practical sense infinite – then the principles of inclusion and exclusion must be justified. I contend that these principles should include those derived from a realist ontology from which a grounded concept of the educated person can be developed (Nash, 2003b, 2002b).

The realist argument with 'constructivists' about the school science curriculum is not, of course, a substitute for a comprehensive analysis of the criteria and practices that legitimate and maintain subject hierarchies and student subjects. An investigation informed by Bourdieu's notion of an economy of practices might provide some useful insights into these relationships, which, of course, are not structured by the given nature of the physical and social reality. It is not even likely, although this chapter argues for a greater recognition of this principle, that realism can provide a *sufficient* basis for curriculum design. There is no space here to develop these ideas, but their importance can hardly be overlooked.

The concept of the educated person in modern societies is, more often than not, transparently related to the economic and political structures that prevail in capitalism, but this is a form of '*misrecognition*', as Bourdieu would say, that realism is capable of subjecting to critique no less vigorous than that in which irrealist 'critical' traditions take pride. Bourdieu's exploration of symbolic power, including the maintenance of control through symbolic violence and the crucial function of misrecognition in the maintenance of class relations of domination and subordination, insists emphatically on the class-linked arbitrariness of school knowledge and its related pedagogic forms. These questions, therefore, of reality, knowledge and truth – which is to put them in ontological order – have a truly fundamental importance and must be included in any thorough enquiry of differential access to education. They situate the study of the curriculum – if not perhaps 'curriculum studies' in its narrowest sense – as a central element in the sociology of education. Bhaskar's critical realism, for example, is grounded in the transcendental argument that if modern science is right then a realist ontology is necessary; if that is so, then the school curriculum (especially in science) should be based on that reality; if that is so, then the transmission of knowledge is not as arbitrary as Bourdieu's and Bernstein's theories assume; and it follows that the implications of all this for the reproduction of educational inequality become a matter of urgency. Is it not possible that relativist discourse, which is manifestly at odds with the characteristic practical realism of working-class thought, might actually contribute to the prevailing sense many working-class students have that school is *unreal*? The question of class inequality in access to education and the involvement of the transmission of knowledge in its generation is one of profound importance. The insights of such seminal thinkers in this area as Bourdieu and Bernstein will continue to stimulate enquiry. The task might be a little easier, however, if we are able to reconcile the *arbitrary* with the *necessary* and work towards their principled reconciliation in so far as that end may be possible and desirable in educational practice.

References

Baudelot, C. and Establet, R. (1981). France's capitalistic schools: Problems of analysis and practice. In C.C. Lemert (ed.), *French Sociology: Rupture and Renewal since 1968*. (New York: University of Columbia Press): 203–11.

Bernstein, B. (1971). On the classification and framing of educational knowledge. In M.F.D. Young (ed.), *Knowledge and Control: New Directions for the Sociology of Education* (London: Collier-Macmillan): 47–69.

Bernstein, B. (1995). A response. In A.R. Sadovnik (ed.), *Knowledge and Pedagogy: The Sociology of Basil Bernstein* (Norwood, NJ: Ablex): 385–424.

Bhaskar, R. (1993). *Dialectic: The Pulse of Freedom* (London: Verso).

Bourdieu, P. (1974). The school as a conservative force: Scholastic and cultural inequalities In J. Eggleston (ed.), *Contemporary Research in the Sociology of Education* (London: Methuen): 32–46.

Bourdieu, P. (1977). *Outline of a Theory of Practice* (Cambridge: Cambridge University Press).

Bourdieu, P. (1984). *Distinction* (London: Routledge).

Bourdieu, P. (1990). *In Other Words: Essays towards a Reflexive Sociology* (Cambridge: Polity Press).

Bourdieu, P. (1991). *Language and Symbolic Power* (Cambridge: Polity Press).

Bourdieu, P. et al. (1999). *The Weight of the World: Social Suffering in Contemporary Society* (Stanford, Calif.: Stanford University Press).

Bourdieu, P. and Passeron, J.-C. (1977). *Reproduction in Education, Society and Culture* (London: Sage).

Bunge, M. (1974). *Treatise on Basic Philosophy, Vol. I: Semantics I: Sense and Reference* (Dordrecht, The Netherlands: Reidel).

Bunge, M. (1996). *Finding Philosophy in Social Science* (New Haven, Conn.: Yale University Press).

Collier, A. (1994). *Critical Realism: An Introduction to Roy Bhaskar's Philosophy* (London: Verso).

Corrigan, P. (1990). *Social Forms/Human Capacities: Essays in Authority and Difference* (London: Routledge).

Danermark, B., Ekström, M., Jakobsen, L. and Karlsson, J. Ch. (2000). *Explaining Society: Critical Realism in the Social Sciences* (London: Routledge).

Danzig, A. (1995). Applications and distortions of Basil Bernstein's code theory In A.R. Sadovnik (ed.), *Knowledge and Pedagogy: The Sociology of Basil Bernstein.* (Norwood, NJ: Ablex): 145–70.

Dowling, P. (1998). *The Sociology of Mathematical Education: Mathematical Myths/ Pedagogic Texts* (London: Falmer Press).

Doyle, L. and Harris, R. (1986). *Empiricism, Explanation and Rationality* (London: Routledge & Kegan Paul).

Edwards, T. (2002). A remarkable sociological imagination, *British Journal of Sociology of Education*, 23(4): 527–535.

Forsnot, C.T. (ed.) (1996). *Constructivism: Theory, Perspectives, and Practice* (New York: Teachers College Press).

Kirk, R. (1999). *Relativism and Reality: A Contemporary Introduction* (London: Routledge).

Halliday, M.A.K. (1995). Learning and the theory of codes. In A.R. Sadovnik (ed.), *Knowledge and Pedagogy: The Sociology of Basil Bernstein* (Norwood, NJ: Ablex), 127–43.

Hasan, R. (1995). On social conditions for semiotic mediation: The genesis of mind in society. In A.R. Sadovnik (ed.), *Knowledge and Pedagogy: The Sociology of Basil Bernstein* (Norwood, NJ: Ablex): 171–196.

Hasan, R. (2002). Ways of meaning, ways of learning: Code as an explanatory concept, *British Journal of Sociology of Education*, 23(4), 537–48.

Holton, R. (2000). Bourdieu and common sense. In N. Brown and I. Szeman (eds), *Pierre Bourdieu: Fieldwork in Culture* (Lanham, Mass.: Bowman & Littlefield), 87–99.

Jenkins, E.W. (1996). The 'nature of science' as a curriculum component, *Journal of Curriculum Studies*, 28(2): 137–50.

Kirk, R. (1999). *Relativism and Reality: A Contemporary Introduction* (London: Routledge).

Lane, J.F. (2000). *Pierre Bourdieu: A Critical Introduction* (London: Pluto).

LiPuma, E. (1993). Culture and the concept of culture in a theory of practice. In C. Calhoun, E. LiPuma, and M. Postone (eds), *Bourdieu: Critical Perspectives* (Cambridge: Polity Press): 14–34.

Margison, S. (1997). Is economics sufficient for the government of education?, *New Zealand Journal of Educational Studies*, 32(1): 3–12.

Maton, K. (2000). Languages of legitimation: The structuring significance for intellectual fields of strategic knowledge claims, *British Journal of Sociology of Education*, 21(2): 147–67.

Matthews, M.R. (1995). *Challenging New Zealand Science Education* (Palmerston North: Dunmore Press).

McEneaney, E.H. and Meyer, J.W. (2000). The content of the curriculum: An institutionalist perspective. In M.T. Hallinan (ed.), *Handbook of the Sociology of Education* (New York: Kluwer Academic/Plenum): 189–211.

Moore, R. and Muller, J. (1999). The discourse of 'voice' and the problem of knowledge and identity in the sociology of education, *British Journal of Sociology of Education*, 20(2), 189–206.

Nash, R. (1999). Bourdieu, 'habitus', and educational research: Is it all worth the candle?, *British Journal of Sociology of Education*, 20(2): 175–87.

Nash, R. (2002a). A realist framework for the sociology of education: Thinking with Bourdieu, *Educational Philosophy and Theory*, 34(3): 273–88.

Nash, R. (2002b). The educated *habitus*, progress at school, and real knowledge, *Interchange*, 33(1): 27–48.

Nash, R. (2003a). Social explanation and socialization: On Bourdieu and the structure, disposition, practice scheme, *Sociological Review*, 51(1): 43–62.

Nash, R. (2003b). Progress at school: Pedagogy and the care for knowledge, *Teaching and Teacher Education*, 19(7): 755–67.

Nimiluoto, I. (1999). *Critical Scientific Realism* (Oxford: Oxford University Press).

Olneck, M. (2000). Can multicultural education change what counts as cultural capital? *American Educational Research Journal*, 37(2): 317–48.

Osborne, M.D. (1997). Balancing the individual and the group: A dilemma for the constructivist teacher. *Journal of Curriculum Studies*, 29(2): 183–96.

Page, R. (1998). Aspects of curriculum: 'Making kids care' about school knowledge. *Journal of Curriculum Studies*, 30 (1), 1–26.

Readings, B. (1996). *The University in Ruins* (Cambridge, Mass.: Harvard University Press).

Robbins, D. (1991). *The Work of Pierre Bourdieu: Recognising Society* (Milton Keynes: Open University Press).

Robbins, D. (1999). Bourdieu on language and education: Conjunction or parallel development? In M. Grenfell and M. Kelly (eds). *Pierre Bourdieu: Language, Culture and Education: Theory into Practice* (Berne: Peter Lang): 313–33.

Rudolph, J.L. (2000). Reconsidering the 'nature of science' as a curriculum component. *Journal of Curriculum Studies*, 32(3): 402–419.

Smart, J.J.C. (1963). *Philosophy and Scientific Realism* (London: Routledge & Kegan Paul).

Stengel, B.S. (1998). 'Academic discipline' and 'school subject': Contestable curricular concepts. *Journal of Curriculum Studies*, 29(5), 585–602.

Walkerdine, V. and Lucey, H. (1989). *Democracy in the Kitchen: Regulating Mothers and Socialising Daughters* (London: Virago).

Witz, K.G. (1996). Science with values and values for science education. *Journal of Curriculum Studies*, 28(5), 597–612.

Young, M. (1976). The schooling of science. In G. Whitty and M. Young (eds), *Explorations in the Politics of School Knowledge* (Driffield: Nafferton Books), 47–66.

Young, (ed.). (1971). *Knowledge and Control: New Directions for the Sociology of Education* (London: Collier-Macmillan).

Chapter 8
Social Capital, Class Identity and Progress at School: Case Studies

Introduction

An earlier article (Nash, 1998) described how relative educational progress is associated with certain dispositions – notably ambition, confidence of success and tolerance of schooling – and suggested that these characteristics are related to classed constructions of self-identity. This chapter extends the argument through an exploration of how social capital, conceived as a set of familial and age-peer resources, has a fundamental role in the development of identity in young people. The family resource framework adopted by realist accounts of the causes of social differences in access to education is indebted to Bourdieu's (1990) analysis of key family assets as forms of capital: financial, cultural and social. The first of these may have a fundamental status in orthodox Marxist interpretations, and the second may have been granted an overarching position in cultural studies (particularly where minority ethnic culture is concerned), but it is the third, a once almost neglected social capital, that has attracted the most significant recent interest. Coleman's (1988) influential paper is largely responsible for this interest and, as the significance and priority of Bourdieu's thesis is not acknowledged there, it is appropriate to mention that the concept does originate with that seminal thinker. 'Social capital' seems likely, in fact, to gain a more extended reference in sociology, and perhaps in economics, to networks of sociality and the range of benefits they provide to a society (Woolcock, 1998). In this conception, 'social capital' becomes akin to 'economic infrastructure', or 'technological expertise', which, on reflection, is rather how 'capital' and 'cultural capital' might be understood by mainstream economics. The point of Bourdieu's analysis, that assets can be regarded as 'capital' to the extent that they may be invested in a given field of practice to bring a definite return, and that, as forms of capital, they are subject to exchange and interconvertability, is obscured by revisionist interpretations of social capital. It goes without saying that concepts cannot be protected from this sort of appropriation, and there must be some significance in the fact that economics has discovered its want of a concept with which to analyse the benefits that accrue to society from the functional networks of reciprocal relationships, particularly those of kin, neighbourhood and civil society more generally, that enable people to go about their business with a justified measure of confidence and trust in the goodness and fairness of others. Nevertheless, this is not quite the concept of social capital used in Bourdieu, or in our research (Nash, 1993), and before the concept is lost to us it may be worthwhile to explore the ways in which familial social capital has its own important contribution to make to social reproduction and the consequent maintenance of social inequality. For familial social capital, notwithstanding the temptation to offer a mechanical interpretation in terms of the more or less direct assistance available to families, in the form of information about schools and occupations, for example, as a result of their 'connections', has a much more significant role. What seems most important about familial social capital, and that contributed by age-peers, in the processes of reproduction is its power in the developmental process to constitute social identity (Poole, 1994).

Secondary school students from middle-class backgrounds are somewhat more likely than those from working-class backgrounds to hold and maintain the dispositions associated with success at school. Meehan et al. (1996: 216) include centrally among these dispositions and practices, 'timeliness, orderliness, neatness', answering and responding to different sorts of questions, test-taking and note-taking strategies, knowing how to get information from the school, and being able 'to talk to teachers at school, while confining street talk and behaviour to the street'. They argued, no doubt correctly (although the reported research findings are unconvincing), that such a repertoire can be taught to working-class students in suitable educational contexts. The correlation between academic attainment and social class (about 0.35; Nash and Harker, 1998) is regarded as technically moderate, and the variance within social classes, and perhaps also within families, is substantial, but it is nevertheless the case that middle-class students are far more likely than working-class students to experience success at school. Five times as many students with higher professional origins obtain a university entrance-level bursary, or better, than those from low-skilled and non-employed families (ibid.). There is firm evidence that these dispositions have their origin in the family and are the consequence of socialisation practices that result in the formation of recognisable social identities available to young people. This process of identity constitution is, in fact, a general result of social capital realised within the family and to a variable extent within the peer group. There are grounds to believe that the transmission of social capital within the family is realised in this form; it acts as a resource providing adolescents with a sense of social position and status that, provided that it is accepted, is a powerful source of the particular aspirations, the confidence that these can be attained, and the will to pursue them within the regulatory forms of the school, associated so strongly with success.

Cultural and social capital are inextricably tied together in the process of identity formation. Indeed, if cultural capital is taken to include the entire body of taken-for-granted knowledge, the concepts and practices of a *classed* mode of life, then the effects of social position are already included. The point of this analysis is to afford those effects their due independent recognition by focusing attention directly on social resources. Middle-class and working-class people are embedded differently in social relations: with those of economic production (the fundamental constitution of class); family and kin; neighbourhood, civil society; and the apparatuses of the state itself. In as much as these relations are a source of social identity they merit attention in tandem with cultural capital. I have argued elsewhere (Nash, 1999a) that middle-class familial cultural capital, conceived as a specific form of literate knowledge, makes its most important contribution in the early development of a distinctive, and highly efficient, type of mental formation.

The two girls introduced in this chapter, Lottie from the middle class and Kylie from the working class, attended different schools. Both institutions were decile 3 schools and thus predominantly working-class in composition (they are designated 1 and 23 in Nash and Harker (1998)). School 23, attended by Lottie, is a large, metropolitan school with a multicultural roll. Almost half its students are Polynesian with two-thirds of those being Pacific Islanders. School 1 is a smaller, urban school. More than a third of its students are Maori and 10 per cent are Pacific Islanders. In both schools students of European descent make up about half the roll.

Lottie's parents were both employed. Her father was a health professional and her mother a secondary school teacher. As she was interviewed in the company of three of her friends, it may be useful to provide brief information about their backgrounds also. Elizabeth was the daughter of a senior business manager (she confessed that School 23 had been her second choice: her letter of application to a girls' grammar school had been lost in the mail!); Vanessa's father was an intermediate school principal; and Anna's father was a self-employed skilled worker. Anna, however, had some social standing in her own right for she had already made a name for herself as a photographic model, and it would be an error to overlook the importance of this in the development of her social identity. Our data file, obtained from school records, lists Kylie as being from a single-parent family dependent on a benefit. When we met her in the fifth form her family circumstances had changed and she lived with her mother and stepfather. Her stepfather was employed in a manual occupation, but at what level of skill we do not know. Kylie had a number of close friends, also working-class girls, and one of these is mentioned in the course of the conversation with her. The interviewer asks Kylie about the fate of Jackie who had abandoned her fifth-form studies mainly because she was desperate to leave home (an oppressive and dangerous environment), and, as she could not obtain an Independent Youth Benefit, had to work full-time for her living. In her distress she approached the school for support and advice only to be turned away because she was no longer enrolled and so not entitled to make a legitimate claim on school resources. This proved to have almost fatal consequences for Jackie: but we have decided to relate Kylie's story, and it is in this context that she discusses her friend's plight. The interviews were conducted by Sarah Major.

To relate such stories, as Wetherell, Stiven and Potter (1987) point out, requires extensive reporting of speech in order to sustain the arguments developed. The transcription follows Opie's (1995) attempt to avoid the constraints imposed by orthogrphical conventions designed specifically for written language. It represents the girls' speech rhythms more accurately and requires fewer assumptions about the structure of the sentences. Brief pauses in speech, whether due to punctuation or noticeable hesitancy are signified by / and longer pauses are shown by // where the additional slash represents at least two seconds. Material deleted from the transcript is indicated by bracketed dots. The girls in these conversations reveal how social relationships in their families are affected by their class position, and the focus is on properties of these relationships and their link to social capital: when the talk is about money, for example, it is not the possession or want of money itself that is the focus of our analysis, rather it is how that comes to shape the nature of the interactions that exist within their families in such a way that a sense of *social being* within a class location is generated.

Lottie: A 'Positively Adjusted' Middle-class Girl

Lottie was just 16 when she was interviewed in her sixth-form year. It seems important to note that Lottie's responses to items included in a Quality of School Life (QSL) instrument, although they place her in a positively disposed group, do not indicate a student with a particularly favourable set of attitudes. Like many middle-class students she belonged to the cluster of 'critical aspirers' – students who, while rather critical of their school, and certainly of teachers, hold high aspirations and usually achieve their ambitions (Nash, 1998). Nevertheless, it is a little surprising to find that she indicated *definitely agree* to being restless, and tired of trying in some subjects, and only *agree* to items expressing a belief in success at school and stating favourable perceptions of teachers. 'I learn most things pretty quickly' was actually ticked *disagree*, and 'I really like to go' with *strongly disagree*. This hardly seems to signify a positive disposition at all, but she recorded her aspiration to enter university without equivocation. She also reported that she owned more than 50 books, that she enjoyed reading, and gave a lot of time to it. This is very much the pattern of the critical consumer of education – not openly disaffected, but far from inclined to offer the conventional responses of one 'colonised' by the school (Woods, 1979). Lottie did succeed at school and made relative progress while doing so. Her School Certificate marks were impressive, particularly in science and English, her Sixth Form Certificate results were in the highest band, and she left school, to enter university, with an outstanding 394 bursary marks. The interviewer initiated one discussion – going to the heart of things – on class differences, by asking, 'Some families are better off than others/ Would you say your family is better off/ or less well off?' The comments of her friends have been retained when they are necessary to understand Lottie's responses:

> Lottie: Yeah/ I think we are// It's really weird/ my family is/ so different to my friends' families/ 'cus// well one of my closest friends and my boyfriend both have// ah what do you call it?/ Well ex-boyfriend sorry/ sorry! *[laughter]*/ have like/ They live with either one parent/ and they've got// They live with their/ parent and/ that parent's boyfriend or girlfriend?/ So that/ when they come to/

my house/ it's really weird for them/ because I have such a normal family/ Like I have a/ really/ normal/ parent/ mother/ and child/ and it's like really/ standard family/ and so it's really weird for them but/ I really like it actually/ I mean sometimes I complain because/ my parents are really caring/ and really/ really/ really/ over-protective?/ But in other times *[laughter]*/ it's really good because …

Elizabeth: Are they really over-protective/ are they?

Lottie: Really over-protective// It's good because/ it is a home it's not just a house/ it's/ my home/ It's like/ a real family/ So/ at other times it's really good. *[…]*

So do you think you have quite a good relationship with your parents?

Lottie: Yeah. *[…]*

Elizabeth: I do/ my mum/ My mum definitely.

Lottie: Yeah definitely more my mum.

Elizabeth: Dads are kind of// well to me/ sort of/ you know/ just/ *[…]* Over there you know/ Or/ they don't really talk/ well mine doesn't anyway.

Lottie: Definitely talk to my mum heaps/ I always talk to my mum. *[…]* Well I've never had a problem with money/ 'Cus my parents do a lot of saving/ like a lot of the people I know/ their parents don't/ save/ They just spend all their money/ all of it/ and they/ Well as far as they know/ they don't have savings and things/ My parents have got a lot of/ money in savings/ so/ we've always got/ not heaps of money/ but we/ We never would be in a state where we didn't have enough money. *[…]* Realistically/ I mean there's/ so many things I want/ I'm a very/ wanting person *[laughs]*/ I mean/ you know like a/ there's heaps of/ things I want/ but I mean/ it's not because/ It's just because I don't need them that I don't have them/ it's not because we don't have enough money for them/ Well/ that as well/ I mean/ some of the things they couldn't afford but/ yeah.

This conversation expresses in an almost paradigmatically the reality of life for many middle-class students, in this case girls, to such a degree that comment seems redundant. The closeness of their relationships with their mothers; their rather distant and occasionally mildly grumpy fathers; the somewhat constricting but in the end deeply comforting sense of being protected; the feeling that they live, even if a little contradictorily, in a 'standard', two-parent family, in a 'really nice homey environment', 'a home not a house'; and the security of their of knowledge that, even though a consumer society might have made them 'wanting people', 'realistically' they want for nothing; all of these qualities of their home environment they recognise and appreciate. They are aware, moreover, that there are more important ways in which to be 'better off' than to possess a large income, and the quality of the social relationships in their households, the way in which 'little things', Vanessa says (in a section not reproduced here), 'don't get turned into big things', is illuminating. When they do confront differences in real wealth between themselves and some of their classmates they acknowledge that this is a 'touchy subject', and the experience of attending a school with a large proportion of working-class students is recognised as one that has brought them a more direct appreciation of how they and others live. The girls were asked, 'Do you think that money is a difficult area for people to talk about?'

> Lottie: Definitely/ there are so many people that haven't got enough money.

> Elizabeth: And/ just/ one thing you can say wrong like/ it'd make them feel like/ really …

> Lottie: It's a really touchy subject actually.

> Elizabeth: Really/ you know/ and/ you'd probably end up feeling just/ really stupid.

> Lottie: Yeah. *[…]* There is a conception that/ because we go to a public school/ we're lower/ Because I was playing a hockey game recently/ and/ a Cheltenham International mother/ we happened to win/ and/ the Cheltenham mother was really angry that her school/ and this is her exact words/ 'had lost to a bunch of ruffians'/ And our team/ is not a bunch of ruffians/ I mean if you just looked at us/ we're not/ We don't look rough at all/ I mean *[laughs]*/ we're just average girls/ and it/ They really do think/ that because we go to a public school we're lower than them// Especially the mothers/ I think it's more the parents than the children.

Middle-class students who attend predominantly working-class schools have adjustments of their own to make. Lottie was a confident young woman, beautifully secure in her knowledge of her standing in the world (exactly the disposition this analysis is concerned with), and more amused than indignant at the attack on the character of her schoolmates as a 'bunch of ruffians'. This declaration – doubtless made in trying circumstances – was so inaccurate that Lottie, whose sense that they were 'just average girls' was an incontestable matter of fact, reports it with unconcerned detachment. Being middle-class herself Lottie was unlikely to be affected personally by outright class hatred, but she was aware that it exists, and that to many of her team-mates the comment must have rankled. The girls' thoughts on private education are worth hearing: they were asked, 'So do you think that students at/ private schools/ do you think they do get a better education?'

Lottie: Mm/ in some cases. *[…]* If/ I mean if they go there/ and they've just got/ If they want to get it/ they can get a really good education/ but I mean a lot of them/ just because they've got money doesn't mean they're bright or even hard working they just don't want it/ But/ the resources are there to get/ a really good education at those schools/ Especially places like Cheltenham International/ 'cus they've just got everything/ offered to them. *[…]*

Anna: Well sort of/ I think it gives them a false idea/ that everything's going to be sort of like/ there for them.

Lottie: Yeah/ handed to them/ yeah.

Anna: When they get out and/ you know/ to work and everything?/ But/ those/ the people who go to those schools are/ more likely to get a bigger shock/ you know/ and not being able to/ cope with stuff and actually/ where you go to get a job/ or something/ unless/ they all know friends of friends who can/ whose dad will … *[noisy debate]*

Lottie: Yeah and they usually do.

Anna: Get a job.

Lottie: And if they go to uni/ I mean we're all going to the same uni/ it's not a private uni/ So/ I mean/ they're/ all there/ they might get better marks in bursary/ and they might not even/ but we're all/ going to go to the same place.

Even these middle-class girls express a certain resentment at the favoured treatment they think likely to be extended to students from private schools by employers as a result of the business connections of their fathers – an evident recognition of the power of social networks to become social capital. At the same time, one of the reasons for Lottie's sanguine reaction towards certain inequalities in the provision of schooling is revealed by her observation that follows that, 'we're all going to the same uni/ it's not a private uni'. Moreover, it really does not matter much what bursary mark one obtains since entry to university is (in the great majority of courses) open regardless. In the event, it is difficult to imagine how she could have attained a better bursary mark than she did, but the analysis is unaffected.

One obvious area of practice in which the importance of social capital is made visible was discussed with some amusement by Lottie and her friends. Families have always thought it necessary to monitor their unmarried daughters' social interactions with men because patterns of social reproduction have depended on their ability to place daughters in a marriage appropriate to their status. These girls understand that this is still so to some extent, even though the strategic imperatives informing such practices are no longer so acute, and that the age-old strategies of family reproduction continue to be practised with degrees of deliberation and oppression that vary from community to community within our society. The girls engaged in this conversation are intelligent and well-educated European girls – and they know what is going on. 'Do your parents take an interest in who you're friendly with?' the interviewer asks, and they are amused because all girls of their age can tell stories about their parents' attempts to monitor and control their interactions with boys, but their responses are unequivocal:

Lottie: Definitely.

Vanessa: Mm.

Lottie: Absolutely definitely.

Vanessa: Who we're boy-friendly with!

Lottie: Yeah *[laughter]*/ that's even more important. *[…]*

What sort of people do they/ approve or disapprove of?

Lottie: Just people who are really nice/ my parents like/ if you've got a nice face and you're really nice// not people who really sort of/ I don't know. *[…]* Yeah/ they definitely have an opinion// It doesn't/ really matter all that much/ I think/ they don't so mind who I'm friends with it's just/ my boyfriends/ really/ I don't know why/ I think/ maybe they think my boyfriend's got a bigger influence over me/ which isn't/ actually true.

Is it actually one/ particular boyfriend?/ Or boyfriends?

Lottie: Oh I mean they don't/ They don't/ don't like them/ Oh! *[laughs]*/ Apart from a few. *[laughter]*

Vanessa: Nobody likes him!

Lottie: But they always/ They always like to meet/ my boyfriends/ and like have them over at our house heaps/ to get to know them/ and some/ boyfriends aren't very/ social to parents/ *[…]* I've only met/ yeah one of my boyfriends' parents/ But that wasn't because/ of my decision/ they just/ never introduced me *[…]* I have no problem with meeting/ parents/ doesn't bother me in the slightest. *[…]*

Do you take any notice of what your parents think/ of friends?

Lottie: No/ but *[…]* I mean you wouldn't/ change friends because of it/ but it still/ you/ like when they/ *[…]* Yeah/ if you bring that person home and you know your parents don't like them/ it's like really uncomfortable/ whereas I like to bring them home and just/ not have to feel like/ 'Oh I wonder what my parent/ my/ mum's thinking of/ what she's saying'/ or/ 'he's saying'/ or something like that/ So it's just really uncomfortable?

Lottie disclaims any social reservations when it comes to meeting the parents of her boyfriends, and thus attests not merely to a lack of shyness, but to a positive affirmation of a social ease with class roots. The active parental monitoring of their social networks, which has gone on throughout their childhood, takes on a different level of significance as girls mature. Working-class girls are sometimes less closely monitored in these respects, but perhaps just as often they are subjected to attempts to impose a stricter surveillance that is almost invariably doomed to failure. When girls are sexually active at the age of 14 and 15, a practice more common in the case of working-class than middle-class girls, this is almost always without the knowledge, and still less the consent, of their parents. It puts such young women in a double jeopardy: they risk both pregnancy and the wrath of their parents.

The real key to success at school, particularly at this level, is *wanting* to succeed. Lottie's reflections on her aspiration are characteristically middle-class. The ambition itself, for a clever girl, is not *classed* in this way, but the reasons she expresses for holding it certainly are. This is a crucial distinction invisible to statistical analysis of reported aspirations. The interviewer asked, 'What do you think influences your future?':

> Lottie: It's a mixture of things// I know my parents would be really disappointed if I didn't go to/ university/ of course they wouldn't hold a gun to my head and say/ 'You have to go'/ But they'd be/ really disappointed so I guess that's had something to do with it/ I've just always expected that that's just what I'm going to do when I leave school// What I want to do at university is probably influenced by just what I'm interested in/ which is/ the languages/ and history side of things// But I've had influences from seeing like friends/ leave school/ or/ Not just friends/ people I know leave school and see/ that/ now they're on the outside they say life is really good/ they've got this job/ They've got no real/ They've got nothing really to look forward to in life/ They've no ambition except to go from one/ well/ not lousy job/ but one/ not very/ fulfilling job to another/ Just/ keep going throughout their lives/ Particularly one girl I knew who left/ I don't know how she managed it/ but she said she left at the end of fourth form/ and/ I work with her/ I used to work with her occasionally at/ the part-time shop I have/ except she does it/ she does it part-time as well as other jobs/ and all she does is just move on from one job to another job to another job and never really achieving anything/ So that's one/ another big motivation/ I don't wanna/ have just/ stupid little/ unfulfilling jobs.

So tell me about your future/ do you see yourself having a/ a career of some sort?

Lottie: I can't really picture myself having a career/ all I want to do is travel/ really/ and/ live in lots of different places and/ just/ do something with languages but/ I don't know what yet/ *[...]* I don't see myself having a family/ I know lots of people say that when they're young/ and then they end up doing it/ but/ I don't really think it's/ it's my kind/ or it's not what I want/ anyway. *[...]*

Does the university fees thing affect you Lottie?

Lottie: No not really because/ I still want to do the same subjects/ and I still want to get/ even if I don't end up going to university I still want to achieve well at school/ so I mean/ But/ it is really scary I think// I mean it just means/ 'cus if I don't get to university I really don't know what I could do/ So/ I think it's really scary that/ they're proposing that kind of/ changes.

Lottie's parents, she says, would be really disappointed if she decided not to go to university, and she would prefer not to see them disappointed, but they would not, she says, 'hold a gun to my head'. They would be persuasive in a great variety of ways, no doubt, but the real measure of their success is to have brought her up in such a way that the aspiration was her own. Lottie had acquired from her parents' class location, though processes of direct and indirect transmission, those powerful structures of cognition and modes of practice that gain their value as 'capital' within the educational system. For it is not only the full range of experiences, including the specifically educational, provided by her parents directly, that must be included here, but the network of social relations, with their structured opportunities for extension, in which she was embedded. Even Lottie's part-time job on a Saturday market stall selling Third World jewellery – and the proprietorial reference to 'the part-time shop I have' is exact – creates contexts for the augmentation and elaboration of her social capital. Lottie had developed all the dispositional qualities of mind associated with scholastic success and it is entirely characteristic of middle-class students that she felt no compelling need to formulate a specific occupational aspiration. No direct goal of that kind pushed Lottie forward, as is so often the case for working-class students; on the contrary, what was 'really scary' to her was the unimaginable possibility of not entering university. Working-class students know that the alternative is likely to be working in an office or shop, and 'just keep[ing] going throughout their lives', and Lottie knew that, too, but for her it was not a real alternative; the fate touched her – for Lottie's capacity for empathy and human understanding was genuine and well developed – but it was a fate she could not imagine ever being hers.

Kylie: An 'Alienated' Working-class Girl

Kylie was unmistakably disaffected with school. The fieldworker recorded several conversations with Kylie in the company of her friends, but the material presented here is based on an individual interview held a month or so before School Certificate examinations when she was still 15 years old. When Kylie completed the QSL instrument a year earlier she indicated *definitely disagree* to all the items stating that teachers were fair, just or listened to her; that learning was fun; that she could succeed at school; or was seen as important, or looked up to; and checked *definitely agree* to the item 'I could do better if I tried'. This is a very negative set of responses, it placed her in the most alienated cluster, and it is worth the effort to find out what was going on in her mind. Kylie lived with her mother, her brother, her stepfather and her stepfather's son. In the event, her School Certificate marks were within the range set by her third-form test scores and in that respect she was successful, but there is no record of her returning to school for sixth-form study and the trajectory indicated by her QSL responses was in that respect fulfilled. She was articulate, open with the interviewer, and spoke frankly about the stresses she experienced in her attempts to manage the conflicting demands of her life. Oddly, perhaps – but then we often found that students said what was on their mind given but half a chance, the most revealing conversation with her developed from a question about her thoughts on intelligence. She was asked, 'Why do some people do better than others at school?/ Do you think some people are just naturally bright?/ Or?':

> I think it really depends on/ a lot/ on your family life as well/ yeah/ There might be brighter people/ but they've been over the years probably helped/ a lot more than a lot of people have and/ um/ I think that you know/ a lot of parents must spend a lot of time with their kids helping them and a lot of parents just can't/ so they get stuck/ And then when you're at home there's/ there's nothing much you can do/ You can't ask the teacher/ so there's your parents/ but if they're not home you're stuffed/ you can't do anything/ Like if I get stuck on my science work/ my mum or my stepdad they don't know anything about science so/ I'm the only one/ 'cus I've got a brother that's doing School C as well/ but I can'-t ask him because he doesn't do science so I'm sort sitting there going *[sighs]*/ So it's quite frustrating.

Very difficult isn't it/ So do you have friends that talk about subjects?

> No/ I think we sort of try to forget it mostly/ out of school time/ Oh/ I get very anti-school sometimes/ Like if I've been studying for ages and doing heaps of work I get very anti-school *[laughs]*/ It's real horrible. *[…]* If your parents can't afford things/ and they can't afford to give you pocket money/ well all the time you do have to work/ And/ not all the time it's for things that you want/ it's for things that you need/ I mean/ they might have problems finding the school fees/

you might have to help them out and/ you know/ I mean it's really expensive especially this year/ and especially when I've got a brother the same level as me/ My parents have got to pay exam fees/ school fees/ books and uniforms and things like that/ it's really expensive/ and/ you know/ I just feel I'm out of place/ It makes you feel guilty/ and um/ you know/ you've really got to get yourself a job/ or it's all sort of just dumped on them/ It's not very fair/ It's so expensive/ it's not really sort of free education any more/ you know/ It's really expensive/ Like you have to pay over a $100 nearly every year/ Yeah/ and that's not for/ that's not for your exam/ that's just for the school year/ you know/ you have to pay it/ And then you've got to pay your exams on top of that/ and I think that's about $60 or $70 or something/ I mean it may sound not/ not very much for a whole year/ but a lot of the time it is for a lot of people/ it's a lot of money/ 'cus they just can't afford to/ you know/ spend that much money// And then/ you know/ the school helps you out/ but a lot of the time parents don't want them to help out because they feel like/ it's charity and that/ I just// it's horrible *[laughs]*.

Yeah/ do you find that's quite stressful for families?

Yeah/ I had a fight with my mum the other day over it/ Yeah/ 'cus/ one of my teachers kept on asking me if I hadn't paid my fees yet/ And um/ Mum thinks that the teacher has no right to do that/ you know/ if they've got any problems ring her/ I had a big fight with her about it/ 'cus she just got real stressed out and uptight about it/ 'Cus um/ the teachers were saying something about/ you know/ taking me out of classes and things like that/ I don't know/ but/ you know/ Just because you can't pay we lose out/ and it's not our fault if parents can't afford to pay for it/ well it is in a way/ but it's really bad/ It's/ like everything just has to be paid for by a certain date/ otherwise you can't do it/ and I don't think that's fair.

What happens if you don't pay?

Well/ we've been told that if we don't pay it by a certain date/ like our exam fees/ we can't enter it.

Do you know when that is?

I'm not sure/ I'm not sure when it was/ I just can't remember/ but/ there is a certain date/ and we had to pay by then/ I don't know if that was just the teachers warning just to pay/ or whether it is actually the way they do it// But it's not very fair. *[…]*

Jackies left.

Jackie said that/ Mr Roberts said they're not allowed to help her out any more/ It's got nothing to do with the school/ I feel it's/ you know/ it could have helped her out// and at school or anything.

Do you think her main problem was a financial one/ because she left home?

Yeah/ she sort of really had to leave home/ you know/ and I think it *[leaving school]* had a lot to do with financial reasons/ I mean she's not getting any money from anywhere/ She's got to wait/ you know/ ages to get the Independent Youth *[Benefit]*/ And then they're not very happy about giving it to you anyway/ So/ I think it was basically a financial thing/ because she has to/ you know/ to pay for a place to stay or/ and things like that/ and she said that// school doesn't pay you to stay at school/ you've got to pay for that/ She couldn't afford to stay anyway I don't think/ But Mr Roberts says the schools not allowed to help her out even emotionally or anything like that/ so I think that's really bad.

What are the social structures that hinder Kylie's progress? The family resource framework suggests that one should examine those causally associated with social class, financial wealth, cultural capital and social capital. In the first place, Kylie was poor. Not only was she poor but she was affected by a sense of alienation as a result. She felt that she could not expect her mother (still less her stepfather) to meet the costs of her schooling without feeling guilty, and one can see that Kylie's mother, who preferred not to suffer the stigma of being a 'charity case', was also hurt by the experience of poverty. The stress and frustration was, to some extent, turned within the family injuring the relations between Kylie and her mother. This young woman, not quite 16, actually worked four evenings a week in a fish and chip shop – some 15–17 hours after school in a hot and tiring job – but she was disciplined enough to dedicate an hour before school and an hour after work to her homework. In the second case, there was the relative lack of educational knowledge within the family and she speaks with a sigh of frustration at this absence. There is no direct mention of the third element, social capital, but again, there is an absence to be noted. In fact, there was a real absence here in Kylie's life: her father lived in Australia and she tried to put aside a small sum from her wages each week so that one day she could join him. Her mother was under stress, her stepfather was pretty much a stranger, her brother was actually her stepfather's son (until recently just another face in the class), and on Saturday (the only day she had free) she took the opportunity to get out of the house. Like a number of working-class young women, Kylie aspired to become a flight attendant, a job still seen as touched with glamour, and spoke of entering a course to gain a recognised qualification for that position. A schoolgirl, Kylie was already a working woman, she smoked, she was used to drinking alcohol, she was familiar with the night-club scene, and she was in all respects at home in the classed and gendered subculture of her friends. Most of the girls in her group were sexually active and had been so for a year or more.

Kylie was conscious that the position she was in – struggling to pass School Certificate while working 16 hours a week in a fish and chip shop – was *unfair*. Several times she echoes the words, 'it's horrible', 'it's really bad', 'it's so unfair'. The obligation to help out with the household finances, or feel guilty if she did not, was recognised as a burden over and above the actual lack of money itself and as one imposed by her class location. But it was difficult for Kylie to find anyone to blame: when the school demanded examination fees (acting as an agent for the Qualifications Authority) she says, 'it's not our fault if parents can't afford to pay for it' and then feels that she must concede that, 'well it is in a way'; and when the school was unable to provide any form of assistance to one of her friends who had left home to live independently, she could see that the state was responsible for the school's inability to act. Nevertheless, the fact that there seemed to be nothing and no one to hold responsible for the system that oppressed her – even the Social Welfare officials who administer the Independent Youth Benefit must be personally blameless – actually added to her level of frustration, and saw it directed sometimes inwards to her family, and sometimes externally to the school where it was merely understood as the expression of an alienated personal disposition. Kylie was not well-disposed to school – as an earlier commentary on this conversation (Nash and Major, 1996) stated – and a more careful reading reveals evidence of a deeper alienation than was first suspected. Those repeated comments that she felt, 'very anti-school sometimes' need to be given their appropriate weight. Kylie told us that she was regarded as good student at primary school and, as she was a little above average ability, good-looking and articulate, this recollection may well be trusted, but at secondary school her marks began to decline.

There is an extraordinary subtle process of negotiation that takes place between the school and its students and a once imperceptible distance steadily opened up as Kylie made her career through the institution. She was not seen as academic, she did not aspire to university, no one 'took her aside' and she manifestly failed to identify with the institution: 'I feel very anti-school sometimes'. Kylie sensed that she was being pushed out of school and, once again, she was able to recognise something about the process that was not quite fair. Kylie would not have been identified as a student with high aspirations; her hand would not have shot up when the teacher asked those who hoped to enter university to identify themselves; the school, generally, does not think much of girls who want to be air hostesses. It thinks even less of the practices typically adopted by working-class girls, even though these are the common practices of the community, as they declare their status as adults. In this context, therefore, Kylie struggled with her sense of alienation. In other conversations with her, more relaxed and culturally at home in the company of her friends, we heard her talking 'teenage stuff' – parents, teachers, boyfriends, night clubs, music, fashion – in forms of discourse that, of course (in so far as the school recognises them as signs that its own values and concerns are being rejected), act to work against her.

What social structures have generated these dispositions? In a realist conception of social science (Bunge, 1996, 1998), they are the structural properties of social class, the examination system, the labour market, and the cultural properties of those theories, beliefs and values inherently, through an association of interest, linked to them. There is, in the discourse used by Kylie, the tone, to use a French term, of *ressentiment* with a distinct class origin (Bourdieu, 1990). It is not envy: Kylie did not wish to see others worse off so that she might feel better (Elster, 1989), but her resentment did arise from the perception that the burdens imposed on her were the result of her class position, had not been *chosen* by her, and were unjust. The shortage of resources, of income, of cultural capital and of people to help her – social capital – that held her back, even in this mechanical form of analysis, should be seen as class limitations on her actions. Such *ressentiment* is not the only discursive response available to working-class students in Kylie's position, but it is not uncommon, and it has its origin in class injury (Sennett and Cobb, 1973) that is, above all, a sense of injury due to the want of familial social capital. Kylie felt that the institutions of society had no place for her, that they did not recognise her, and it is in this sense that the lack of social capital should be recognised as being at the root of the sentiments that dominated her class-formed habitus.

A Realist Concept of Cultural Capital

Lottie and Kylie, like all of us, are embedded within social structures, constituted by actual relations between people, and with properties distinct to their nature (Archer, 1995). The families to which Lottie and Kylie belong, for example, have certain real properties on which they can be distinguished: stability, wealth, the extent and density of their social networks, and so on, all of which have tangible effects on these girls' adjustment to school. Many of these properties are, in fact, subsumable under the concept of 'social capital' in its central Bourdieusian sense of social resources with the power to provide a return in a given field of practice. The importance of this last comment cannot be overestimated. The classed identities adopted by Lottie and Kylie are recognised as such and, while fundamentally derived from familial and age-peer resources – social capital – are mechanically associated with success and failure in an institution anything but neutral in its reaction to the social practices they generate. In some respects, Lottie did not think much of the school she attended; when its students came under attack – and her own social status badly misperceived – she was loyal to the institution, but she was not much impressed by the quality of the teaching she received. Yet, her ambivalent attitude to school, reflected in her QSL responses, had no effect on her high aspirations, and certainly did not affect her educational progress. There must be many lessons to be learned from this. Not the least may be that responses to questionnaire instruments need to be interpreted with care – and not only with respect to the individual but with respect to the groups they constitute. There is no reason to suppose that Lottie misrepresented her sentiments when completing the QSL instrument; on the contrary, her frankness in this respect enables the analysis to be driven forward. It is rather that the connection between holding uncritical responses of acceptance of the regime of schooling, a firm belief in ones success, and a sense of high personal status within the school (the latter rarely reported, in any event, by European fourth-form girls in large, multicultural schools) is mediated in complex ways by the active work of the school. Statements made in conversation require no less care in their interpretation, and perhaps care of a form that cannot be prescribed in a mechanical way, but one that can only be demonstrated with more or less skill (Hammersely, 1995). How much of that skill has been demonstrated in these analyses is for the reader to determine. The point of the exercise is to show how children come to have a changing, that is ever-developing, sense of who they are and what they can become, derived from the *classed* discourses they encounter. Some young people break with their class of origin, they are able to accumulate their own effective resources, including social capital, but for the most part they do not (Nash, 1999b). Lottie has become a middle-class girl just as surely as Kylie has become a working-class girl. They were never asked to place themselves in those terms, and their responses would leave this analysis unaffected, for it is the special task of sociology, not theirs, to understand what they have become and what structures of social relations have been responsible for that. (This is not to say that these girls did not understand how their possibilities for action were structured by social properties – it is clear that they did have some sense of that, and it is an educational task to deepen and extend this form of self-knowledge – but it is to say that forms of 'denial' or 'misrecognition' would not diminish the force of the analysis.) Their sense of position, the concept they hold of their place in the social order and the affect that locks it into place, is a consequence – *the* consequence – of the differentiated social capital they have inherited and acquired.

Lottie and Kylie are as vivid in my mind as anyone I know, and reflecting on their transcripts I hear their voices as they engage with the interviewer in these conversations. No real difference in accent can be detected, and there are no perceptible differences in those features of language that supposedly mark middle-class and working-class speech (perhaps the areas discussed were inappropriate to their realisation), but there is a difference nonetheless: in Kylie's voice one can hear the tones of grievance and tiredness, and in Lottie's the resonant expression of self-assurance and confidence. How are teachers to recognise the real frames of mind in which students express their responses to school? There is something to be learned from their questionnaire responses: there is infinitely more to be learned from their conversations (Nash, 1997). Even the tone of voice can be important in this context. Lying deeper than the fragmented analysis of these girls' respective success and failure in terms of their aspirations, academic self-concepts and willingness to tolerate school (and Lottie herself could only just tolerate it) is a more fundamental structure – a structure of society itself that does indeed become part of the structure of their socialised personalities – social class. These girls have learned who they are in a set of social relations in which people act – in some instances with conscious design – in a manner that teaches them who they are (Elias and Scotson, 1994). And it is not so much the literate resources of class, cultural capital, although so vital in developing and maintaining effective concepts of knowledge, nor yet the financial resources of class, although so directly important as purchasing power, but social capital itself that is revealed as the most critical family resource. If we are to work with the concept of social capital, then let us be clear why it is so important.

References

Archer, M. (1995). *Social Theory: The Morphogenetic Approach* (Cambridge: Cambridge University Press).

Bourdieu, P. (1990). *The Logic of Practice* (Cambridge: Polity Press).

Bunge, M. (1996). *Finding Philosophy in Social Science* (New Haven, Conn.: Yale University Press).

Bunge, M. (1998). *Social Science under Debate: A Philosophical Perspective* (Toronto: University of Toronto Press).

Coleman, J. (1988). Social capital in the creation of human capital, *American Journal of Sociology*, 94: 95–120.

Elias, N. and Scotson, J.L. (1994). *The Established and the Outsiders* (London: Sage).

Elster, J. (1989). *The Cement of Society: A Study of Social Order* (Cambridge: Cambridge University Press).

Hammersley, M. (1995). *Social Research and the Problem of Educational Inequalities: A Methodological Assessment* (London: Falmer).

Meehan, H., Villanueva, I., Hubbard, L. and Lintz, A. (1996). *Constructing School Success: The Consequences of Untracking Low-achieving Students* (Cambridge: Cambridge University Press).

Nash, R. (1993). *Succeeding Generations: Family Resources and Access to Education in New Zealand* (Auckland: Oxford University Press).

Nash, R. (1997). *A Year in the Sixth Form* (Palmerston North: ERDC Press).

Nash, R. (1998). Progress at school: Modes of adaptation and realist sociology, *New Zealand Journal of Educational Studies*, 33(1): 67–79.

Nash, R. (1999a). Realism in the sociology of education: Explaining social differences in attainment, *British Journal of Sociology of Education*, 20(1): 107–25.

Nash, R. (1999b). *School Learning: Conversations with the Sociology of Education* (Palmerston North: Delta Studies in Education).

Nash, R. and Harker, R.K. (1998). *Making Progress: Adding Value in Secondary Education*. (Palmerston North: ERDC Press).

Nash, R. and Major, S. (1996). *'When we're educated': Preparing for the Future, Voices from a New Zealand Sixth Form*, vol. 3 (Palmerston North: ERDC Press).

Opie, A. (1995). Developing a picture: Assessments with older clients with disabilities and their caregivers. In R. Munford and M. Nash (eds), *Social Work in Action* (Palmerston North: Dunmore Press): 201–22.

Poole, F.J.P. (1994). Socialisation, enculturation and the development of personal identity. In T. Ingold (ed.), *Companion Encyclopedia of Anthropology: Humanity, Culture and Social Life* (London: Routledge).

Sennett, R. and Cobb, J. (1973). *The Hidden Injuries of Class* (New York: Vintage Books).

Wetherell, M., Stiven, H., and Potter, J. (1987). Unequal egalitarianism: A preliminary study of discourses concerning gender and employment opportunities, *British Journal of Social Psychology*, 26: 59–71.

Woods, P. (1979). *The Divided School* (London: Routledge & Kegan Paul).

Woolcock, M. (1998). Social capital and economic development: Towards a theoretical synthesis and policy framework, *Theory and Society*, 27(2): 151–208.

Chapter 9

Pedagogy and the Care for Knowledge: Reproduction, Symbolic Violence and Realism

The New Zealand Progress at School project (Nash and Harker, 1998) was designed as a study of school effects to investigate the conditions of success and failure in secondary education. The research utilises a family resource framework, broadly inspired by Bourdieu (2000), but accepts the contemporary realist theory of science developed by Bunge (1998) and Bhaskar (1993). The longitudinal Progress at School research monitored the secondary school attainments of about 5,400 students at 37 New Zealand secondary schools, primarily in order to investigate school effects on attainment. It has been a productive project, which has generated an abundance of empirical data and sustained a deep engagement with social and educational theory (Nash, 2002, 2003). One of the most difficult theoretical areas has concerned the nature of pedagogy and the relationship between knowledge and the structures of the world. There is a tension between our commitment to scientific realism and Bourdieu's anthropological relativism that some attention to the theme of care as a principle of pedagogy might enable us to relax. Bourdieu's influential theory maintains that social reproduction is effected through forms of cultural reproduction mediated by the school, that education is inherently a matter of symbolic violence, and that school knowledge has a necessarily arbitrary character. In as much as the school is established to transmit the knowledge of a dominant class, so the argument goes, it can be expected that students from inferior classes will encounter particular difficulties in acquiring what it has to teach (Bourdieu, 1973; Bourdieu and Passeron, 1977). This theory has been widely accepted, but there are implications raised by a realist deliberation on the *care for knowledge* that will repay examination. If the theses of scientific realism are correct, then the definitive knowledge of the school may not be adequately characterised as a reflection of the cultural *arbitrary*, but as actually *necessary* if an individual is possess accurate knowledge of what the world is like. This is to say that academic knowledge may be defined improperly by a term – which is simply an anthropological given – that seems to undermine the possibility of establishing a universal curriculum based on modern science. This realist case, which will necessarily require some discussion of the nature of knowledge, will be made in the context of an empirical study of teaching practice. It will also, in a way that may not be too strained, argue that a care for knowledge is an aspect of the care for students that has properly been relocated by some contemporary authors as central to the pedagogic relationship. This is a matter of great significance: if the processes of social reproduction, as Bourdieu's theory has it, are to be interrupted by *pedagogic action*, then the care for knowledge may be as important as the care for students. A care for students, in fact, may entail a care for knowledge.

Pedagogy and the Language of Care

The presence of the language of care in contemporary writing on pedagogy should be recognised as the resurfacing of an older tradition. Texts written to instruct teachers on the nature of their craft once frankly identified the essential characteristics of a good teacher as certain dispositions of mind. Their authors were not shy to emphasise the importance of love and care. As one entirely representative text put it, first among the essential qualities of the teacher is a love of children (Salmon, 1914: 10):

> The man or woman who does not feel deep and abiding love for children as children, who does not watch with interest the unfolding of their minds, who is not ready to share in their games as well as their tasks, and who does not sympathize with the most troublesome, who does not recognize the infinite possibilities of their natures, has no right to be a teacher.

The emergence of a scientific approach to pedagogy, as the twentieth century progressed, saw this sacerdotal language displaced by a technical discourse marked by the influence of behaviourist psychology. Attention shifted from consciousness, including habituated dispositions, to overt and observable behaviour; whereas the properties of the teacher had been given in terms of *character*, they were now described in accordance with the principles of science; and a moral language appropriate to an era in which elementary education was controlled by the church was replaced by a secular language that reflected the neutral position of the rational state. In this intellectual climate, the belief that a love for children should be an inherent and necessary quality of a good teacher seemed intolerably old-fashioned. Moreover, as this idea was often coupled with the no less traditional view that this disposition, coupled with a little subject knowledge, and a few tricks of the trade learned through practical experience, should constitute sufficient basis for a career in teaching, it encountered a further source of professional resistance. As formal teacher training based in specialist colleges became increasingly established, these 'barbaric' ideas (Hoyle and John, 1995: 51), which in the 1980s actually re-emerged in a recognisable form, were interpreted as a threat to the power of an organised profession. The fundamental disciplines contributing to teaching offered a scientific approach that gave no legitimation to the often non-secular and non-quantifiable lexicon of pedagogy in which 'love' had been central. Although the radical discourse of 'critical pedagogy', with its triple roots in revolutionary Marxism, depth psychology and liberation theology, might have recognised the concept of *charity*, it developed a polysyllabic discourse of 'emancipation' and 'empowerment' having little in common with the traditional language of love and care. For some decades the concept of care, to the extent that it was recognised at all in orthodox professional discourse, was confined to the official-sounding phrases of the legal statute, as a 'professional duty of care'. This effectively puts a crucial element of the relationship between teacher and pupil on the same level as that of the duty of a driver to other users of the public highway. The recent reappearance of *care* as a term of art in the literature of empirical social science in education is, therefore, an event of some significance.

Noddings's (1984) argument that care for students' educational and moral welfare is central to the teaching relationship has provided a useful discourse for the elaboration of these concerns. Valenzuela (1999), for example, is thus able to argue that the failure of many Latin-American students in the US high school can largely be explained by their withdrawal from a system that demonstrates its lack of care for their education and social well-being. All too conscious of the fact that the school denies the worth of their culture, they respond by refusing to accept what the school offers on its restricted terms. If the school does not care about them: they will not care about the school. It is more than time that these basic concepts of love and care were restored to their central place in the pedagogic relationship. McNeil (2000: 139), in her illuminating study of teaching in successful Texas magnet schools, also noticed this quality and observed that, 'caring took the form of accountability, of openness to questions, of fairness in assignments and in assessments, and an acceptance of all the students'. This may be accepted: but there was something else these good teachers cared about: they cared about knowledge. The introduction of poor-quality, mandated textbooks, principally designed to enable students to achieve adequate grades on standardised tests, was resisted by most self-respecting teachers. In this context, McNeil relates how a biology teacher, Ms Bartlett, openly criticised the official textbook and instructed her students – 'Here is the right formula' (ibid. 211) – to copy the correct version into their notebooks. Why did Ms Bartlett do this? It is because she cared as a teacher not only for her students, but also for knowledge itself. At the very least, one could say that her care for her students extends to caring that what they learn in her class should be useful, reliable and worth knowing. It might be argued, indeed, that, unless teachers care for knowledge, there is no reason why they should care whether their students become knowledgeable or not.

There was an episode in the Progress at School research that pushed our thinking forward. The following extract is from a conversation held with a 19-year-old Maori girl then in her first year reading law at university. She had attended a girls' school where she demonstrated impressive progress in all her subjects and achieved a position of academic and social eminence. The interviewer asked her, 'Do teachers have an influence on whether you do well?'

> In our third and fourth years, yeah, depending on how they treat you makes …
> Well, like, even for me, if a teacher gives me the time to – of what they're doing
> – if they, you know, just step outside of their own space and help you, and makes

you feel like, important, in that class, I will do it better in a class that's like that than if a teacher just says, 'Right, write out, do this, do that', and sat down. I just would not be interested, unless I had an interest in that topic anyway. […] Mr Norton he was our science teacher, he was, you know, white as the day, but he used to get up there and, *te reo*, [*speak Maori*] and he used to hard out go round at us in Maori. And he used to do summer schools, Maori classes, and things, just so he could talk to us. It wasn't that hard for him to go along and do it, but just the effort that we had seen him make, that made us respect him so much more. Like when he said something we did it all right, and that was just the respect we had for him. Whereas, you know, if some teacher who said to us, 'Oh will you fellows shut up', you know, we'd say, 'Oh get real', you know? It's just a whole different respect thing, and he had it, because of the … We just felt – I don't know – glad that he had just done that for us. It made you feel, far, we are important! And a lot of us did really well in science, too, in our fourth form. And like, even when I left in my seventh form, I went back to him and said, you know, 'Thanks for everything, see you later', because he impacted me, from these first two years.

It is unusual for students to speak with such enthusiasm about their teachers, and this discourse is obviously interesting in other respects, but the notable point in the context of an empirical research program was Becky's observation that the girls in her class 'did really well in science'. Do students actually learn more from teachers they respect? It was possible to compare the performance of the 16 Maori students in Becky's bilingual class (the fourth- and fifth-form class lists were available) with the 32 in mainstream classes. In English and mathematics there was no significant difference in the mean scores, but in science, where the mean score of those in other classes was 36.5, that of Becky's class was 44. This is a difference of more than half a standard deviation and statistically significant. The performance of these groups in mathematics and science is particularly interesting because the size and composition of the groups was exactly the same, and there is no apparent reason why the Maori girls in Becky's class should have gained distinctly superior science marks to those in other classes. The best explanation must be that offered by Becky: they excelled themselves because they had a teacher who evidently cared, in a way they recognised as noteworthy, about them and their education. It can seem almost impossible to specify the characteristics of a good teacher, except in self-evident tautologies, but the discussion will attempt to move beyond this through an investigation of *care* in the pedagogic relationship. The obvious sense in which 'what made the difference' in *this* pedagogical relationship was a respect for the symbolic forms of the students' ethnic culture, should not be overlooked, but it may be useful to situate that particular manifestation of care as one with its roots in a more general context. The care for knowledge itself can be distinguished from the care for students and requires its own analysis.

Pedagogy and the Care for Knowledge

The study of pedagogy is more than usually fragmented by the disciplinary struggle for dominance in this field. If the resulting patchwork is colourful, the overall pattern is hard to discern and some focusing remarks may be helpful. One may say, with Appel (1997), that pedagogy remains an alien term in the lexicon of teachers. Simon (1980) commented more than 20 years ago on the lack of serious interest in pedagogy as the definitive practice of education and it is still possible for students to emerge from a college of education without a clear idea of its core meanings. A brief introduction to the central meanings as they have emerged in the work of Bernstein (1971), Bourdieu (2000) and Friere (1974) will provide a necessary context for the analysis. The discussion does not allow 'pedagogy' to be used as a synonym for 'teaching method', where the reference is to such technical characteristics of classroom practice as the use of textbooks, worksheets, individual and group learning schemes, and so on. In this context, Bernstein's (1971) rigorous analysis of the central concepts for the study of the transmission and acquisition of knowledge remains invaluable. In his discourse, 'pedagogy', refers to the way knowledge is transmitted, and belongs with 'curriculum' as the way knowledge is organised, and 'evaluation' as the way knowledge is realised. This theoretical concept of pedagogy, which is designed to allow investigation into the structural principles that regulate a pedagogic system, directs attention to the pedagogic relationship and the social conditions that regulate the transmission of knowledge. The position developed in this chapter will identify, however, not a principle (a conceptual object of discourse), but an active disposition of the self, with an embodied nature, as the definitive property of the pedagogic relationship. This influential analysis, particularly as it forges links with Bourdieu (Stabile, 2000), is crucial the analysis developed here. The pedagogical relationship necessarily involves the application of technical expertise, but it is not defined in terms of those techniques, but rather as the property of a social relationship of a certain kind.

If teachers are to care about knowledge they need to be clear about two principles: first, they must possess criteria that will enable them to distinguish between what is worth knowing and what is not, and second, they must transmit knowledge in such a way that it is acquired by processes appropriate to its nature. Teaching is, of course, practised in a regulated curriculum framework, but this does not mean that the question of what should be taught can be relegated to the taken-for-granted and placed outside the legitimate concern of teachers (Nuttall, 1999). Moreover, although questions about the transmission of knowledge and questions about its organisation can be separated, and represented by the concepts of pedagogy and curriculum, the discussion of pedagogy does require some clarity about the epistemological foundations of knowledge. There is much good sense in the apparently simple idea that knowledge is what is known (Bunge, 1998). This formulation has, among others, the virtue of allowing the epistemological concepts of 'truth', 'certainty', 'justification', and so on, to be treated as properties of knowledge rather than as intrinsic to its definition. This makes it possible to speak of knowledge as true, partially true or entirely false, and as held securely or tentatively, as the case might be. If the pedagogic relationship is defined as being to do with the transmission of knowledge, and if knowledge is defined in terms of truth, then the implications for pedagogy would certainly be over-restrictive. There would be no teaching unless that taught was demonstrated to be true. This realist concept of knowledge, however, is difficult to reconcile with a position that has attracted widespread support in the sociology of education. The difficulty, of course, is Bourdieu's theory of cultural and social reproduction in as much as it posits the mobilisation of symbolic power as the crucial mechanism in the generation of social differences in educational achievement. In the words of Bourdieu and Passeron (1977: 5) '*pedagogic action* (PA) is, obviously, symbolic violence insofar as it is the imposition of a cultural arbitrary by an arbitrary power.' A concept of pedagogy acceptable to critical realism must be able to contribute to the resolution of these questions.

As Robbins (2000: xiii) has pointed out, Bourdieu saw society as a series of arbitrary cultures 'which were in competition with each other and in which dominance was secured, not as the result of any intrinsic merit or superiority, but one of *force majeure*.' In the broad anthropological sense, all knowledge can be regarded as arbitrary within a given society. Human societies have a wide range of practices. In the area of family organisation, for example, the established forms may prescribe endogamy or exogamy, monogamy or polygamy, primogeniture or ultimogeniture, and matrilocality or patrilocality. These practices are arbitrary in the sense that all can be adopted; they are functionally equivalent in as much that as one is as 'workable' as another; and it is certain that the routines of human societies, unlike those of the great apes, are not genetically determined. The practices that constitute and reproduce society can be analysed, in the structuralist tradition, in terms of their fundamental *principles*, which are naturally acquired through the process of socialisation and which are then basically maintained as learned habits. These core principles will – it is possible to say almost necessarily – be transmitted from generation to generation as embodied dispositions. Such knowledge, moreover, has the property of symbolic violence in as much as it is the cultural property of a particular group and mobilised in the struggle for dominance. What is widely taken as a Bourdieusian theory of educational reproduction is based on the insights that in capitalist (or perhaps industrialised) societies, the knowledge of the dominant and dominated are arbitrary cultural products. Grenfell and James (1998), for example, argue that classed knowledge, readily assimilated by those for whom it is designed, is rejected as alien by those from the dominated classes. There is no need to suppose that school knowledge is organised and taught with the conscious intention of excluding those with an inferior habitus; nevertheless, as Bourdieu (2000) argues, it effectively achieves that end. This entire theory requires, of course, a thoroughly relativised concept of knowledge.

However, the question remains. What must be taught by teachers who care about knowledge? This question, of course, is posed with reference to our current era and global scientific culture. There is a realist answer to this question. Bhaskar's (1993) critical realism is founded on the 'transcendental' assumption, or observation, that modern science, particularly biology, chemistry and physics, has succeeded in demonstrating, if as yet incompletely, the material nature of the world. Scientific realism, promoted rigorously by Bunge, also accepts that the theories of modern science are fundamentally correct. The implications of this realist view of science for teaching merit some discussion. It suggests that students who are not taught the demonstrated facts about the world, and the techniques by which those they can be known, are being deprived of what might be regarded as the birthright of a person living in our era (Matthews, 1995). In the humanities things are not quite the same, but perhaps they are not fundamentally different either. If the established practices of a society, in all their forms, are arbitrary in the broad anthropological sense, there may be systems of analytical thought that are, at least, considerably less relative. The tools of conceptual and logical analysis and the literate habits of mind they generate in those who study these subjects may be regarded as necessary to the education of any one in a modern society. It is arguable, in this sense, that some knowledge of the human condition may be identified as that of a common culture. French and English history, for example, are cultural arbitraries, and yet to be a citizen of France or of the United Kingdom, and to know nothing of its history is not to be educated in the widest sense even about a central component of one's identity (MacIntyre, 1984). If there is *arbitrariness* at one level, there is *necessity* at another. One cannot be a citizen, in other than a formal and legalistic sense, of a modern democratic society without the knowledge necessary to an Aristotelian practical grasp of that status. The knowledge that gives us the capabilities of a useful member of a society should be regarded, in this sense, as necessary. Moreover, sound judgement, optimism, care for knowledge and so on are not to be regarded as arbitrary capabilities, but as ones necessary to human flourishing. There is little doubt that Bourdieu, despite the implications that have been drawn from his work, himself endorsed this position of the Enlightenment (Lane, 2000). There is obvious sense in which knowledge is constructed by societies that are always located in time and space, and there is an equally obvious sense in which the knowledge required to live in different societies is to some extent always specific, but this should not be allowed to sustain the view that all knowledge is socially arbitrary. What is necessary must be argued on the grounds of the ontology of human beings, what is necessary to human flourishing, and on the nature of science as a practice able to reveal the ontology of the physical world (Nash, 1999).

The pedagogic relationship is, furthermore, one of respect for the way in which knowledge is transmitted. A teacher must offer instruction in such a way that students are provided with the conceptual tools necessary to critique its origins and assess its truth. Teaching is not the transmission of propaganda. To instruct students in the doctrine of a party, in the broadest sense of that term, in such a way that acceptance of the doctrine is its essential purpose, is to engage in the work of disseminating propaganda. To teach students that the earth is a globe in orbit around the sun is, indeed, to provide them with real knowledge. And yet, should that knowledge be taught as a doctrine, without reference to the methods of scientific demonstration by which it is known, then students have not gained their knowledge in a context that makes it open, as far as they are concerned, to an appropriate test or demonstration. If the students have not been taught *propaganda*, they have certainly been taught by the *methods* of propaganda, and are so prevented from realising their knowledge in the right way. The practice of teaching, therefore, requires a standpoint of authenticity towards knowledge – a teacher must not hold an attitude of cynicism towards knowledge and its worth to students – and it involves a form of instruction that encourages logic, evidence and debate. There was moral outrage in New Zealand, and rightly so, when a prison inmate convicted of violent crimes was reported to be acting as a 'facilitator', or tutor, on an 'anger-management' course, and suspected of doing so for the purpose of making a favourable impression with the parole board (New Zealand Press Association, 2000). Even if the instruction he provided actually altered the behaviour of those in his class for the better, we would be reluctant to accept this as evidence of good teaching, or of teaching at all. The entire proceeding is a deeply inauthentic and a mere sham. The crucial importance of these principles in contested areas of the curriculum, such as evolutionary theory, should be evident. The task of the teacher is not to instil belief, but to enable knowledge to be gained with the tools intrinsic to its conditions of demonstration. These principles of the pedagogic relationship may be recognised, moreover, in the professional *dispositions* of teachers. The following section will examine the practices of a teacher in a somewhat routine Year 11 science lesson that will disclose these effective dispositions of pedagogic action as well as any other. It is not that the problems to be solved are unique to school science, but this is a certainly a subject where they are particularly acute.

Reflections on a Science Lesson

The Progress at School research adopted an integrated 'numbers and narratives' methodology (Nash and Harker, 1998). Fieldwork observations were carried out in several schools, in one school for two years, and a number of techniques were developed to record information about the contexts of learning in classrooms. One of the most successful was to interview students a short time after a lesson to describe their experience. The fieldworkers, who had experienced the same lesson, were often able to elicit some rich and illuminating data. The following conversation took place with a 16-year-old, working-class Maori student with standardised 'ability' test scores almost a standard deviation below the mean. School learning did not come easily to Yolanda, no one expected her to enjoy much success, and low grades and nominal 'failure' were a continual experience; yet she persisted at school and sustained a lively interest in her classes. She was, in fact, one of those students who make relative progress at secondary school, and, although she never succeeded in passing a science test, she completed school and found employment in a clerical position. It was a deserved achievement.

Yola, what were you learning today in science?

What were we learning today? We were learning about electrical appliances and how, what runs through them, what current, and how to graph them on axes and … Oh, and he's going to tell us about plugs tomorrow.

Sounded quite good, didn't it?

So we know how to do it without getting an electrician.

That was quite funny when he was looking at your graph and Dick's graph. Did Dick copy your graph?

Yeah. [*laughs*] Yeah, he did. And Mr Prasad says, 'Oh those are very good graphs', and Dick goes 'Shush!'

He must have guessed though, because he said something like, 'These graphs both start at the same point', but he kept his cool, he didn't give it away, did he?

But Dick attempted to do it. I just gave it to him anyway.

Did you do the experiment yesterday?

Yes, that's right, we did the experiment yesterday with an ammeter and voltmeter, lamps and – what else did we have? – and a switch, but we didn't use it. And we just had to slide the – up and down to see how much current was flowing through the wires. She doesn't know what I'm talking about! [*Referring to her friend Marisse who has joined them*]

[*Marisse*] Yes I do! [*laughs*] Shut up!

And what did it show, the graph?

What did it show? It shows that when voltmeters and current meters both increase or decrease both at the same time. So, yeah, that's what it showed.

What was that E over I equals R?

Yeah, I don't remember those things very well, the formulas. I don't know.

[*Marisse*] Her teacher gets up and teaches them. All my teacher does is, 'Oh here's a page, do page 58 copy it out'. Don't get any instruction on really how to do it. I'm surprised I passed my test.

I've never passed a science test in my life.

Can you describe how Mr Prasad teaches?

Can I describe? Well, sometimes, it depends. It depends on the teacher. I mean, some people don't think he's good, but I think he's a good teacher, and I like the way he teaches, because he talks, you know, and he instead of saying, 'Copy this out' and telling us, you know, 'Do it', and just not … He explains it. He shows you every detail that you want to know. He goes through it in stages and like, not even after he's done it the first time, he goes, he refers to it again and again, and it's, you know, going through your head all period, so by the time you're finished, you know half of what he's talking about anyway. Today he took our papers in, and he showed us how the current on the voltmeter was 'increasing-at-the-same-time-or-decreasing-at-the-same-time'. What else did he show us?

Did you pick up that 'line of best fit'?

Yeah, that line of best fit thing. Oh, I dunno. Oh, I knew kind of what he was talking about, and it just shows which one is connected with each, yeah. He went over that work we did, what we had to fill in with the reliever, that sheet we'd copied down. That's what we always do when he's not here. But it's OK, because when he comes back he explains what we've been doing, because we don't understand it. He's a good teacher. He is disciplined, but you can be funny with him.

Jack with that fuse!

Yeah. Mr Prasad goes 'What is this fuse used for?' and Jack goes, 'It's used in a car', and he's not answering the question, you know, 'What does it do?' And he's going completely off the track. Quite funny.

But he [Mr Prasad] kept asking him.

Yeah he did.

So why do you use fuses?

Why do you use fuses? So that you don't damage your machines and stuff. The fuse is high resistance. No problems!

The fact that Yolanda failed to gain a better-than-nominal pass mark in the School Certificate science course she was studying does not mean she had acquired nothing of any value from her instruction in basic science. In this lesson, one of a unit on electricity, she had learned something about the nature of electrical circuits and the properties of electromotive force. Through demonstration and guided experimentation she had observed the character of Ohm's law in a context where its everyday practical application in the design of fused circuits was emphasised. Yolanda describes Mr Prasad as a good teacher, and her account of his teaching practice is worth some analysis. The students worked in groups, completing their own worksheets, and were able to take measurements using the apparatus provided for that purpose. Yolanda seems to understand the functions of an ammeter. Mr Prasad is specifically praised for his insistence on explaining information. He 'shows you every detail', 'goes through it in stages' and not once but 'again and again'. He tests whether students have learned the information. Yolanda notes with amusement how Jack, a student in her group, recognised a fuse as one used in a car engine, but his teacher wanted to know its function and persisted until, presumably, the required response was given. Mr Prasad's energetic teaching is contrasted with another that students openly regard as inferior and practised by inexpert or, as Marisse's tone implies, lazy teachers. This teacher does not expect students to learn by asking them to turn to a page of the textbook with the direction, 'copy this out', or by instructing them to 'do it', as if they already knew what to do, while perhaps, sitting at his desk busy with something else. In Marisse's words, Mr Prasad, 'gets up and teaches'. Yolanda is able to give an adequate description of her teacher's practices and evaluates them with reference to the way they contribute to her own learning.

Good, or effective, pedagogy, as the following section will show, is defined in behavioural terms as having clear lesson plans, demonstrating good organisation, providing opportunities for practical activity, giving adequate explanations, and the careful marking and subsequent discussion of student papers. At this level, these are, indeed, the marks of a good teacher. Yolanda says little about modes of control, 'he is disciplined, but you can be funny with him', but there is no doubt that Mr Prasad was relaxed and able to maintain control. It is less easy, however, for Yolanda to analyse her teacher's behaviour at a deeper level. She might have said, it is not unimaginable, that 'the thing about Mr Prasad is that he really cares about science', but that she did not say those words does not mean that we cannot read them in her account. There can be little doubt that Yolanda understands that her teacher's practices are informed by the principle that scientific knowledge, its theoretical bases and its practical application, is worth the effort of learning. It is because of this principle that Mr Prasad insists that it should be learned. It is not sufficient that Jack should be able to recognise a starting motor fuse, nor yet, perhaps possess the routine 'practical' information that they should be replaced every 50,000 kilometres in accordance with the operating manual, rather he must know what it does and how it works. He must also learn that questions about mechanism cannot be sidetracked, particularly by those interested in mechanics, by the evasions of nominalism. Jack knew that the fuse is used in a car, and he answered the question within the framework of his taken-for-granted knowledge, but the teacher refused to accept that answer, thus, incidentally, rejecting the particular 'construction of reality' and the grounds on which it is likely to be based, and insisted on a realist explanation at the level of mechanism.

This information is, perhaps, available to Mr Prasad's students only within the taken-for-granted view of their own discourse. Mr Prasad, however, had a degree of self-knowledge characteristic of reflective teachers (Schon, 1983; Pollard and Tan, 1987). His own comments on his teaching are eloquent testimony to this assertion:

> I've never met a young person I didn't like. There's something about every one of them that you can respond to as an individual. They all want to learn – none of them want to fail or be ignorant – and they can all learn. Everyone in this class will learn something worthwhile. They won't all get to university, not even all those who want to get to university will do that, but they will get something from being here. […] I treat them all the same in the sense that I expect them to learn what they can. […] It is to do with respect, yes. I respect them as people who are here to learn, and they respect me as a teacher. That's the nature of the relationship, the contract, if you like. I think of them as people who will be that much better for knowing something about the principles and applications of science. That's what we learn about. […] Of course, I have to talk about the examinations, and the unit standards we have to think about now, and I'm always relating things to the everyday life they know, circuits and fuses, and so on, but they have to know that what I really want is for them to know *this*, to know science. They should know what things are like, how it all works, how it all fits together. This is the world we live in, the world we are part of, and this is *me*, this is what I know. You don't have to be Einstein to get that. […] At one level they certainly understand that. They know that they're better off not being ignorant – you listen to them: even kids who have given up on school don't like being called 'dummies' – and they can separate that idea out from not getting enough marks to 'pass', if that's what happens.

Lively teaching able to engage students' interest in a curriculum that continually makes reference to a wide range of practical applications can provide students with a sense of *knowing*. Knowledge is what is known, and what is known is known to people. It is particularly important to grasp the point that it is people who know – not books or computers. This sense of actually knowing – the sense of satisfaction that comes from being able to demonstrate the properties of the world – needs to be systematically inculcated by the forms of scientific education. Mr Prasad asserts the value of mathematics and science as worthwhile knowledge and as qualities intrinsic to the educated person. To be educated means to possess the concepts and methods that reveal the structures of the physical and social world. Students rarely ask why they need to learn that the earth is a sphere in orbit about the sun, nor do they commonly ask what 'use' this knowledge is to them, and yet they are likely to ask why they need to learn the fundamental laws that would enable them to observe for themselves, should they wish, that these facts can be demonstrated. These points will be elaborated in a concluding discussion of the production of classed knowledge, the responses it evokes, and how it might be possible to liberate education from what seems to Bourdieu the inevitability of symbolic violence.

Discussion

Educational policymakers are increasingly persuaded, rightly or wrongly, that schools, if staffed by competent and effective teachers, have a considerable power to interrupt the processes that generate unequal outcomes between social groups. If this project is to succeed, the universal pedagogy that Bourdieu proposed – although never specified by him in any detail – will need to possess both a care for students and a care for the definitive knowledge of realist science. The argument that all knowledge is *arbitrary* must be challenged in as much as it threatens to inhibit this development. The arguments must be worked through. There is no dispute that school knowledge is *classed*. Young's (1976) critical investigation of the development of school science in England, for example, argues that science was introduced to the school curriculum late in the nineteenth century in order to increase the supply of trained scientists by preparing students with the necessary qualifications for entry to a university science course. Consequently, the subjects of school science – physics, chemistry, biology – developed under university control as bodies of pure knowledge consisting of abstract laws, methodological principles and lists of facts having little relation to each other or to areas of practical application. In this way, the academic distinction between the high-status, pure knowledge of theory and the low-status, impure knowledge of practice in those subjects was imposed on the schools. The economic division of labour is driven by the imperative of efficiency and divorces conception from execution, theoretical knowledge from practical application, mental from manual work, and directive from directed labour. These relationships and their continued effect on structuring access to knowledge should always be remembered. This does not alter the fact that, if a realist otology is correct, some knowledge taught by the modern school is not arbitrary, in any useful sense, and might better be recognised as necessary. The characteristic responses of students with different class origins to knowledge, and particularly to scientific knowledge, may be clarified by this discussion.

Working-class students, for example, are more likely than are middle-class students to recognise the exchange value of school knowledge as a reason more central to its acquisition than its use value. Working-class families accept the value of skilled knowledge, as for example in craft expertise, within a framework of thought deeply rooted in the realist ontology of material practice. It is in this context that working-class parents and students make their demand for the educational credentials necessary to access vocational courses. The school, of course, responds to that demand as a source of motivation, but in so doing it typically makes little systematic attempt to restructure the students' view that the curriculum it provides as abstract, theoretical, and intrinsically useless for everyone not intending to be a 'rocket scientist'. The instrumental concept of knowledge is thus continually emphasised in its exhortations to succeed in gaining its academic credentials. In a subtle irony, schools may thus fail in their educational task not because they give too little emphasis to credentials, but because they give too much. To know the world as it is should be recognised as being in itself a form of power: not a power *over* nature but over oneself in relation to nature. Bringing together the sciences in terms of their value, giving some attention to their history, and demonstrating to students the critical value of such knowledge, in as far as it is within their grasp, can provide a conceptualisation of great benefit. Through computer simulations, debates, scientific clubs, and other activities designed to demonstrate the fundamental unity of science and the practical integration of its fields of application, students might gain a fuller appreciation of the value of their scientific education. The mystique attached to certain areas of science has the effect of closing off access to areas of knowledge that need to be opened to working-class students. Mathematics with calculus is more 'more highly thought of', as the students say, than the 'alternative' mathematics offered to 'low ability' students, because it is more useful to any one of the myriad of technologies that sustain industrial civilisation and in areas of application that are not confined to the sphere of work. Students need to gain a sense, also, that mathematical and scientific knowledge is valuable, which is applicable in the most direct sense, in fields other than the strictly vocational. An informed participation in many areas of organised life, as a citizen and as a member of different communities, can be enhanced only by a scientific education. Debates touching on environmental and planning issues are often effectively closed to those incapable, for want of knowledge, of understanding the concepts and methods of modern science. The task of the school should be to conceptualise science within this wider framework, affirming its value and declaring its areas of relevance within the wider social, economic and political parameters structuring the lives of its students. Where such knowledge and this sense of its worth is not part of the taken-for-granted framework of information within the students' families, the school may need to assume the responsibility to provide this conceptualisation. This may be admitted as an integral element of caring about knowledge in such a way that its status as symbolic violence is negated.

Simon (1980) commented more than 20 years ago on the lack of serious interest in pedagogy as the definitive practice of education, and the study of pedagogy is more than usually fragmented (Appel, 1997). It may be too soon to anticipate the development of an integrated theory of pedagogy, and still less a universal pedagogy in which those attributed an 'inferior' cognitive habitus will have a genuine opportunity to acquire necessary knowledge, but the re-emergence of an intellectual context in which it is possible to reflect on the qualities of care in teaching should certainly be welcomed (Gauthern, 2000). If this chapter is successful in provoking reflection on the proposition that a care for students should extend to a care for knowledge then it will have achieved its modest purpose.

References

Appel, S. (1997). The teacher's headache. In Appel, S. (ed.), *Psychology and Pedagogy* (Westport, Conn.: Bergin and Garvey): 133–84.

Bernstein, B. (1971). On the classification and framing of educational knowledge. In M.F.D. Young (ed.), *Knowledge and Control* (London: Collier/Macmillan): 47–69.

Bhaskar, R. (1993). *Dialectic: The Pulse of Freedom* (London: Verso).

Bourdieu, P. (1973). The school as a conservative force: Scholastic and cultural inequalities, trans. by J.C. Woodhouse. In J. Eggleston (ed.), *Contemporary Research in the Sociology of Education* (London: Methuen): 32–46.

Bourdieu, P. (2000). *Pascalian Meditations*, trans. R. Nice (Cambridge: Polity Press).

Bourdieu, P., and Passeron, J–C. (1977). *Reproduction in Education, Society and Culture,* trans. R. Nice (London: Sage).

Bunge, M. (1998). *Finding Philosophy in Social Science* (New Haven, Conn.: Yale University Press).

Friere, P. (1974). *Pedagogy of the Oppressed* (Harmondsworth: Penguin).

Gauthern, D. (2000). The art of mentoring: Teaching that engages the soul, *Waikato Journal of Education*, 7: 171–6.

Grenfell, M. and James, D. with Hodkinson, P., Reay, D., and Robbins, D. (1998). *Bourdieu and Education: Acts of Practical Theory* (London: Falmer Press).

Hoyle, E. and John, P.D. (1995). *Professional Knowledge as Professional Practice* (London: Cassell).

Lane, J.F. (2000). *Pierre Bourdieu: A Critical Introduction* (London: Pluto).

MacIntyre, A. (1984). *After Virtue: A Study in Moral Theory*, 2nd edn (Notre Dame, Ind.: University of Notre Dame Press).

McNeil, L. (2000). *Contradictions of School Reform: Educational Costs of Standardized Testing.* (London: Routledge).

Matthews, M.R. (1995). *Challenging New Zealand Science Education* (Palmerston North: Dunmore Press).

Nash, R. (1999). *School learning: Conversations with the Sociology of Education*, Delta Studies in Education 3 (Palmerston North: Delta Press).

Nash, R. (2002). Numbers and narratives: Further reflections in the sociology of education, *British Journal of Sociology of Education*, 23(3): 397–412.

Nash, R. (2003). Social Explanation and socialization: On Bourdieu and the structure, disposition, practice scheme, *Sociological Review*, 51(1): 43–62.

Nash, R. and Harker, R.K. (1998). *Making Progress: Adding Value in Secondary Education* (Palmerston North: ERDC Press).

New Zealand Press Association (2000). Prisons to stifle 'look good' tricks, *The Dominion* (11 August 2000): 3.

Noddings, N. (1984). *Caring, a Feminist Approach to Ethics and Moral Education* (Berkeley, Calif.: University of California Press).

Nuttall, G. (1999). Learning how to learn: The evolution of students' minds through the social processes and culture of the classroom, *International Journal of Educational Research*, 31(3): 142–256.

Pollard, A. and Tann, S. (1987). *Reflective Teaching in the Primary School* (London: Cassell).

Robbins, D. (2000). *Bourdieu and Culture*. London: Sage.

Salmon, D. (1914). *The Art of Teaching* (London: Green).

Schon, D. (1983). *The Reflective Practitioner* (Basic Books: New York).

Simon, B. (1981). Why no pedagogy in England? In B. Simon and W. Taylor (eds), *Education in the Eighties* (London: Batsford): 124–45.

Stabile, C.A. (2000). Resistance, recuperation, and reflexivity: The limits of a paradigm. In N. Brown and I. Szeman (eds), *Pierre Bourdieu: Fieldwork in Culture* (Lanham, Md.: Bowman and Littlefield).

Valenzuela, A. (1999). *Subtractive Schooling: US–Mexican Youth and the Politics of Caring* (Albany, NY: State University of New York Press).

Young, M.F.D. (1976). The schooling of science. In G. Whitty and M.F.D. Young (eds), *Explorations in the Politics of Knowledge* (Lewes: Falmer Press): 47–61.

PART 4
Secondary Effects and Statistical Modelling

Chapter 10

Controlling for 'Ability':
A Conceptual and Empirical Study of
Primary and Secondary Effects

Observed class disparities in access to higher education are due partly to the fact that working-class students are less likely than middle-class students to gain the necessary entrance qualifications, and partly to the fact that school leavers with different class origins tend to enter higher education in different proportions even when their qualifications are the same. In Boudon's terms, there are both primary and secondary effects of social stratification to be explained. Boudon (1974) maintained that the latter were more important than the former, thus effectively relegating theories of primary effects, the most dominant being IQ theory, to a minor role, and attempted to make sociology the central discipline in the explanation of IEO (inequality of educational opportunity). Boudon also maintained that opportunity cost models of transition from one stage of the educational system to another were more consistent with the demonstrated facts than rival theories of class-cultural habit. The real target of Boudon's critique is, of course, Bourdieu's influential theory of cultural reproduction (Bourdieu and Passeron, 1990). This could hardly go unnoticed and may even be one of the reasons for the indifferent reception it has received from sociologists of education. In any event, although Boudon's thesis gained widespread support when initially proposed, interest has waned to the point where, perhaps, but for the contribution of his compatriot Duru-Bellat (2000), it would be possible to argue that our discipline has all but forgotten Boudon. The concepts of primary and secondary effects have, however, retained an important status in contemporary social mobility research (Breen and Goldthorpe, 1995) where the influence of Boudon's theoretical and methodological work persists. It is also of some interest to note that at least one French associate of the emerging school of critical realism has attempted to assimilate Boudon's sociology to that ontological doctrine (Hamlin, 2002).

This introduction will provide a context for a detailed conceptual and empirical investigation into the distinction between primary and secondary effects and its utility in the explanation of social disparities in educational achievement. This dual argument, which is essential if its critical intentions are to be realised, requires, first, an analysis of the key concepts and, second, an empirical analysis of relevant data. The British Cohort Study 1970 (BCS70), which is more than suitable for this purpose, is used with acknowledgements to the ESRC Data Archive and the National Centre for Social Research.

Primary and Secondary Effects: Their Identification and Cause

A secondary effect is identified when a table depicting outflow–inflow rates for students with a given level of qualification shows class origin to be associated with class destination. It is also possible, by a modest extension of the concept, to regard class differences in relative achievement levels at different times as evidence of a secondary effect. If the proportion of working-class students in the upper fifth of an achievement distribution at age ten is, say, 15 per cent, and at 16 it is 10 per cent, then it might be argued that a secondary effect has been detected in as much that the deviation is, on this evidence, not due to intellectual ability. Such evidence might be taken, in fact, to indicate a lagged secondary effect. The secondary effect is allocated to sociology in as much as it is not a primary effect, and, in so far as a secondary effect is not accounted for by 'motivation' or 'values', then it is explained by a rational action model. The concept thus seems to have a methodological definition.

There appears to be enough ambiguity in Boudon's position, however, to open the possibility of an alternative interpretation. According to Hamlin (2002: 42), for example, Boudon defines primary effects 'as expectations and aspirations which are not mediated by cultural inequality, but by individual properties such as IQ, school achievement, etc.' If this substantive definition is accepted, then it must be supposed that secondary effects, by contrast, are defined as expectations and aspirations that *are* mediated by cultural inequalities, and through collective properties, such as a selective educational system, and so on. But this is all highly problematic. First, it seems odd to define an *effect* by providing what amounts to a list of *causes* and, second, it might be argued that IQ, school achievement and so on are mediated – that is generated in contexts with a defined character – by social and cultural inequalities in quite the same way as are expectations and aspirations.

The source of the confusion is this: in as much as one of the primary effects of socialisation is evidenced in demonstrated cognitive dispositions, and in as much as these dispositions are effective in the production of differentiated educational achievement, then it can be said that these primary effects are a cause of differential educational achievement, and so an effect is a cause. But the potential for ambiguity and confusion in so muddling the concepts of cause and effect should be apparent. If the causes of observed primary and secondary effects are to be open to investigation, rather than regarded as already explained by definition, it becomes necessary to distinguish between the methods used to estimate the magnitude of a secondary effect and to describe the mechanisms of its generation. The problem of explanation in Boudon's theory is acute. The whole point of the distinction between primary and secondary effects is to isolate that quantum of inequality of educational opportunity, so-called, that cannot be accounted for by demonstrated prior attainment. Of the multitude of causes that might be involved, prior ability is procedurally ruled out. There is rather more to Boudon's explanation of IEO, however, than this limited achievement.

Secondary Effects and the Rational Action Model

Boudon's sociology rests on individual foundations, and his application of decision theory to this area is intended to provide an alternative explanation to class value or socialised habit theories. The strength of secondary effects, Boudon, argues is not due to preferences derived from distinctive class values, but is the product of a decision-making process that can be modelled in the terms of cost–benefit analysis. The central argument is that opportunity costs vary according to class position because middle-class families must encourage their offspring to enter courses leading to the highest levels of professional status or else fail to maintain their status, whereas working-class families are able to accept the 'compromise' of a lower professional destination and still enjoy the satisfactions to be experienced from the relative degree of upward mobility so conferred. Boudon launches a three-pronged defence of this substantive thesis. In the centre, there is a drive against the capacity of conventional statistical methods – the principal target is path analysis – to offer an explanatory narrative of inequality of educational opportunity. The attacks on the wings, independent to the point of being contradictory, assert on one flank that secondary effects are unlikely to be generated by classed occupational preferences, and on the other that, even if simulation models cannot demonstrate that rational decision-making is the actual generative mechanism, the assumption is justified in so far as the models have a useful function. These arguments will be confronted in turn: the central thrust is the most powerful.

Boudon is thoroughly familiar with quantitative methods and it is as a competent insider that he expresses reservations about the explanatory logic of variance analysis, which disguises significant relationships apparent in tabular presentations of data and criticises the explanatory syntax supported by the models of causal sociology (Boudon, 1981). In order to explain the correlation between class position and educational achievement it is necessary, he maintains, to abandon the schema that suggests that a series of factors interpose themselves between class and educational success with a cumulative effect depending upon their variable weights. The critique is likely to be inaccessible to those without a statistical education. It may be useful to give a narrative account of the processes of leaving school that will show the nature of these problems.

Let it be supposed that, as a matter of fact, the differential tendency of working-class students to enter higher education is sometimes due to a classed preference for a lifestyle associated with forms of labour and sometimes due to decisions based on relative opportunity costs. It is possible to imagine, for example, that the differential tendency is such that, when students have similar school qualifications, 60 per cent of those with middle-class origins and 40 per cent of those with working-class origins proceed to higher education. Now suppose, further, that half of the 20 per cent of working-class students whose actions in aggregate reveal a secondary effect decide their future on the basis of class values ('I prefer working with my hands') and half because additional education seems not worth the cost ('I'm concerned about the debt, and not sure how I could repay it if I don't get the job I want'). Although this state of affairs can be described in straightforward terms, a theoretical model able to accommodate such a level of complexity is difficult to construct (hence the preference for the 'simplifying' assumption of rational action), and it is impracticable to express the relationships in regression-based path models. Boudon thus effectively relinquishes the attempt to estimate the contributions of different variables central to the project of quantitative sociology. Factorial models, he proposes, should be replaced with decision-making models in which agents with different social origins are recognised as likely to find in their class position a point of reference from which the advantages and disadvantages of deciding on one educational course or career rather than another are taken into account. Boudon's critique in this respect is sound. The flank attacks, however, are somewhat less convincing.

The case against 'value theory' – perhaps the idea that working-class kids get working-class jobs because that is the kind they want – rests on an argument that seems less than convincing. If it is a matter of classed values, he asks then, why do only some, rather than all, working-class students want middle-class jobs? All empirical research shows this to be the case, for among the boys there are 'ear'oles' as well as 'lads' (Willis, 1977). Boudon insists, therefore, with reference to a representative analysis, that the very fact that 'a significant proportion of lower-class youngsters put a high value on education and a significant proportion of middle-class gave it a low value' constitutes evidence that the 'value' perspective is questionable, 'for we must ask why an important minority would deviate from the basic value patterns associated with social class' (Boudon, 1974: 23). This objection, however, must surely apply with equal force to Boudon's own thesis, as it leaves unexplained why a 'significant proportion' (often the majority) of working-class students, rather than none, should reach the rational conclusion that the benefits of entering higher education outweigh the costs. To argue that, where there is no risk, students have the same aspirations regardless of social origin, and that classed values are therefore irrelevant, is actually circular in as much that the estimation of risk is made after the fact. If the calculation is sound for one, then it is sound for all: such a view seems, at least, as plausible as the idea that a classed value should be held by all members of a class.

Then there is Boudon's assertion that an explanation in terms of economic decision-making is simpler than the alternative value or cultural theories, and therefore to be preferred in a mature science, in as much that no 'unnecessary' mechanism is introduced to the model (Menger, 1963). But this application of Ockham's razor seems blunted by the fact that the proposed simulation models have only limited explanatory power and, of course, the concept of science that is prepared to accept a substantive explanation that misrepresents reality, merely because it is simple, is not one that appeals to realists. In fact, the grounds for supposing that Boudon's interpretation of a model – that is an outflow–inflow table using actual or simulated data – supports the thesis that secondary effects are caused by decision-making reduces to the observation that such a thesis is as consistent with that supposition as any other. Such models assume what they need to demonstrate. Boudon's attempt to maintain both that models need not describe the real mechanisms of their generation, and that they do, is a telling contradiction. If the first assertion is true, then the second is redundant: if the second is true, then the first is redundant. Simulation models can always be based on Boudon's theoretical assumptions, but as they cannot provide information that enables those assumptions to be tested, whatever utility they may have must lie elsewhere. The argument that the concepts of primary and secondary effects are valuable in the construction and testing of models of social disparity in education is, perhaps fortunately, quite independent of these considerations. A final point may be offered on the nature of structural and non-structural variables in sociological explanation.

Many sociologists (Saunders, 1995; Marshall and Swift, 1996) accept that Boudon's approach enables the effect of structural and individual variables on educational achievement to be distinguished and assessed. Hamlin, as the discussion has shown, argues that this is actually the substance of the distinction between primary and secondary effects. The matter may, however, prove somewhat more complicated. If the methodological definition proposed is accepted, then it is given by the procedure that primary and secondary effects can be identified and the respective contribution they make to the observed social difference in the specified outcome given a precise quantitative expression. This is not at all the same, of course, as estimating the magnitude of individual and structural properties – to suppose that this is even a useful distinction – on the generation of IEO or inequality/difference. The discussion of structural and individual properties in the explanation of complex social processes raises complex problems. The conventional discourse, characterised by the distinction between dependent and intervening variables, and so on, is fraught with conceptual difficulties that cannot be resolved in its own terms. There is no space here for an elaborated discussion of these matters, and a summary statement on the nature of explanation must suffice.

Sociological explanations almost always take the form of a structure–disposition–practice scheme in which social properties provide a context for the emergence of dispositions to act within the established practices of a social group. Once it is understood that social events, processes and states of affairs require an extended narrative with this form, it should become clear that any attempt to construct a model in which indicators intended to point to structural and individual properties competing for variance must misrepresent the processes involved.

The character of the discussion now shifts from conceptual enquiry to empirical data analysis. Boudon is aware that the mechanisms responsible for the classed distribution of achievements and destinations presented in a table are not self-explanatory. It is somewhat disconcerting to note Boudon's (1974: 31) comment that, 'we are not able to ascribe empirical quantitative measures with the concept' [of secondary effects], as the models developed here to estimate the magnitude of primary and secondary effects are a straightforward extension of his arithmetical models. The data-set is so rich that it has been possible to examine three distinct transitions, from an assessment of scholastic ability at ten to O level, from O level to A level, and from A level to degree.

Table 10.1 Educational qualifications, social class, and ability: Numbers and proportions

	Quality of O level	N.	Prop. poor A level	Prop. good A level	Prop. who have degree	Prop. with A level who have degree
High ability						
SES 1	None	68	.044	.206	.0	
	Poor	97	.423	.010	.103	
	Good	443	.185	.535	.686	
						.830
SES 2	None	64	.109	.109	.016	
	Poor	80	.475	.025	.138	
	Good	298	.218	.393	.540	
						.733
SES 3	None	135	.007	.044	.0	
	Poor	121	.264	.033	.045	
	Good	229	.236	.349	.424	
						.579
Average ability						
SES 1						
	None	241	.029	.017	.004	
	Poor	266	.229	.019	.041	
	Good	486	.294	.311	.440	
						.608
SES 2	None	530	.017	.025	.0	
	Poor	387	.160	.023	.047	
	Good	452	.184	.290	.343	
						.564
SES 3	None	1354	.010	.008	.001	
	Poor	727	.149	.008	.048	
	Good	567	.203	.228	.266	
						.488
Low ability						
SES 1	None	66	.015	.000	.0	
	Poor	35	.171	.000	.029	
	Good	16	.125	.000	.125	
						.335
SES 2	None	226	.004	.000	.0	
	Poor	61	.164	.016	.033	
	Good	26	.192	.153	.231	
						.382
SES 3	None	905	.012	.003	.0	
	Poor	192	.208	.005	.021	
	Good	53	.132	.113	.170	
						.192

Details of Sample and Variables

The British Cohort Study (BCS70) data-set consists of successive surveys of all children born in one week of 1970. It is not possible to review the large number of educational research studies that have drawn on this extensive data-set. McNiece, Bidgood and Soan (2004) provide a recent commentary on the value of national longitudinal studies to research, and Bynner and Joshi (2002) present evidence relevant to the discussion of equality and opportunity in education. The analysis offered here is based on a sample of 8,125 students for whom data on social origin and school attainment is available. Information was taken from the ages 5, 10, 16, 26 and 29 studies, and from cohort members, their parents and teachers as appropriate. In order to gain data on degree qualifications, cohort members were included at age 26 or 29 and, where both questionnaires were completed, the latter was taken as definitive. Where responses to these questionnaires were not available recourse was had to the age 16 data, and whatever information could be gleaned about examination success, from cohort members, parents or teachers at that point was utilised. The object of the exercise is to establish not simply students' level of completed educational attainment, highest qualification obtained, but their O level, A level and degree qualifications, so that their educational trajectory may be tracked. The variables in the model must be described:

> *Social class*: Social class, or socio-economic status (SES), is indicated by father's occupation in 1980, or 1970 when that was missing, using an approximation of the Goldthorpe scale introduced by Savage and Egerton (1997) as a modification of an earlier version (Savage et al., 1992). The current analysis collapses the scale to three: SES 1, the 'service' classes, referred to as the salariat; SES 2, the 'intermediate' classes; and the manual working class. This scheme allocates 21.2 per cent of the valid population to SES 1, 26.6 per cent to SES 2 and 52.2 per cent to SES 3. The full scale was, however, included as a categorical variable in logistic regression analyses.

> *Achievement at ten*: A version of the British Ability Scales (BAS) was administered to cohort members at the age of ten. This instrument was designed within the discourse of IQ theory and is textually recognisable, with verbal and non-verbal subscales, as a test of that kind. It is technically a well-produced instrument and, when the four subscales are summed, generates a near-perfect normal distribution with a characteristic standard deviation (SD). The mean for the sample used in this analysis is 76.9 (SD, 14.1). The mean BAS score for each class is: SES 1, 84.3; SES 2, 78.5; and SES 3, 73.1. For the purposes of estimating the relative size of primary and secondary effects, on the basis of Table 10.1, the BAS score has been divided into the upper quintile (high ability), the three middle quintiles (average ability) and the lower quintile (low ability).

Achievement at O level and A level: It is not a straightforward matter to determine the level of educational attainment reached by respondents. Information was taken from the age 29 questionnaire, which provided better details on A level performance than the age 26 questionnaire, but age 26 responses were used in cases where that was the only source available, and sometimes, particularly for O level and lower qualifications, responses at age 16 were used. The information is self-reported and subject to error (as illustrated by the fact that many respondents gave a different year at which they left school on the ages 26 and 29 questionnaires), but the use of various sources does not seem to bias the analysis. O level performance is divided into two performance categories: 'good', being four or more O levels with A–C grades, and 'poor', being any other O level attainment. A level performance is 'good' when respondents have two or more passes at grades A–C, and 'poor' when their attainment is lower. Students with no O levels, including those with CSE or GCSE qualifications, those for whom 'no qualifications' is an indicated response, and those for whom there is no information on their school qualifications, are classified as having no O levels. The mean BAS score of students with missing information on qualifications is almost identical to that recorded for those with no O levels. It is a safe assumption that that great majority of these students, 1,311 in total, left school at 16, and it seemed appropriate to include them as having gained no O levels.

It is relevant to note at this point that the evidence for secondary effects rests on the assumption that the levels of attainment used are an adequate control for the cognitive dispositions demonstrated in the successful performance of schoolwork. An examination of mean BAS scores with respect to the transition between O level and A level allows this assumption to be tested. These levels of attainment are similar to those presented in official data-sets utilised by Boudon, and it is important to recognise that they are not fine enough to control for prior ability as assessed by the BAS score. Middle-class students with good O levels, for example, have a mean BAS score of 88.6, but the mean for working-class students is only 82.7. In the case of good A levels, the respective social class means are 93.1 and 85.9. These are substantial differences – at A level the gap is about 0.5 SD – and call into question the assumption that these crude achievement categories are an adequate control, between social classes, of students' ability for academic learning. The result of this, which should be borne in mind throughout the following analyses, is to *overestimate* the apparent magnitude of any secondary effect detected.

Degree: Cohort members were asked to provide information on post-school qualifications on the age 26 and 29–30 questionnaires, and these sources have been used to determine the award of a degree qualification.

Other variables are defined, in as much detail as space allows, in the appropriate sections.

Transition One: From BAS Score to O Level

The decision to begin the analysis at age ten is arbitrary and imposed primarily by considerations of length. Feinstein (2003) has reported, using the BCS70 datset, significant associations between cognitive performances at 22 and 42 months with occupation at 26 years. This may be borne in mind in the course of the discussion. The task is to determine the proportion of students in each social class that can be expected, on some plausible assumption, to reach a given level of educational achievement. A simple rule of thumb, adopted by Gray and Moshinsky (2003) in pioneering work of the 1930s, is to use the mean IQ of the higher achievement group. Floud and Halsey (1961: 212), analysing selective entrance to secondary school, fixed the 'hypothetical qualifying IQ at the point where the number of grammar school boys below that level is equal to the number of modern boys above it'. A somewhat more defensible technique is to take the minimum IQ as the cut-off point determined by the proportion of students in the higher achievement group.

It is interesting to note that these methods give different results when applied to the study of BCS70 O level achievement. Halsey's approach is the most liberal: at BAS 80 points there are approximately as many students with a greater score without good O levels as there are students with a lower score with good O levels. When students with scores above 80 are compared, however, the mean score of those with O levels is 0.4 SD higher than that of those without good O levels, and on the assumptions of the model this method seems a rather poor control for ability. Gray and Moshinsky's method is the most conservative: it gives a value of 91, which generates groups differing by only one BAS point and is thus a better control for ability, but it seems an over-rigorous criterion to apply. The proportional cut-off method gives a value almost at the mid-point of these extremes, and thus appears to be a good compromise. As 30 per cent of all students gain good O levels, the BAS cut-off value is 85. When the means of those above this score are compared, the means of the groups with, and without, good O levels are 94.9 and 92.3 respectively, and although this difference (0.18 SD) is not trivial it can be accepted, and students who score above 85 are thus assumed to have the potential, other things being equal, to achieve good O levels. A model based on these data can now be constructed.

Table 10.2 presents a model of the O level achievement of students according to their class origin. The model shows the proportion of students in the high BAS quintile at age ten. It is clear that the proportion of high-ability students is associated with class origin, and the number of Intermediate and Manual students excluded from the high quintile by the Salariat level indicates the size of an important primary effect. Not all students in the high ability quintile achieve good O levels and there is a general loss (in the case of Salariat class students, 354 - 258 = 96) to be recorded. This loss may be regarded as a secondary effect in as much that all students in the highest fifth of the ability range might be expected to obtain good O levels. The estimated number of good 'O' Levels that would be obtained by Intermediate and Manual class students were they as successful as Salariat class students, enables the class secondary effect to be calculated. The estimates are 9 for Intermediate and 29 for Manual class students. By the assumptions of this model, which examines only students in the upper fifth of the ability distribution at ten, in order for there to be equality in their O level achievements it would be necessary for another 205 Manual class students to match the Salariat level. And for them to do that, 241 would need to have the level of competence for academic work demonstrated by those in the highest BAS quintile, and their rate of success would need to rise from 47 per cent to 73 per cent to give another 176 (rather than 114). The model may be useful in providing an indication of the relative importance of primary and secondary effects in the transition from BAS scores at ten to good O levels at 16. There seems little doubt that the primary effect, due to exclusion at age ten, is by far the more significant. This analysis deals only with the upper fifth of the ability range at age ten. In some ways this is a drawback, because there is evidence that secondary effects are strongest in the mid-ability range (Payne, 2001), although her analysis is concerned with post-16 achievement, but there are good reasons to consider the fate of the most able students. The next stage of the analysis is to examine whether there is any evidence for the proposition that the secondary effect is caused by processes other than rational decision-making.

Table 10.2   Model of primary and secondary effects for high ability quintile children, 10–16 years

Social Class (SES)	High ability quintile	Class difference being in high quintile	Four or more 'O' Levels, A-C grade	Predicted 'O' Levels by Salariat class proportion	Secondary loss: No O-level	Secondary effect (Loss calculated by Salariat class proportion)
1	354	N/A	258	N/A	96	N/A
2	172	182	116	125	56	9
3	113	241	53	82	60	29

Six variables (see below) have been selected from those available as relevant to the hypothesis under test. The BCS70 study made a somewhat less extensive investigation of the cultural activities of cohort members' families of origin than might have been expected. The most direct questions of this kind put to parents, concerning the number of times children aged five were read to each week and whether they read books at age ten, are included. Mothers were also asked at what age they expected their child to leave school and this was also found to be a significant predictor. The teacher variables include ratings at age ten of classroom behaviour, from which a factor score reflecting the child's tendency to pay attention, persevere or become distracted was derived; an assessment of the child's vocabulary, also indicated by a factor score; and the mother's level of interest in her child's education. A logistic regression model using these indicators correctly predicts the outcome category of 69 per cent of 1,402 cases. Adding the full category social class scale increases the prediction by just 0.5 per cent.

Variables at Ages Five and Ten Used to Predict Relative Progress between BAS Score and O Level, with Exponents Showing Odds

> *e131*: (1.11) mother's statement of number of days child is read to each week (age 5), eight-point scale.

> *m86*: (1.55) mother's report on child's book reading (this and all others at age 10), 3-point scale.

> *m134*: (1.58; 2.89; 1.68 treated as categorical) mother's statement of age at which child is expected to leave school, 4-point scale.

> *j097*: (1.49) teacher's estimate of mother's interest in child's education, 4-point scale.

> *Vocabulary*: (1.33) derived factor score: teacher's rating of child's vocabulary, variables j065 to j068 (vocabulary simple or advanced, simple/advanced language structure, assimilation/use of new vocabulary, organisation of child's thoughts).

> *Attentive/distracted*: (1.25) derived factor score from teacher's rating of child's behaviour as attentive or distracted, variables j152, j155, j139, j151, j138, j174, and j127 (easily distracted, pays attention in class, shows perseverance, squirmy and fidgety, becomes bored during class, completes tasks, child is daydreaming).

The conclusion seems clear: these variables point to effective processes, at home and at school, that are just those 'traditional' sociology of education always thought were involved, that generate social disparities in educational achievement. It is fascinating to discover that each additional day a child is read to at five increases the odds of making relative progress between ten and sixteen, in the sense defined here, by 10 per cent even when the effects of all the other variables are taken into account. Again, reading books at ten increases by 55 per cent the odds of success for those whose mothers respond 'often' rather than 'never or hardly ever'. These findings do not suggest that rational decision-making has much to do with the relative decline of students with the ability to obtain good O levels.

Transition Two: From O level to A level

The examination of progress as indicated by school examination performance at ages 16 and 18 has been focused on institutional and gender differences and based on hierarchical regression models (Yang and Woodhouse, 2001). The approach taken in this section has different concerns and employs an elementary analytical technique. From the data displayed in Table 10.1, it can be found that, if there are 1,000 high-ability SES 1 students, there will be 319 high-ability SES 3 students. Of the former, 729 will get good O levels, and of these 390 will get good A levels and 7 will get poor A levels. Considering the SES 3 students, 151 will get good O levels, of whom 53 will get good A levels and 5 will get poor A levels. If high-ability SES 3 students got O and A levels with the SES 1 propensity, there would be 233 with good O levels, who would get 25 good and 2 poor A levels. It thus seems that for every 1,000 SES 3 students another 72 would get good A levels. But if the primary effect is thought away – that is if there were no class differences in the age-ten test scores – then altogether there would be another 681 working-class students with the same ability as those from the salariat. Although this is an unsophisticated analytical method, there may be some insight to be gained from it and there is no reason to suppose that the calculations misrepresent the actual state of affairs. Jackson et al. (2004) provide counterfactual estimates from a mathematical integration model based on the full ability range that suggest, for 1987 and 1996 youth surveys respectively, that when GCSE and GCE grades in English and Mathematics are taken into account an additional 110, and 90, in a 1,000 working-class students might be expected to remain at school after 16 rather than leave at that age. It is one thing, of course, to enter the sixth form, and another to leave it with good A levels: the manual:salariat class differential in that respect is about 2:1. There is no theoretical reason to suppose that the causes of that relative decline are different from those responsible for the variation in transition rates.

The second component in the analysis is to determine whether the transition from good O levels to good A levels or no A levels is associated with courses of action other than opportunity cost decision-making. If it can be shown that those who choose to discontinue their studies, or fail to achieve an expected level of qualification, are characterised by a distinctive pattern of 'values' or class-cultural dispositions, then the hypothesis that a rational action model describes the real processes involved is to that extent not supported. This is exactly what the results of a logistic regression analysis do show. Students with good O levels who fail to obtain A levels can be distinguished from those who obtain good A levels by their low occupational aspirations, dissatisfaction with school and poor ability to concentrate as assessed by their mother. A logistic regression analysis, using variables to indicate these characteristics predicts the outcome of 71 per cent of 1,155 cases successfully: adding social class to the model does not improve the prediction.

Variables at age 16 used to predict relative progress from O level to A level

Occupational aspiration: (7.12; 2.07; 1.65; 1.88; 0.91 treated as categorical) six-point scale (degree, teaching/nursing/management, intermediate, small business, high-skilled manual, low-skilled manual), derived from jb27a1– jb27a15 and adding jb29a1 (family business).

Poor concentration: (1.86) factor score derived from mother's rating of teenager's behaviour, pa6.3, pa6.19, a6.13 and pa6.15 (fails to finish things started, has difficulty concentrating, inattentive/easily distracted, cannot settle to do things).

Dislikes school: (1.37) factor score derived from jb14a, jb14b, jb14c, jb14d, jb14e, jb14f, jb14h and jb14g (feels school is largely a waste of time, quiet in classroom and get on with work, thinks homework is a bore, finds it difficult to keep mind on work, never takes work seriously, does not like school, always willing to help the teacher, plans pointless, takes things as they come).

When students with good O levels are considered, those who hope to get a degree are seven times more likely to have good A levels than those who aspire to manual work, almost twice as likely when their mother's assessment of their disposition to concentrate is one (SD) better than average, rather than one SD worse than average, and about 75 per cent more likely when their level of satisfaction with school is one SD higher rather than lower than average. These estimates are additive in the sense that each makes its contribution but also subtractive in the sense that, in as much as not liking school and holding low aspirations are correlated, the one takes something from the other. The importance of aspirations in this model has some theoretical interest. Aspirations are the result of decision-making of a kind that is perhaps not best thought of as rational, but it is a decision that has a considerable effect on how students conduct themselves at school, and that low aspirations are associated with non-cognitive dispositions is a fact not to be neglected. We are perhaps justified in concluding, nevertheless, that relative academic decline between O level and A level has somewhat more to do with 'values', or at least to dispositions of a relevant kind, than to rational decision-making on grounds indifferent to such personal dispositions.

Transition Three: From A level to Degree

Table 10.3 provides information from which an estimate of primary and secondary effects can be made with respect to the transition from A level to degree. It will be noted that the percentage of cohort members with poor or good A levels obtaining a degree is somewhat greater for those from middle-class backgrounds in comparison with other groups. A model of 1,000 SES 1 students with A levels indicates that 715 will get degrees: according to the data, there will also be 463 SES 3 students with A levels who get degrees. Were the secondary effect from A level to degree, eliminated SES 3 students with A levels would increase their number of degrees by 54 per cent. It should be noted that taking the base for calculation as those with A levels, rather than those with good A levels, gives a high estimation of the secondary effect. The data, in this respect, are now 15–20 years out of date, and contemporary working-class transition rates to degree qualification have increased (Payne, 2001). Nevertheless, the modelled improvement of more than half is very considerable, and it implies a 6-per-cent increase in the number of working-class young people obtaining degrees, but it does not follow that policies directed at the elimination of secondary effects is necessarily the most effective means of improving rates of class access to higher education. Boudon supposes that they are the result of rationally considered choices, made in contexts where opportunity cost structures differ for middle- and working-class students, and that being so it would seems to be a matter of providing additional incentives of sufficient weight to affect the decision-making processes of working-class students. What the cost of such policies might be is so far unquantified. What might make a difference to secondary effects at this level has not been adequately discussed from either a theoretical or practical viewpoint (Jackson et al., 2004).

Table 10.3 Degree qualifications and social class: Numbers and proportions

Social Class (SES)	N. with A-level	A-level Propn.	Good A-level Propn.	Degree Propn.	Poor A-level with degree Propn.	Good A-level with degree Propn.
1	758	.441	.544	.315	.302	.537
2	564	.266	.504	.167	.193	.504
3	628	.147	.392	.063	.111	.385

Conclusion

The whole point of Boudon's approach, as Duru-Bellat (2000: 543) demonstrates, is to support the thesis that, 'the impact of attainment during early years on the subsequent career is not particularly strong'. This is consistent with the all but universally accepted position in the sociology of education that no intellectual group differences exist at birth and that the relative achievement gap between social classes and cultural groups emerges and widens in the course of schooling. Nevertheless, there are sociologists of education sceptical of the value of Boudon's analytical distinction. If social inequalities are created by the educational system, then class disparities in achievement are interpreted as evidence of inequality of educational opportunity, and whether the school excludes students with 'inferior' cultural capital, or merely allows them to withdraw on the objectively grounded, and to that extent rational, belief that educational success for people like them is at once improbable and expensive to attain, is an indifferent matter of detail. Within the most widely accepted theory of cultural reproduction, to distinguish between primary and secondary effects may seem theoretically unnecessary and even politically ill motivated. Bourdieu and Passeron (1990), for example, regard all 'choices' as being made within a context where rates of class exclusion are built in to the generative habitus and, therefore, while aware of the phenomenon, do not recognise the concept of secondary effects.

To suppose that differences in educational attainment at an arbitrary point are the product of primary socialisation, moreover, may seem a concession to 'deficit theory'. This is all the more certain if the index used to control attainment is presented as a test of 'ability' or 'intelligence', which is bound to provoke vigorous criticism. These objections, however, do not invalidate the conceptual distinction or the method of identification proposed. A primary effect, methodologically identified, is not demonstrably caused by primary socialisation any more than a secondary effect is demonstratively caused by rational decision-making. There is no reason why the school rather than the home, for example, should not be responsible for a primary effect noted at a given point. Nor does it matter what tests of attainment are used for the purposes of identifying a secondary effect. The distinction may be more difficult in practice than many have supposed, but the analyses presented above are offered as an illustration of what might be a worthwhile line of enquiry. There is room for methodological pluralism in this field (Moore, 2004).

Is anything crucial to Boudon's position lost by this revisionist discussion? The argument, accepted, for example, by Goldthorpe (1996), that the presence of secondary effects is evidence that cost–benefit decision-making is involved in their production, or that models based on that assumption can be accepted regardless of whether this is actually the case or not, lacks real conviction. It seems, moreover, that in contemporary Britain – although BCS70 cohort members were born some time ago now – the socialisation processes involved in cognitive development, which are likely to be responsible for most of the observed primary effects, are somewhat more important, in the transitions examined, than those that generate secondary effects. The conclusion that primary effects outweigh secondary effects is also reached, following their analysis of an earlier data-set, by Jackson et al. (2004). Boudon's insight that a two-component process of differentiation is involved may thus be accepted as sound and potentially useful. The processes must be continuous, for schooling can be divided into as many fragments as one wishes, perhaps from year to year, and the consequences of each apparent decision, whether reached formally or informally, feed back into subsequent learning to create a seamless course through the system, but they may be distinct in form. Even if the suspicion that primary and secondary effects might, more often than Boudon thought, have the same causes proves justified, that does not negate the validity of the conceptual distinction. It could be important to know, in the general and in the individual case, whether the decision to withdraw from education is due to an effective disposition of mind – some specific intellectual competence or cultural preference – or to a more or less rational decision made in consideration of the relative costs and benefits involved.

References

Bourdieu, P. and Passeron, J.-C. (1990). *Reproduction in Education, Society and Culture*, 2nd edn (London: Sage).

Boudon, R. (1974). *Education, Opportunity and Social Inequality: Changing Prospects in Western Society* (New York: Wiley).

Breen, R. and Goldthorpe, J.H. (1995). Merit, ability and method: Another reply to Saunders, *Journal of Sociology*, 29: 575–82.

Bynner, H. and Joshi, H. (2002). Equality and opportunity in education: Evidence from the 1958 and 1970 birth cohort studies, *Oxford Review of Education*, 28: 405–25.

Duru-Bellat, M. (2000). Social inequalities French secondary schools: From figures to theories. In S.J. Ball (ed.), *Sociology of Education: Major Themes, Vol. II, Inequalities and Oppression* (London: Routledge/Falmer): 536–49.

Feinstein, L. (2003). Inequality in the early cognitive development of British children in the 1970 cohort, *Economica*, 70(277): 73–96.

Floud, J. and Halsey, A.H. (1961). Social class, intelligence tests, and selection for secondary school. In A.H. Halsey, J. Floud and C.A. Anderson (eds), *Education, Economy, and Society: A Reader in the Sociology of Education* (New York: The Free Press): 209–15.

Goldthorpe, J.H. (1996). Class analysis and the representation of class theory: The case of persisting differentials in educational attainment, *British Journal of Sociology*, 47(3): 481–512.

Gray, J.L. and Moshinsky, P. (2003 [1938]). Ability and educational opportunity in relation to parental occupation. In L. Hogben (ed.), *Political Arithmetic* (London: Routledge): 377–417.

Hamlin, C.L. (2002). *Beyond Relativism: Raymond Boudon, Cognitive Rationality and Critical Realism* (London: Routledge).

Jackson, M., Erikson, R., Goldthorpe, J.H. and Yaish, M. (2004). Primary and secondary effects on class opportunities in educational attainment: The transition to A-level courses in England and Wales, Paper prepared for the meeting of the ISA Research Committee on Social Stratification and Mobility, Neuchâtel, Switzerland, May 6–8.

McNiece, R., Bidgood, P. and Soan, P. (2004). An investigation into using national longitudinal studies to examine trends in educational attainment and development, *Educational Research*, 46: 119–36.

Marshall, G. and Swift, A. (1996). Merit and mobility: a reply to Saunders, *Sociology*, 30(2): 375–86.

Menger, C. (1963). *Problems of Economics and Society* (Urbana, Ill.: University of Illinois Press).

Moore, R. (2004). Cultural capital: Objective probability and the cultural arbitrary, *British Journal of Sociology of Education*, 24: 445–56.

Payne, J. (2001). *Patterns of Participation in Full-time Education after 16: An Analysis of the England and Wales Youth Cohort Study* (London: Department of Education and Skills).

Saunders, M. (1995). Might Britain be a meritocracy? *Sociology*, 29: 23–41.

Savage, M., Barlow, J., Dickens, P. and Fielding, T. (1992). *Property, Bureaucracy and Culture: Middle-class Formation in Contemporary Britain* (London and New York: Routledge).

Savage, M. and Egerton, M. (1997). Social mobility, individual ability and the inheritance of class inequality, *Sociology*, 31: 645–72.

Willis, P. (1977). *Learning to Labour: How Working-class Kids Get Working-class Jobs* (Farnborough: Saxon House).

Yang, M. and Woodhouse, G. (2001). Progress from GCSE to A and AS Level: institutional and gender differences, and trends over time, *British Educational Research Journal*, 27: 245–67.

Chapter 11

Explanation and Quantification in Educational Research: The Arguments of Critical and Scientific Realism

Introduction

The debate over 'qualitative' and 'quantitative' research methods, particularly in as much as this has to do with the possibility of statistical modelling and forms of explanation, may have gained a new source of energy from the contemporary influence of *critical realism* on social theory (Bhaskar, 1993). Two recent texts, Scott (2000) and Willmott (2002), may suffice to show that this influence has been extended to the discussion of theory and method in educational research. These works give additional support to Manicas's (1998) critique – reproduced in a standard reader on critical realism – of the positivist assumptions of quantitative methodology and of causal explanations based on regression analysis that also takes its examples from educational research. The semantic opposition of 'quantitative' and 'qualitative' is a self-evident mistake, as many have pointed out, but the institutionalised methodological division of research approaches legitimated by these terms is deeply rooted in philosophical theory, and it is in this context that the critique joined by critical realists merits some attention.

The practice of critique is difficult and whether it is best directed at an ideal-type reconstruction or as a concrete text is often a nice point. The problem with the former is the likelihood that no one will admit to holding the position described, while the problem with the latter is that the text is easily declared to be unrepresentative. It will become clear that this chapter has adopted, in due acknowledgement of the risks, the second strategy. There is something very important and *practical* at stake in all this: What information do we need to have in order to explain the events, processes and states of affairs educational research is concerned with? How can that information be obtained; and what form must explanations take in order to be useful?

The structure of the chapter may be found complex: it will argue from the standpoint of *scientific* realism that the rejection of quantitative modelling by *critical* realists, taking Scott as a leading representative of this position in education, is unsound. This project will require a brief comparison of the contrasted realist positions in the philosophy of science, and a concrete illustration of the problems posed by non-realist forms of quantitative explanation that their shared critique of positivism attempts to resolve. Critical realism and scientific realism are closely related positions, but, whereas many critical realists have concluded that statistical modelling must be rejected, scientific realists maintain that quantification is necessary to science and that the conventional epistemological assumptions of applied statistics can be surmounted. Scientific realists, for example, argue that the assumptions of positivism, often implicit in statistical modelling, are not inherent to quantification itself and that statistical techniques may be used to enhance realist explanatory narratives. The thesis presented here does not claim to be original in disputing these matters with critical realism from a position of scientific realism. Kemp and Holmwood (2003), for example, convincingly argue that regular events occurring in the social world provide an ontological basis for quantification and non-positivist explanations. And Byrne (1998) similarly concludes that the rejection of statistical methods by critical realism is an error incompatible with the complexity and chaos of the way real societies work. It seems important, however, that these issues should be raised in the specific context of educational research, and perhaps also in a context that will show why all form of realism share serious reservations about the language of positivism adopted by conventional approaches to statistical explanation.

Realism about the things of the world is a common-sense doctrine and it might be expected that a realist approach to educational research would broadly accept the established approaches that guide the conduct of scientific research and its related techniques of quantification. This is, as already indicated, largely so in the case of scientific realism, but critical realism has rejected the standard models of statistical research and explanation as incompatible with its philosophy. One would need to be bold to summarise the elements of critical realism – Collier's (1994) discussion requires an entire book – but Bhaskar (1998) has provided a short introduction that may be taken as authoritative. There are, he maintains, three core elements: (i) the things of the world cannot be reduced to the domain of the empirical; (ii) the domain of the real is more extensive than the domain of the actual; and (iii) the nature of the world is stratified in such a way that, although one kind of mechanism may be grounded in another, it cannot necessarily be reduced to the elements from which it has emerged. Critical realism, it may be noted, is also a moral philosophy: it argues for an ontological ethics based on human well-being, and rejects the fact-value distinction (Collier, 1999).

As a philosophical movement, critical realism asserts that the entities of the world possess causal powers by virtue of their existence, and that the explanation of events, states and processes should be made with reference to the properties that confer such powers. The application of this philosophy to the social sciences, including sociology, psychology and economics, is being worked out by several authors, many of whom are linked to the Centre for Critical Realism at the University of Warwick. Bhaskar (1979) argues for a form of naturalism, an approach to science that recognises the fundamental unity of the world, grounded in the specific and emergent properties of physical and social entities. The recognition of a single ontology at this level enables Bhaskar to insist that, although the social world is an open system 'characterized by the complete absence of laws and explanations conforming to the positivist canon' (Bhaskar, 1998: xv), there is no obstacle to the identification of systematic patterns of a kind that will allow the possibility of empirical controls for the purposes of scientific enquiry. Moreover, although Bhaskar understands that the social world is constituted as a result of meaningful activity, he explicitly rejects the idea that sociology is limited to the investigation of social events and processes where the intentions of agents can be ascertained, or that sociological explanations must necessarily be made in the light of such knowledge. The subject matter of sociology, on the other hand, certainly includes the beliefs that have been generated within a society and which affect the activities of its members.

Critical realism is particularly conscious of the reflexive manner, the so-called *double hermeneutic*, in which social theory in its own right can have a dialectical influence on social practice. It is a wide concept of realism that takes 'absence' as a definitive case of the real. As Bhaskar's critical realism has developed it has made increasing use of the concept of dialectic to express the complex nature of entities and the relationships between them. Social life is thus constituted by material transactions with nature, by interpersonal relations, by the emergent social structures of such relations, and by the stratified constitution of the self. The explanation of social events, processes and states of affairs requires an account of the mechanisms by which they have come into being.

Bhaskar does not attempt to distinguish his critical realism from scientific realism, particularly in so far as realism establishes ontology as the necessary foundation for the practice of physical science, and all the indications are that he regards his position as a development within scientific realism. There may be no need to detail the points of difference between Bhaskar's critical realism and what might be called the standard doctrine of scientific realism, but it may be useful to indicate where the most significant deviations of critical realism from the general position are to be found. Bunge (1998) is among the most assertive contemporary advocates of scientific realism and, although in some respects idiosyncratic, there is no realist philosopher of science more systematic and his position may be taken for this purpose as a benchmark. Scientific realism cannot be described as a *movement*, as Bhaskar's critical realism has become, and in nominating Bunge as a representative there is no intention to overlook the contributions of other realists in this field, some of whom have already been noted, but it will be consistent with the approach taken here to focus on the stance developed by this writer.

Bunge's philosophy is no more readily summarised than Bhaskar's, but the important differences, in the context of this discussion, have to do with Bhaskar's introduction of the concept of dialectic (which Bunge dismisses as worthless); an apparent support for explanations in terms of powers (where Bunge prefers properties); a tendency to argue that an effect demonstrates not only the existence of a causal power but the nature of the entity with that power (which Bunge regards as an inadequate demonstration); and a noticeable rejection of explanations supported by quantitative methods (which Bunge regards as essential to a mature science). There is, for want of a better term, an unmistakable tough-mindedness to Bunge's philosophy of science, apparent, for example, in his uncompromising materialism – he specifically rejects Popper's World 3 (Bunge, 1981), which Archer (1996) has incorporated within her realist sociology – and, perhaps even more obviously in his intolerance of anything he considers to be non-scientific, including hermeneutics, psychoanalysis and postmodernist treatments of 'discourse' – all of which approaches, in the case of some writers more than others, have actually been sympathetic treatment by critical realists. Scott, for example, treats 'discursive formations' as real mechanisms. Although Bunge's blend of moderate empiricism, bluntness of expression, intolerance for theories that some critical realists are willing to indulge (psychoanalysis, hermeneutics, dialectics, and so on), and preference for mathematical expression thus makes it unlikely that many critical realists will give it much attention, his work may be regarded as closer to the recognised stance of scientific realism.

There should be no doubt that the critique of statistical thinking has the authoritative endorsement of leading advocates within the critical realist camp. Writers accepted as critical realists have provided a trenchant critique of quantification in social science, dismissive in its implications, that is likely to be regarded as the definitive position of realism in its most general sense. Yet it would be a retrograde step should the view of quantification held by many writers influenced by critical realism become identified as the definitive *realist* position, for *scientific* realism has a very different stance on quantification. Bunge argues, for example, that the social sciences need more, not less, quantification, and that of a more rigorous and precise kind. This final break gives the current chapter its theme. It is proper to mention in this context, however, that Bunge, in these respects not noticeably idiosyncratic, does not accept the conventional concept of measurement in social science, recognises the concept of emergent social entities, rejects the Humean concept of causality and, although maintaining a strong preference for scientific explanations based on established laws, finds the classical deductive–nomological model of explanation inadequate. This account has focused on certain manifest differences between critical and scientific realism, as these respective positions are developed by Bhaskar and Bunge, but it should go without saying that both share the common ontological ground of realism: they do not dispute that the entities of the social world are constituted by social relations, that these emergent entities have properties in accordance with their being, and that the explanation of social events, processes and states of affairs requires an account of the real mechanisms that bring them about.

It is not altogether surprising, in the light of this commentary, to find that Scott and Willmott, drawing on critical realism, have developed themes at once hostile to quantitative analysis – and in Scott's case at least – openly sympathetic to certain postmodernist influences. Scott's work will be given close attention in this discussion as a text more systematic in its argument and located in an influential social research publication series. As I made clear, to respond to a specific author and text is often an appropriate way to deal with the objection that positions subjected to critique have no substantive existence or influence. Scott is an eminent figure in curriculum studies and an active participant in the wider British debate on educational research. Whether or not the interest in critical realism will continue to gain ground remains to be seen, and there is no need to overestimate the current impact of this philosophical tendency on mainstream educational research, but it might be thought that Scott's attack on quantitative models in this field is worth examination in their own right. There are serious matters to discuss that go right to the heart of what it is to conduct an effective scientific investigation and to construct an adequate scientific explanation. This account, as should already be evident, must be concerned with the fundamental philosophical principles at stake, but it must also engage with the detailed arguments of statistical analysis. For this latter purpose the UK PISA (Programme for International Student Assessment) 2000 sample of about 9,000 15-year-old students provides a resource that may give the illustrations – of the interrelationships between social class, wealth, literate resources and attainment that constitute Scott's own examples – some substantive value in their own right.

Scott's Critical Realist Objections to Statistical Modelling

Scott mobilises three arguments against mathematical modelling. There are, as he recognises, several approaches to mathematical modelling, but the critique is broad-based and distinctions between them are regarded as less significant than their common epistemological foundations. The first argument has to do with the characteristics of open and closed systems; the second with the distinction between association and causation; and the third with the dimensions of intensionality and extentionality in the social world. Scott argues that the open character of the social world, which follows from the meaningfulness of social action, ensures that the associations reported by statistical analysis cannot be interpreted as revealing determined causal relationships. A systematic response to these arguments might be expected, but this is not necessarily the most effective procedure to adopt, and two of the arguments are rather easily dealt with.

The fact that the social world is an open system does not rule out the potential usefulness of quantitative models. Bhaskar (1998) accepts this point, in a discussion of Lawson's (1997) use of such models in his own critical realist approach to economics, and there seems little more to add in this context. A similarly brief response can be given to the argument that intensionality – the dimension of meaning – makes explanations based on quantitative modelling inappropriate. Bhaskar acknowledges that social science must attempt to explain social events, processes and states of affairs regardless of whether the intentions of action, that is to say the meanings actors give to their actions, are known. To insist otherwise would unnecessarily restrict the scope of social science, for the intentions and interpretations of agents are not always available and, even then, cannot be taken at face value. The problems raised by the concepts of association and causation are, however, much more serious. Scott's critique is basically sound in this area, but the matter requires a more extended discussion, and the implications are open to debate. In some respects, moreover, Scott's objections are actually not the most telling that can be brought against quantitative modelling. The short answer to his case is simply that explanations supported by mathematical models do not need to make many of the assumptions he believes are necessary and, so the chapter will argue, can be accommodated within scientific realism. This response may be elaborated through an analysis of a key example he gives of poverty and its effects on examination performance.

Scott argues that the association between poverty and educational attainment should not be regarded as one that reveals a causal relationship. In an open system, he asserts, a low income does not determine level of attainment because, among other things, the meaning given to poverty is not identical for different people and groups and, consequently, the association cannot be regarded as causal. As he writes (2000: 44): 'The measures which are usually used to determine the relationship between poverty and achievement in school are approximations or proxies to the real variables which are implicated in the causal mechanisms which may or may not be operationalized.' This statement requires a little decoding. The term 'real variables' must refer to the properties of real social entities, and 'implicated in the causal mechanism' must refer to components of the causal mechanism, where 'mechanism' is identified here with a process that may or may not be activated. The observation that causal mechanisms may or may not be operationalised conveys the idea that a mechanism does not work unless, as it were, it is first switched on. In this context, it might be said that the presence of books in a home indicates certain literate capabilities of parents that may be utilised – but then again may not be – to instruct children in the arts of reading.

Scott develops his theme by arguing that, among other possibilities, poverty might cause poor examination performance due to lack of space, which means that children cannot do homework; poorer diets, which mean that children cannot concentrate and so learn less quickly; low levels of cultural capital, which means that children cannot access 'pedagogical interactions'; and low levels of parental emphasis on the importance of education, which means that children do not try as hard as they could. How quantitative evidence might be analysed within a realist framework will be examined for particular example with reference to the PISA data. Scott argues that poverty is a *proxy* for the real variables, by which it is clear that he means not an indicator variable of any kind, but a specific lived process. The argument here, by distinction, is not simply that an indicator variable may be a proxy for another, as a proxy for household income might be constructed from a selected list of household items (which is exactly what PISA does), but that poverty as a state of affairs is a proxy for an effective process, or mechanism, at a specific organisational site of the kind necessary to the construction of a complete explanation. This failure to distinguish between an indicator variable and the processes it points to, a confusion of model and reality, is one for which realists have no excuse. The constraints of thought imposed by positivist concepts, however, are so powerful that they can limit even those who possess the theoretical key by which their bonds may be released. Scott's insistence on process as mechanism is sound in as much as, other things being equal, explanations that contain such information are to be preferred to those that do not, but it will be argued on realist grounds that this position should not be accepted without reservation and that it can have unwelcome implications for sociology.

The aim of sociology is to provide explanations of social events and processes. A complete explanation will include an account of social structures (properties of organisations), individual dispositions to act and established practices (Nash, 2003). The best accounts of social processes are thus multilayered and, in their attempt to reflect the complexity of the world, offer narratives that *integrate* rather than *disintegrate*, as is typically the case with reductionist models, many of which actually threaten to eliminate the structural level entirely (Mayer, 1997). The arguments necessary to examine the relationship between levels of explanation are highly complex and there is no suggestion here that the search for an effective process mechanism is inadequate in virtue of its reductionist character. When a kindergarten head teacher sees poverty as a barrier to learning because children arrive at school 'hungry, badly clothed, unwell, unhealthy' (Groser, 2003), she holds a position realists may support and endorse. Poverty is the state of being poor and as such it may be the cause of some other social state including relative educational attainment. At the level of the family, the state of being poor is a cause of low attainment whenever the lack of money directly or indirectly affects the capacity of children from poor families to learn at school. It is not necessary to know exactly how this happens in order to demonstrate the fact that it does.

Let us suppose that one of the conditions created by a low income is that children are left in poor-quality childcare with the result that cognitive development is inhibited. This will not be true of all poor families, but that does not mean that it is poor-quality childcare rather than the effects of poverty that is the cause of underachievement with that origin (although it might well be useful to know that information). What we are dealing with is a hierarchy of linked causal processes. It would be pointless to construct explanations in terms of structural properties that exclude process mechanisms at the level of disposition and practice when these are known. But by the same token it is arguably no less satisfactory to reject the causal nature of structural properties when these are responsible for the generation of the effective dispositions and practices involved at those levels. Scott's argument actually leads to a kind of reductionism that does not reflect the realist intuition of the sedimented character of social reality and is for that reason inadequate. There should, of course, always be an argument relating the variables and properties they represent in an appropriate way, but there are times when that mechanism must be postulated rather than demonstrated. A good case, for example, can be made for the argument that low-quality childcare is causally more likely to be experienced by low-income families, for it is all many can afford. These relationships, of course, are ones that can be tested most satisfactorily only by quantitative research, and the implications of that must be faced.

The argument that poverty can be regarded as a real state of affairs with causal properties may be compared with the position taken by Jackson and Pettit (1992: 119), who distinguish, in an argument entirely compatible with the principles of scientific realism, between process and program explanations. In their words: 'The process explanation relative to any given level identifies the actual causes and relevant causal properties. The program explanation identifies a condition such that its realization is enough to ensure that there will be causes to produce the event explained: if not the actual causes, then some others.' Jackson and Pettit may be unwilling to regard poverty as a causal property, but they would surely recognise it as a condition that will ensure that directly causal events do occur. These authors note that, 'structural explanations explain, when they explain, by introducing factors which program for the realisation of the conditions explained' (ibid. 117). Poverty is a structural condition, and may be included in an explanatory model precisely because it is a condition that is likely to give rise to processes that will generate effective practices of the kind required to bring about the observed events. All of this suggests that a critical realist may argue that poverty is a state of being to which causal powers can be attributed. Jackson and Pettit, for example, argue that high unemployment means that an increase in the number of working-class youths short of money makes it more likely that events will occur that will raise the crime rate, and this is also to argue that poverty – shortage of money – is a causal element in the whole process. But this is not quite the same as to argue, as Scott does, that poverty is a proxy variable standing for something else. This position, moreover, is not reductionist, as Scott's is, because it recognises that poverty is a state of affairs that has whatever powers it has by virtue of the fact that it programmes for certain dispositions and generates certain practices. Pettit (1993) is inclined to argue that when a process explanation has been obtained a program explanation is redundant, but the realist notion of a hierarchy of social states and entities is not incompatible with this position. There is no need to accept that states of affairs, which are emergent at the level of the program, do not have the causal powers attributed to them. This will be an appropriate point at which to explore these ideas with substantive illustrations, based on the PISA UK data, of what can be learned from a quantitative analysis considered from the position of scientific realism.

As the following sections present data from the PISA study it will be necessary to provide basic information on the sample and variables included in the analysis.

The PISA Sample and Some Core Variables

The UK Programme for International Student Assessment (PISA) data-set provides information on about 9,000 15-year-old students. The data can be downloaded free together with all necessary documentation and command files from the official website (Organisation for Economic Cooperation and Development [OECD], 2001). The study is a characteristic product of the international educational research community and is principally designed to facilitate international comparisons of educational standards. All the data are obtained by tests and questionnaires completed by principals, teachers and students. The analyses reported in this analysis use attainment in English and certain data from the student questionnaire. We are interested in socio-economic status, cultural capital and poverty, and the first task is to define the variables:

> *Reading attainment*: Several estimates of reading attainment are provided by PISA. The analysis reported here uses the Warm estimate of reading attainment, which is the most useful for within-country analyses and recommended as the measure appropriate for reporting individual attainment. The estimate has a nominal international mean of 500 (UK, 522.6) and a standard deviation (SD) of 100 (UK, 100.3).

> *Socio-economic status*: The PISA SES indicator is based on the International Socio-economic Scale (Ganzeboom, De Graaf and Trieman, 1992). Information about parental occupations is obtained from the student questionnaire, and the analysis given here uses the highest reported occupation of a student's parents. Index values have been grouped into quintiles for the purposes of Table 11.1. SES 1 designates those in the upper fifth of the distribution.

> *Number of books in the home*: The student questionnaire asks students to estimate the total number of books in the home. The item informs students that there are about 40 books per metre of shelves and that magazines are not to be included. The categories provided are: none; 1–10; 11–50; 51–100; 101–250; 251–500; more than 500. The analysis presented in Table 11.1 divides the scale at the point closest to the median, resulting in groups with <100 books and >100 books. This is adopted as an indicator of 'cultural capital', although other indicators could be used, and a scale intended for this purpose, constructed of a number of items about family practices in relation to cultural consumption, is included in the PISA data-set. The number of books in home, however, has the advantage of transparency. As far as the substantive analyses presented in this chapter are concerned it makes very little difference what index is used.

> *Wealth*: PISA provides a scale based on household goods to indicate family wealth. Students are asked to report the presence in their home of a dishwasher, a room of one's own, educational software, an Internet connection, and number of cell phones, televisions, computers, motor vehicles and bathrooms.

The statistical relationships between these variables will be explored in substantive analyses presented for the purpose of illustrating the core theoretical arguments in the discussion of realism and its critiques. Of course, it is not to be taken for granted that anything much can be learned about the relationship between family resources of wealth and literacy and educational attainment from the PISA data. The data are obtained from student questionnaire responses, and the degree to which these can be accepted as a trustworthy source of information of actual states of affairs is open to question. The 'measures' used, which are much better referred to as indicators, are also accepted in the form given by PISA analysts, and this involves a further set of assumptions. There are, indeed, to adopt a conventional term, likely to be serious measurement problems. The SES scale, in particular, is less than ideal, but then it is a great deal better than nothing. These matters are not, however, the focus of the debate, which at this point is concerned to show that the quantification of relevant evidence is necessary to support hypotheses about the processes that constitute the link between structural properties, in this case poverty, and the properties of people and the social properties that adopt. As Kemp and Holmwood (2003: 179) conclude, 'While ... statistical regularities, by themselves, establish a causal link, it is also important to acknowledge that the search for such patterns can be an important part of the process of identifying causes operating in the social world'. The procedure advocated is fundamentally that of science itself, and the rewards of the comparative method (that is to say Mill's method of difference) can often be achieved with no statistical technique more problematic than counting. It is also important, however, within this realist defence of quantification, to draw attention to the difficulties posed by the residues of positivist language in statistical modelling.

A Quantitative Investigation of Poverty, Overcrowding and Attainment

The search for the generative mechanism, where that is a social process, must often require quantitative forms of investigation. Scott's supposition that poor families have less room to live in and therefore find it harder to complete their homework with the consequence that they learn less and so gain lower achievements examinations, moreover, can be treated as a set of related hypotheses open to test. It should immediately be clear, however, that without the use of statistical methods there seems no way to test any such hypothesis. One would have to show, for example, that poor children living in overcrowded homes achieve less at school than poor children from homes with adequate space. It is significant that Scott does not discuss how his suggested mechanisms might be shown to exist by any method other than direct observation. It follows, therefore, that he is also unable to investigate the contribution different but related process mechanisms might make, but there is no reason why cramped living conditions, poor nutrition, lack of 'cultural capital', or parental press for education should not all be involved in the generation of class differences associated with an index of poverty and to various degrees that could, in principle, be assessed.

One way to discover whether the causal processes suggested by Scott actually exist is to treat the suggestions as hypotheses and subject them to test. Consider, for example, the suggestion that poverty has its effects because low-income families often lack the space to provide children with a quiet place to study and that as a consequence their attainments are lower than would otherwise be the case. Some elements in this causal chain can be tested with the PISA data. If the hypothesis is correct then we should expect that children from low-income homes, in comparison with others, often lack a quiet space to study, spend less time on homework and have lower attainments. The first thing to note is that only 13 per cent of students in the lowest quintile of the Wealth distribution actually report that they have no quiet place to study. The hypothesis is already looking a little shaky. The next step is to look at the differences between poor students with a quiet place to study and those without, and it turns out that they are relatively minor. The proportion of poor students reporting that they have no time for homework, with and without a quiet place to study, is 7 per cent and 13 per cent. In the remaining categories the figures are, respectively: less than one hour, 33 and 28 per cent; 1 to 3 hours, 53 and 45 per cent; and more than 3 hours, 10 and 12 per cent. The most one can say about this is that the trend is in the expected direction, but it is hardly convincing support for the hypothesis.

The final step is to examine whether the mean reading attainments of these students are actually different. It so happens that, with the exception of those who report having 'no time' for homework (in which case it would seem not to matter whether they have a quiet space in which to do it or not), the differences are not significant. We find that the means of those who do less than one hour of homework, with and without a quiet space, are 489 and 484; in the remaining categories the means are: 1 to 3 hours, 522 and 520; and more than 3 hours, 540 and 532. Scott argues that quantitative models provide no useful information about the causes of social differences in educational attainment, but the causal mechanisms he suggests as generating the association between poverty and low attainment cannot be observed or tested without reports confirmed by statistical analysis. If one is prepared to accept the self-reports of 15-year-old students as observations (which of a kind they are), then those analysed here give the hypothesis very little support. The difference in educational attainment associated with poverty does not seem to be caused by *this* particular mechanism. There must be some mechanisms involved, to be sure, but they will not be detected without exactly this kind of scientific procedure. It is incoherent to argue that a social process might be involved in the generation of the effect to be explained and yet to deny the value of quantification in testing the validity of that argument.

Socio-economic Status, Cultural Capital, Wealth and Reading

The object of this section is to give a practical illustration of how the approach to quantification supported by realism might enable multilevel explanatory narratives, as opposed to multivariate causal models, to be constructed. This will involve the rejection of positivist concepts but the acceptance of what can be learned from statistical models. If scientific realism is to incorporate the findings of quantitative models, then it must do so within an explicit epistemological framework. The investigation may begin with an examination of the pattern of association between the indicator variables. The PISA variables presented earlier are related, as might be expected, but the level of association is quite moderate. Table 11.1 reports the correlations. It will be observed that the correlations of Reading with SES and Number of Books are similar, and somewhat lower between Reading and Wealth. It is worth noting also that the correlations between SES, Wealth and Number of Books, arguably an indicator of 'cultural capital', are no more than moderate. Even the correlation between SES and Wealth – between variables that are often treated as equivalent 'measures' – is not strong, although it is one of the largest in the set. This pattern raises questions that will receive further comment. It may be added, in this context, that the relationship between these indicators and what they point to is precisely the concern of the entire discussion of this chapter. With respect to the purposes of the illustration, it does not matter whether, for example, Number of Books is a good or a poor indicator of the property of families recognised as 'cultural capital', but it matters critically how that relationship is to be constructed in theory. If this remark seems obscure, it may become clearer as the argument is developed.

Table 11.1 Correlations between reading, wealth, SES and number of books

	Wealth	SES	Nbooks
Reading	.109	.285	.365
Wealth		.350	.232
SES			.350

The multiple correlation coefficients between Reading and the three other variables, SES, Wealth and Number of Books, attempt to express the total variance in Reading scores accounted for by those variables. The multiple correlation coefficient, calculated by a stepwise procedure, shows that each variable has a certain independent contribution to make:

.351	Number of books
.419	SES
.420	Wealth

Does it make sense to ask which of these variables has the greatest effect on attainment? It is question that quantitative models seem to have the potential to answer, and it is certainly possible to obtain answers that seem more or less plausible. The pattern suggests, for example, that Wealth has little independent effect on reading attainment when SES and Number of Books are taken into account. It is a little more difficult to ascertain the degree of independence between Number of Books and SES. When SES is entered into the equation first and Number of Books second, the Multiple Correlation steps are .336 and .419, and it is thus clear that these variables are related to reading attainment scores in similar respects. This interpretation is confirmed by the path analysis showing the relevant beta weights given in Figure 11.1. The model supposes that SES (parent occupation) and Wealth are family resources that enable the purchase of books, as resources of literate practice, and that the pattern of interaction between these variables can be used to support theories about families, their resources and practices, and their consequent effects on reading attainment. The pattern suggests that income level, as such, is a less important resource than certain others presumably associated with occupation. To the extent that income has an effect on reading it does so mainly through the possession of books. This is not quite so true in the case of occupation. What all this means, however, for a narrative of explanation has still to be worked out.

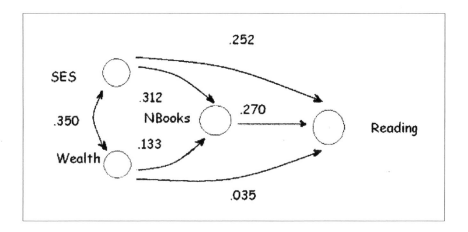

Figure 11.1 A path analysis of the relationship between PISA variables

The statistical models presented here can easily give the impression that the contribution of such variables, and thus the effects on attainment of the structures and practices of families they represent, are somewhat trivial. After all, the proportion of Reading score variance accounted for by these indices of family resources is just 17.6 per cent. The pattern of associations, however, can appear in a much different light when presented in a tabular form (Boudon, 1974).

Table 11.2 shows the mean reading estimates for students categorised by SES, number of books in the home, and an indicator constructed from items included in the Wealth variable. The information is fundamental to the discussion and it will not be redundant to draw attention to some of the most salient points.

Table 11.2 Mean reading estimates by SES: Number of books, and wealth

| | | Number of books in home | | | |
		0–100	N.	101–500+	N.
SES					
	Wealth				
1 High					
	Rich	534	99	587	382
	Inter.	545	258	598	606
	Poor	524	72	606	111
2 High average					
	Rich	522	193	560	360
	Inter.	526	454	576	547
	Poor	526	118	583	138
3 Average					
	Rich	502	173	536	360
	Inter.	513	607	549	443
	Poor	494	242	539	107
4 Low average					
	Rich	488	87	539	103
	Inter.	493	594	542	335
	Poor	495	293	531	135
5 Low					
	Rich	482	89	501	72
	Inter.	476	779	506	329
	Poor	477	529	516	158

Note: SES is derived from Highest International Socio-economic Index and divided into quintiles. Reading attainment is the Warm estimate for overall reading performance. Number of books is divided roughly at the mean of the seven-point category scale. Rich students are defined as those in the upper quintile and poor students those who live in the lower quintile. Students falling between these extremes, in the three middle quintiles, are defined as intermediate in wealth.

In every SES group students with 0–100 books have lower mean scores than those with 101–500+ books in all categories of wealth. The within-class mean attainment difference associated with number of books ranges from 31 in the case of low SES students to 55 points for high SES students. The within-class difference between wealthy and poor students is relatively minor and ranges from 2 points for high-quintile SES students to 13 points for those in the mid-quintile SES category. In the high SES category the difference in mean attainment associated with number of books and wealth is greater than in the low SES category, but there is no trend in the intermediate SES categories: the differences, from SES 5 to SES 1, are: 34, 44, 42, 40 and 63. This pattern is consistent with the regression models. The effect of number of books apparent in Table 11.2, even on a dichotomised scale, can appear dramatic. The mean attainment of 'rich' SES 1 students with 0–100 books is not significantly different from the mean of 'poor' SES 4 students with 101–500+ books. Such information is not immediately apparent from an inspection of regression models.

The value of statistical models depends on the interpretation given to the indicator variables. In the standard, positivist, approach to quantitative analysis, indicator variables are regarded as measures of an underlying concept that is supposed to be more or less adequately assessed by the standards of 'validity' and 'reliability' that prevail in this field. This is not the perspective of realists engaged with quantitative analysis. Bunge (1998), for example, has criticised the conventional approach to the measurement of social variables as fundamentally flawed. The most systematic critique of measurement theory relevant to this discussion merits more attention from realists interested in these problems than seems to be the case. Berka's (1983) materialist theory of quantification argues that whether or not a property can be quantified depends on its nature and thus establishes ontology rather than epistemology as the foundation of measurement. Berka distinguishes between *scaling* and *measurement* proper, proposes that the object of measurement (such as length) and the measured object (such as a stick) should not be conflated, and shows that the concepts of validity and reliability, which carry the burden of the positivist approach to measurement, are inadequate. An indicator of occupations, basically ordered by education and income, reflects the class position of a family; the number of books gives some information about the level of literate resources possessed by a family; and a list of possessions shows that a family has enough disposable income to afford them. What frames of mind they indicate and what practices they support are matters to be settled by investigation and analysis. Such research, of course, must include precisely those forms of enquiry rooted in the qualitative tradition: it is becoming clear that *statistical* explanation is a misnomer as far as scientific realism is concerned.

Indicators of occupational status and number of books in the home, for example, should not be regarded as measures of underlying concepts, but as scales on which homes are ranked by occupations, more or less ordered by income and education, and the number of books they possess. The assessment of attainment – in the PISA data-set not technically a score – is derived from test responses transformed to provide a standardised index of performance. All these indicators point to properties of social entities or individuals, and the business of interpreting the 'meaning' of indicators is actually that of providing an argument that links an indicator to the property it is intended to point to. The relationship between an indicator and the properties it points to, whether these are structural, dispositional or behavioural, is a complex matter that, fortunately, need not be discussed extensively in the case of the illustrative models presented in this section. It can certainly be argued that an estimate of reading attainment, a pseudo-score, points to both a relative performance level and an effective disposition to demonstrate such a performance. Class location is itself given by a complex of social relations, definitively those of to do with the control of capital and labour, and these are relations of power that enable certain practices to be adopted. An indicator of class position, therefore, is one that gains its power to achieve the effects detected by statistical analysis through a great variety of class-associated practices.

What interpretation can a scientific realist place on the statistical analyses presented in this section? The regression equation shows that an increase of 1 standard deviation in SES is associated with an increase of 0.34 standard deviations in Reading. Similarly, an increase of 1 standard deviation in Number of Books is associated with an increase of 0.37 in Reading. The statistical interpretation of this is straightforward, but the substantive interpretation imposes very severe difficulties. The scales are obviously not comparable and standardising them, which is a routine matter, does nothing to solve the real problem. What it means, in fact, is that having a father who is a mechanic and a father who is a teacher is associated to about the same degree with reading attainment as does living in a home with 70 rather than 400 books on the shelves, for these are the approximate ranges covered by one standard deviation on each scale. There is no technical solution to the problems raised by this observation. We know that occupation and number of books have powers of this kind, but how they are actualised, that is through what dispositions and practices, and even at what sites, cannot be learned from this information. Even if the implied equivalence could be given an agreed interpretation, which is not the case, one would still be faced with the problem of constructing a narrative of causal processes, in fact, any substantive interpretation would have to be such a narrative. This is likely to be an area where reality is discontinuous, and subject to breaks with a qualitative effect, rather than linear in character.

Perhaps the most plausible interpretation one can place on the overall analysis made in this section of the relationship between reading, wealth, socio-economic status and number of books is that family practices associated with the possession of books do contribute to the development of certain cognitive and non-cognitive dispositions effective in generating differential reading performance. The explanation in its most complete scheme has a structure–disposition–practice form that requires the adequate description of structures (properties of social entities), dispositions (properties of individuals that lead to action) and practices (established ways of doing things and hence structures of agency). Indicators of social class, wealth or poverty and the number of books reflect structural properties of families, these properties are causally associated with certain dispositions, and these are dispositions that lead to the adoption of certain practices. It is in this way that the number of books in a home is most likely to have a causal connection to the attainment of children.

Jackson and Pettit's argument that a programme explanation is possible, where social class may be argued to be a cause of educational attainment even though the chain of transmission is not clear, may be accepted as legitimate. An explanation having the full structure–practice–disposition form is, however, always to be preferred when it is available. Yet this is not to say, with Scott, that poverty (or wealth) is a proxy variable for unknown resources and for unobserved practices with causal efficiency. The search for mechanism, moreover, requires some philosophical care. Bhaskar's argument that the extraction of surplus value is the hidden mechanism determining the nature of class relations and class-associated practices clearly does not locate the effective mechanism at the level of practice, as in this example. If the realist concept of ontological level is to be respected, at least of the individual and of the social, then accounts that attempt to recognise properties at the level of structures, dispositions and practices are likely, in one respect or another, to represent the effective causal mechanisms sought to explain the events and processes under investigation.

The interpretation of these statistical models, based on regression and on tabulated analyses, points to the need to utilise such models as a basis for obtaining knowledge of the real social processes they represent. The models are not, in themselves, treated as explanations, but as sources of information more or less useful in the construction of complex explanatory narratives. These explanations, moreover, will often require information external to the statistical model that is likely to be generated by so-called qualitative studies. The intuition behind Scott's critique, in all likelihood, is grounded in the fact that the correlations between SES, number of books in the home and attainment, although presented in the language of 'variance explained', provide substantive explanations only at the programme level and leave the processes involved – the specific actions of people with certain dispositions at given sites of practice that actually 'make the difference' – as secret as they ever were. And when it is suspected, as critical realism does suspect, that the language of statistical positivism bears the taint of ideology, the accounts of statistical modelling seem not only inadequate and incomplete but systematically misleading and therefore to be rejected. This is not the more considered response of scientific realism, but it should be understood that the genuine problems raised by this grounded discussion of how statistical models might be interpreted in a realist framework emerge from a common rejection of the positivist epistemology embedded in the conventional discourse of statistical explanation (Nash, 2002).

Conclusion

Realism rejects the account of causation as constant conjunction, opposes the nominalist interpretation of variables, regards models as representations of reality, and argues that explanations should, wherever possible, be given in terms of generative mechanisms. This programme suggests that the identification of causal factors requires a conceptual analysis as well as a technical analysis. If it is the case that there are multiple effective causes, each contributing some determinate effect, then that is a reality that explanatory models should attempt to represent. This is the essence of a realist approach to science. It is a central, if not actually definitive, problem of the sociology of education to provide explanations of how differences in social access to education are generated. There will be no dissent to the proposition that this state of affairs has multiple causes. Scientific realism, therefore, must accept the need for quantitative analysis to establish both the extent of social disparities and the estimation of the relative weights that should be accorded to distinct processes, the evidence for which can be ascertained, in part, by the statistical analysis of indicator variables. The positivist notion that the number of books in a home and other literate resources (such as computers, musical instruments and so on) can be treated as indicators of a 'latent variable' representing, perhaps, a 'concept of cultural capital' that can be constructed as an object of measurement, and represented as a causal factor in the context of a model, is unacceptable in any version of realism. That criticism, however, is not in itself sufficient basis for the rejection of the forms of statistical modelling, illustrated in this chapter by analyses of the PISA data-set, as useful in the construction of realist explanatory narratives.

On the contrary, scientific realism, particularly as articulated by Bunge (a professor of mathematical physics before his switch to the philosophy of science), is entirely compatible with quantified approaches to social science. The critical realist critique exemplified by Scott must, therefore, be considered faulty on several grounds. In summary, the objections to statistical modelling are unsound; the attempt to deny causal powers to poverty as a condition of being is inconsistent with realism; the argument lends support to forms of reductionism that would eliminate sociological variables and, finally, the position reached seems entirely to disallow the scientific testing of hypotheses about the existence of the process mechanisms believed to be responsible for the differences these accounts attempt to explain. If the cliché will be allowed, one might say that the critical realist critique risks throwing out the scientific baby with the positivist bathwater.

Realism constructs explanations of events, processes and states of affairs in terms of the generative mechanisms that give rise to them. In social science, including sociology, history and economics, the most complete explanations will have a structure–disposition–practice scheme where the structural properties of emergent social entities, the dispositional properties of individuals and the actions performed by individuals within recognised social practices are all included in the explanatory narrative. In as much as social structures, so conceived, are actually a level of reality constituted by pre-existing social relations and the results of historic practices, explanations at that level cannot necessarily be reduced to individuals' states of being or to their actions. The implications of this realist conception of the social, its properties, their reflection in indicators, and the construction of statistical models, must be given careful consideration. There are, to be sure, some fundamental problems with the conventional discourse of statistical analysis: the legacy of positivism is so deeply entrenched in its technical vocabulary that the construction of realist explanatory narratives is much difficult than would otherwise be the case.

Scott's critique is, at best, only partially cogent and cannot provide an alternative approach to the explanation of social events, processes and states of affairs. It fails to recognise that employment of the discourse of positivism does not necessarily denote a formal allegiance to the theoretical tenets of positivism. As Byrne, who might be described as an idiosyncratic scientific realist himself, puts it: 'Positivism is dead' (1998: 37). Its bones, however, remain fossilised in the lexicon of applied statistics. The terms quantitative researchers are constrained to use appears to commit them to a Humean concept of cause, and to a view of science that rules as illegitimate any reference to a reality outside its models, but this is not the practical view of most researchers in this field (Patterson and Goldstein, 1991). The same point can be made in relation to correlation and causality.

All textbooks in statistical methods advise students of the distinction between correlation and cause, and usually discuss the relationship between statistical models and the reality they are designed to represent. Although it is true that these discussions are never satisfactory – hardly surprising given that the problems are impossible to resolve with the only concepts available – it does seem unjust to suppose that statistical researchers are necessarily committed to the formal implications of their theoretical language (Batholomew, 1999). It is possible to maintain that the epistemological foundations of statistical modelling do not render its substantive analyses inherently worthless. The conventional theory, so well entrenched as to be regarded by many quantitative researchers as nothing more than 'the language of statistics', nevertheless continues to pose severe difficulties. It is worth being clear about that these are.

The first point is simply that even to distinguish between the model and what it represents is a problem. Scott is hardly alone in having difficulty in speaking of the object of investigation without recourse to the word 'phenomena', or in being driven to use the terms 'variable' and 'factor' to refer both to an indicator and to the property that it points to. The substantive causal process is actually referred to as a variable, although it is plainly not in this discourse. But if the conventional position, which is empiricist and nominalist, prefers to talk about models, where realism prefers to talk about the entities and properties they are about, both face a similar difficulty in making the link between model and the reality it represents. The fact that realism is committed to the world and the possibility of its demonstration does not make the business of its demonstration, when that is a bit more difficult than kicking large rocks, any the easier.

It would certainly help were realist thinkers in this field willing to adopt a set of concepts that makes it possible to speak about indicators rather than 'measures'; of events, processes and states of affairs rather than 'phenomena'; of variables as a reference to terms employed in a model; and of properties when referring to those features of the social world that have provided the data expressed by a variable. These small reforms alone would bring greater clarity to the debate about the nature and conduct of educational research. The problem of linkage – which positivism was designed to bypass, and which quantitative researchers therefore so struggle with – is impossible to resolve with the concepts of positivist theory. In these respects, then, critical and scientific realism are agreed, but in the argument of this chapter that critique supports the case not for the abandonment of statistical models and explanations based on them, but the adoption of a realist epistemology sufficiently robust to improve the multilevel explanatory narratives of a naturalised social science.

These problems have been recognised by scientific realism, which, in Bunge's argument, is able to provide a non-positivist framework for quantitative modelling. Such a framework must allow the structural properties of the social formation – poverty is one among many – to be included in a causal narrative at the appropriate level. This is not to deny, of course, that poverty, as a social state of affairs, has its effects on, for example, educational attainment, as a result of dispositions as states of mind, and through social practices generated in some form as an adaptive response to poverty. Some implications of these philosophical concerns have been explored with reference to statistical models using the PISA data. The primary purpose of these is to ground the discussion in concrete illustrations, but if they make any substantive contribution to the explanation of social differences in education that is a bonus not be despised.

References

Archer, M. (1996). *Culture and Agency: The Place of Culture in Social Theory* (Cambridge: Cambridge University Press).

Bartholomew, J. (1999). The measurement of standards. In H. Goldstein and S. Heath (eds), *Educational Standards* (Oxford: Oxford University Press): 121–38.

Berka, K. (1983). *Measurement: Its Concepts, Theories and Problems* (Dordrecht, The Netherlands: Reidel).

Bhaskar, R. (1979). *The Possibility of Naturalism: A Philosophical Critique of the Contemporary Human Sciences* (Sussex: Harvester).

Bhaskar, R. (1998). General introduction. In M. Archer, R. Bhaskar, A. Collier, T. Lawson, and A. Norrie (eds), *Critical Realism: Essential Readings* (London: Routledge): ix–xxiv

Bhaskar, R. (1993). *Dialectic: The Pulse of Freedom* (London: Verso).

Boudon, R. (1974). *The Logic of Sociological Explanation* (Harmondsworth: Penguin).

Bunge, M. (1981). *Scientific Materialism*, esp. Chap. 8: Popper's unworldly World 3 (Dordrecht, The Netherlands: Reidel).

Bunge, M. (1998). *Social Science under Debate: A Philosophical Perspective* (Toronto: University of Toronto Press).

Byrne, D. (1998). *Complexity Theory and the Social Sciences* (London: Routledge).

Collier, A. (1994). *Critical Realism: An Introduction to Roy Bhaskar's Philosophy* (London: Verso).

Collier, A. (1999). *Being and Worth* (London: Routledge).

Ganzeboom, H.B.G., De Graaf, P. and Trieman, D.J. (with J. De Leeuw) (1992). A standard international socio-economic index of occupational status, *Social Science Research*, 21(1): 1–56.

Groser, C. (2003). Little done to fight poverty says report, *The Dominion Post*, 18 March, A4.

Jackson, F. and Pettit, P. (1992). Structural explanation in social theory. In D. Charles and K. Lennon (eds), *Reduction, Explanation and Realism* (Oxford: Clarendon): 97–131.

Kemp, S. and Holmwood, J. (2003). Realism, regularity and social explanation, *Journal for the Theory of Social Behaviour*, 33(2): 165–87.

Lawson, T. (1997). *Economics and Reality* (London: Routledge).

Manincas, P. (1998). A realist social science. In M. Archer, R. Bhaskar, A. Collier, T. Lawson and A. Norrie (eds), *Critical Realism: Essential Readings* (London: Routledge): 313–38.

Mayer, S.E. (1997). *What Money Can't Buy: Family Income and Children's Life Chances* (Cambridge: Mass.: Harvard University Press).

Nash, R. (2002). Numbers and narratives: Further reflections in the sociology of education, *British Journal of Sociology of Education*, 23(3): 397–412.

Nash, R. (2003). Social explanation and socialization: On Bourdieu and the structure, disposition, practice scheme, *Sociological Review*, 51: 43–62.

Orgnisation for Economic Co-operation and Development. (2000). *Manual for the PISA 2000 Database* (Paris: OECD).

Organisation for Economic Co-operation and Development. (2001). *Knowledge and Skills for Life: First Results from PISA* (Paris: OECD).

Patterson, L. and Goldstein, H. (1991). New statistical methods of analysing social structures: An introduction to multilevel models, *British Educational Research Journal*, 17(4): 387–93.

Pettit, P. (1993). *The Common Mind: An Essay on Psychology, Society, and Politics* (Oxford: Oxford University Press).

Scott, D. (2000). *Realism and Educational Research: New Perspectives and Possibilities* (London: Routledge/Falmer).

Willmott, R. (2002). *Educational Policy and Realist Social Theory: Primary Teachers, Child-centred Philosophy and the New Managerialism* (London: Routledge).

Chapter 12

The Explanation of Social Disparities in Achievement: What has Sociology of Education to Offer Policymakers?

Introduction

What are the causes of mean differences in the educational achievements of social groups within a given society? It might be said that the sociology of education exists basically to answer that question. Whether it has made much progress towards this goal is far from certain, the discipline is deeply fractured by theoretical and methodological disputes, but perhaps something can be gained from the research conversation of the last 30 years. We may assume, at least, that the study of group differences is similar in form whether specified by class location, ethnic origin or gender, and that the explanations provided by theory must be internally coherent and open to empirical test. The investigation of group differences will also draw on information derived from research into the causes of population, that is to say individual, variance in educational achievement, but it will be argued that this is not the optimal approach. A satisfactory model will necessarily provide information about the complex social processes that generate disparities, and perhaps in such a way that the relative importance of specific sites and agents can be estimated. Some may have begun to suspect that the construction of an integrated explanation, incorporating quantitative and non-quantitative modes of analysis, true to the nature of the world, and supported by data generated by the standards of realist science, is much more difficult than policymakers often appreciate. This is an area, in fact, where a more or less elaborated common sense theory is almost certainly correct, but demonstrating that to be so is another matter entirely.

The argument developed may seem ambitious. It integrates conceptual and statistical analysis, in a 'numbers and narratives' approach, to investigate what policymakers can learn from sociology of education about the causes of social disparities in achievement. As Moore (2004) has recognised, there are 'issues' that need *explanations*, and as extra-scientific obstacles to the construction of realist accounts of social disparities in education in access to education are deeply entrenched, these must be overcome. Although reference has been made to class, ethnicity and gender, the empirical analysis will deal with social class as this is where the theoretical and methodological difficulties are most acute. Some relevant peculiarities of the analyses of ethnic disparities are discussed, and the absence of gender as a separate topic indicates nothing other than its relatively unproblematic nature in that respect. The discussion is supported by statistical models that draw on data collected by the PISA (Programme for International Student Assessment) data-set for England and Wales. The explanation of the causes of social disparities in educational achievement faces a number of technical and political difficulties. It will be suggested that there is more to the explanation of social disparities in education than is often supposed. There is no single technique that will enable quantitative estimates to be calculated, complex sociological accounts cannot be derived automatically from statistical models, and the relationship between explanation and the formation of educational policy is problematic in certain important respects. Those who are willing to countenance the hypothesis that family resources and practices must be included in an explanatory account must also be prepared to respond the charge of deficit theory certain to be brought against them. Such are the themes to be explored.

Policymakers and Theories of Social Disparity in Achievement

It seems that policymakers should be interested in explanations of inequality/ difference, particularly when these provide information that can be used to derive estimates of the cost-effectiveness of specific policies designed to reduce its magnitude. Coleman (1966) in the US and Halsey (1975) in the UK both developed an approach to the sociology of education aimed at meeting the needs of educational policymakers by documenting the extent of inequality of educational opportunity – the term used to refer to observed disparities in the mean achievements of social groups – and providing statistical models based on correlations between indicators of properties of individuals and social institutions. In conventional language of quantitative research, the models are designed to explain the causal relations between measured variables and to analyse the variance in achievement test scores. The idea is that if policymakers understand the causes of social disparities in achievement they will be better able to eliminate them. Things are, however, a little more complicated.

Other things being equal, it is useful to know what mechanism brings about that state of affairs. Although this proposition might seem like common sense, it is one that will bear some discussion. If a car refuses to start, then we must isolate the problem – empty fuel tank, dead battery, faulty starter motor and so on – and do whatever is necessary to make it work. On this model, if educational policymakers knew that social disparities in educational achievement were due to system malfunctions – negative teacher expectations, an inappropriate curriculum, flawed assessment procedures and so on, and all to a certain extent – then they should be able to alter these system components in order to bring about an improvement in its outputs. By the same token, if there were convincing evidence that, for example, the achievement difference between middle- and working-class students is largely generated by the actions of parents in the early years of life, then attention might be directed to the provision of family support and early childhood education, rather than to school reforms.

The relationship between what is known about the mechanism of causation and the processes of transformation is, however, not necessarily straightforward. That a state of affairs has a certain cause does not always mean that the removal of that cause is the only way to change that state of affairs. Short-sightedness, for example, is often due to DNA structures, but it can be corrected by optical lenses or laser surgery, and these remedies, moreover, can be applied whatever the cause and even whether the cause is known or not. Policymakers in education may well be in a similar position. It may not matter all that much whether class disparities in achievement arise as a consequence of processes at home or at school if they can be eradicated by pedagogical practice. A school-based programme of pedagogical reform is likely to be similar whether the group disparities it is designed to remove are theorised as being due initial familial socialisation or to its own malfunctioning.

The central question around which all of this discussion revolves, of course, is whether durable cognitive skills acquired in early childhood as a result of classed socialisation practices affect their capacity to master the school curriculum. The evidence for this hypothesis is increasingly difficult to ignore (Feinstein, 2003). The challenge for the educational system is to develop teaching methods, what Bourdieu called a universal pedagogy, with the power to bring children with all entry-level skills to the same standard of achievement within a manageable period of time. Any reference to 'cognitive skills' is likely to be heard as a reference to 'intelligence' and threatens to spin the discussion into the vortex surrounding IQ theory, genetic determination and the practical limits to learning. There is no more bitterly contested area of education than this paradigm instance of 'deficit theory'. These questions, however, are avoided only at a high cost.

Mathematics Achievement, Social Class and Books in the Home

The primary purpose of international educational research is to enable nation states to compare their performance on an agreed common standard of achievement. It is supposed that the sources of variance in educational achievement are to be found in the actions of agents at different sites, and that the independent contribution made by each to the overall variance can be estimated by statistical regression models. Research like PISA is designed to obtain data, by means of questionnaires and achievement tests, necessary to these forms of analysis. The public data-set includes variables on family background (household income, parents' education, educational resources and so on); student properties (intelligence, self-concept, attendance); school properties (type, size, ability composition, grouping practices, teacher–student ratios and so on); and teacher properties (educational qualifications, experience, competence and so on). As the PISA data-set is available for secondary analysis, this discussion will draw on that resource in an attempt to explore some problematic aspects in the investigation of the causes of group disparities in educational achievement. The question central to the sociology of education is, of course, not identical to the question that PISA is designed to answer. It is the thesis of this chapter that what causes disparity in a population, and what causes social disparities in achievement, are two distinct questions. It is perhaps not widely appreciated that the statistical techniques utilised in the study of population variance are not ideally suited to the analysis of group disparities, and there is considerable reluctance to acknowledge that it may be necessary to make a principled break with certain theoretical assumptions behind the standard models.

The research question proposed is this: to what extent is the association between social class and mathematics achievement due to the association between social class and the number of books in the home? There is good reason to believe that durable structures of the cognitive habitus acquired in early childhood and effective in the operations of scholastic learning are developed in environments characterised by a specific relationship to language (Bernstein, 1996). It is plausible to suppose that the quantity of books in a home may indicate, if very approximately, the forms of literate communication in the household. This question as it is posed, however, is less straightforward than it might seem. There are several methods that might be used and they do not necessarily give the same answer.

It is worth being clear about the point of attempting to estimate the extent to which class differences in achievement are associated with the literate culture of the home. The object of site/agency analysis is to isolate the contribution made by parents in families and by teachers in schools to social disparities in achievement. Within the home, for example, it is of interest to distinguish the relative contribution of financial wealth, educational qualifications and social networks. Within the school the separate effects of such properties as curriculum organisation, teaching methods and assessment procedures are all a legitimate focus of attention. Of course, if the aim is to construct an index of those properties of the home that correlate most highly with educational achievements, then it is sensible to include cultural indicators together with occupational status. Socio-economic status if often defined, indeed, to embrace cultural practices, and complex scales combining occupational level and literacy resources, such as the PISA Index of Socio-Economic and Cultural Status (SECS), have this form. Such indices are, not surprisingly, more strongly associated with achievement than scales of occupation alone. The disparity in mathematics achievement between the highest and lowest SECS quintile is 116.7 points (1.25 standard deviations), which is significantly wider than the 69.2 points (.75 SD) for equivalent points on the PISA occupational scale.[1] It is perfectly legitimate to investigate the origins of social disparities in

---

1   One practical consequence of this, incidentally, is that the attempt to control student intake characteristics, as for research into school composition effects, by occupational scales, are likely to be biased: the mean mathematics values for students from the *lowest occupational quintile*, for example, are 472.2 for those at selective schools, and 542.3 for

education, and an index of social class so constructed as to include literate resources cannot be used for the purposes of exploring their effect on observed achievement disparities within or between social classes. It may seem an elementary error, for certain purposes, to construct an indicator of 'home environment' that does not include reference to literate resources and practices, but it cannot be a error to investigate the contribution those properties make to the achievement disparities between social groups, and an index of social class based on occupational grades is not only suitable but necessary for that purpose. The scale of social class used in the current analysis is derived from the ISCO codes (International Standard Occupational Codes) and intended to approximate the Goldthorpe (1996) scheme. The data are not ideal for this purpose as there is no information on the self-employed status of parents, but it is the best that can be done.

Table 12.1 Mathematics achievement, social class and number of books in the home

	0–25 books	26–100 books	101–200 books	201+ books	All	Total
Social Class						
High Service	498.2	524.2	556.6	591.2	557.2	1243
Lower Service	487.6	515.7	546.0	573.5	540.4	1064
Routine non-manual	468.8	496.6	523.8	565.8	512.6	657
Skilled	476.7	495.8	520.9	532.2	501.5	1510
Low skilled	459.1	486.0	507.2	520.9	486.3	1811
Total	471.9	500.4	529.4	562.9	515.9	6285

Note: Mathematics achievement is derived from plausible values divided into quintiles; number of books in the home is collapsed from variable *St19q01*. A five-point social class scale designed to approximate Goldthorpe's scheme, is derived from the ISCO code. The number of books in the home is a four-point scale collapsed from a six-point scale taken from the student questionnaire.
Source: PISA 2003, UK (England). Sample 6285. Social class derived from ISCO codes (variables *bfmj* and *bmmj*) and approximates the Goldthorpe scale.

Table 12.1 presents the relationship between mathematics achievement, social class and number of books in the home. It can be shown by multinomial regression analysis that the odds of a student from the highest social class being in the upper fifth of the mathematics distribution are exactly three times greater than those of

those at non-selective schools. This disparity of 70.1 points (.76 SD), is huge and, given that prior achievement is the declared principle of selection, it is unlikely that much of this difference – if any – has emerged as a result of differential secondary school experiences.

students from the lowest social class being at that level, but when these odds are adjusted for the number of books in the home, they are reduced to 1.3:1.

The most straightforward approach to estimating the contribution added by number of books in the home to the association between SES and mathematics achievement can be calculated from the information given in Table 12.1:

- The total SES disparity is: $557.2 - 486.3 = 70.9$
- The total disparity due to SES and number of books is: $591.2 - 459.1 = 132.1$
- The reduced SES disparity due to number of books is: $520.9 - 498.2 = 22.7$
- Therefore the disparity is cut from 70.9 to 22.7, a reduction of about two-thirds.

The correlations between the three variables used in this examination will provide the necessary basis for those models based on regression analysis:

- Social class – Mathematics achievement = r .308
- Number of books – Mathematics achievement = r .393
- Social class – Number of books = r .298

Mathematics achievement is indicated for the purposes of regression analysis by the principal component extracted from the five plausible values given for mathematics.

These correlations are typical of the genre and all moderate in size. The association between social class and mathematics, for example, accounts for less than 10 per cent of the population variance in achievement, and more than one commentator has drawn the conclusion that social class makes a relatively trivial contribution to the overall variation in educational achievement. The simplest way to control for the effect of books on the association between social class and achievement is to calculate the partial correlation. It is .212 and, as the original correlation is .308, it seems that about one-third of the association between social class and mathematics is due to the association between books and social class. The same conclusion is reached by the mathematically equivalent path analysis, favoured by Jencks et al. (1972), where standardised regression coefficients are used to calculate the direct and indirect effects of social class on achievement.

Regression analysis can also be used to generate predicted mathematics achievement given the number of books in the home, which value can then be compared with the actual means for each social class. This procedure shows the observed disparity between the highest and lowest social class to be 70.9, and the disparity given the scores predicted from the number of books to be 25.2. On this basis it is possible to argue that the social class gap in mathematics achievement has been reduced by about half a standard deviation when the number of books in the home has been taken into account.

There is evidently no statistical technique that will give uncontested information about that part of social class advantage in education is due to a given indicator such as the presence of books in the home. The same data-set gives a range of estimates depending on the mode of analysis preferred. This is, perhaps, the lesson to be learned from this exercise: in order to grasp the nature of the association between indicators it is advisable, wherever possible, to examine the data through regression and analysis and cross-tabulated models (Boudon, 1974a, 1974b).

Sociological and Statistical Modes of Explanation

The general approach to the explanation of social events, processes and states of affairs, under which description social differences in educational achievement can be placed, requires the integration of institutional structures, individual dispositions and customary social practices as distinct properties. A complete narrative of explanation should recognise each of these distinct levels (López and Scott, 2000). We can maintain that: social organisations are an emergent property of the structure of social relations; social organisations accomplish their functions by virtue of being constituted by people with certain cognitive and non-cognitive skills; and conduct within organisations follows established practices. The task for sociology is thus multifaceted. It must describe the relations that constitute social organisations and identify their emergent properties; identify the cognitive and affectual schemes that generate action within established practices; and record those customary modes of accomplishing social tasks with respect to their origins and effects within a given social group. Most accounts of the causes of social events, processes and states of affairs produce structure–disposition–practice narratives of this type, although they are not usually acknowledged in such terms, and this scheme has no claim to originality. Explanations of this kind are, in fact, standard in sociology.

Complex explanatory narratives within this scheme, however, maintain an uneasy coexistence with those derived from statistical modelling. The influential quantitative explanations – those ubiquitous 'at risk' models of rational policymaking – are especially problematic in this context. The principal difficulty is that whereas structure–disposition–practice accounts integrate social properties at distinct levels in a complex hierarchical narrative, 'at risk' models are constructed in terms of 'factors' or 'variables', given the same status as 'measures' and included in statistical models in such as way that they must compete for the explanation of variance. These models may have their uses. Baragwanath (1998: 95), for example, argues that the 'ability of teachers to identify children who fall into the "at-risk" category provides opportunities for early intervention', and expresses a widely held view. The assumptions of such models are, nevertheless, not to be accepted without careful reflection: there is an inherent tension between the forms of explanation provided by 'at risk' models and that provided by a multilevel structure–disposition–practice narrative, but can be overcome only by a realist, rather than positivist, framework for the interpretation of statistical analysis.

There are many difficulties with conventional statistical techniques, but the one that should be the most obvious in this context is often that most overlooked. These models, it will be realised, attempt to quantify variables contributing to the total population variance in achievement, rather than to those associated with the difference between social groups. There is actually no necessary relationship between the proportion of the total variance accounted for by a variable and the contribution it might make to the difference between social groups.

A more or less formal structure–disposition–practice explanation is arguably the key to an integrated sociological theory able to give 'factors' what respective due they have in an account of social events, processes and states of affairs. When indicators of social class and number of books in the home are included in a statistical regression model, of the type that generates 'at risk' profiles, it is an inevitable fact that these indicators will each account for a given proportion of the variance. It is well known to analysts in this field that the results of such an analysis may even depend on the order in which the indicator variables are entered into the equation. The information provided by models of population variance may be useful primarily in being able to point to dead ends. If an indicator is shown to contribute little to population variance, then it is unlikely to point to major causal processes generating substantial group disparities. There is some apparently reliable evidence, for example, that student achievement is unaffected whether classes are streamed or organised by mixed ability, and that being so it is unreasonable to suppose that this property of schools, or classrooms, can be a significant contribution to social disparities in achievement.

Scientific Explanation and Moral Judgement

Some of the most influential contributors to the sociology of education, including Bourdieu and Bernstein, were deeply irritated by critiques that positioned their work as 'deficit theory'. Bernstein expressed his disdain for a debate, 'vociferously and tediously debated in education since the 1960s' (Bernstein, 1995: 402); pointed out that 'whether a theory is deficit or otherwise cannot be reliably inferred from low-level diagnostic statements, but only from an examination of its fundamental problematic' (Bernstein, 1975: 27); and attempted to distance himself from the compromised discourse of compensatory education. Bernstein (1970) argued that the school, in as much that there was no convincing evidence that it made a genuine attempt to transform its curriculum, pedagogy and modes of evaluation, could not be supposed to be providing equality of educational opportunity. It was thus improper to talk of *compensatory* education when *education* of an appropriate kind was not being provided. Bourdieu protested in even stronger language against explanations of inequality in access to education that ignored the effects of class habitus. His comment that '[i]t is essential to checkmate explanations whose highly fantastic nature would be immediately apparent if they did not awaken the oldest phantasms of the Western tradition' (Bourdieu, 1993: 187) may need a little gloss.

What radical intellectuals of the dominant class (and dominant race) fear most in the reception of their thought, so Bourdieu hints, is that they might be perceived as numbered among those who accept the dominant order of the capitalist state and to that extent be complicit in its regimes of oppression. The imperative to censor all expressions that might be tainted with the discourse of 'deficit theory' is all too easy to comprehend. There may be some virtue, nevertheless, in responding with a level head to the arguments of those unable to omit family resources and practices from their narratives of explanation.

Perhaps the first point is that the discourses of science and ethics are not interchangeable. Conventional rhetoric against so-called deficit theory makes no distinction between a scientific model that attempts to describe and explain the nature of the social world and the moral attribution of culpability for its state. This distinction, however, is vital to the development of a consensus on the pathways to meaningful educational reform. It is one thing to argue that, for example, low income and low levels of education, regarded as classed resources allocated to families, are causally associated with educational achievement, and quite another to hold families necessarily responsible for the level of resources they possess. Sociologists who investigate the consequences of poverty are not usually criticised if their research shows increased rates of ill health, poor nutrition and emotional distress, but sociologists who advance the hypothesis that children raised in poverty are likely to develop cognitive and non-cognitive dispositions with a detrimental effect on their school achievements are certain to stand accused of propagating a deficit theory. The 'deficit theory' label is almost confined to education and it is more than time that the grounds for this peculiarity are interrogated.

It is one thing to construct a scientific model to describe and analyse the nature of the world, and another to attribute moral culpability to specific agents and institutions for the state of the world. The standard assumption that that the school has the power to create equality of educational opportunity, the accepted term for the identity of achievement between social groups, should be recognised as the root sources of much of the confusion in this area. If this position is held, then it seems to follow that if the educational system does not provide such equity it has failed to fulfil its prescribed functions. Such failure is both technical and moral, in as much that were there sufficient political and pedagogical will to effect change the results would be different. Once the situation is seen in this way, as it has been by all leading sociologists of education, the implicit charge of culpability on the part of those responsible for the system is difficult to refute. The logic suggests that all theories of social disparity in education carry a moral overburden so that agents at all sites are not only responsible for what they do, but are actually to blame for whatever, as they might be, unintended and unforeseen consequences follow from their collective actions. This is the intellectual and ideological context in which to include any reference to parents and homes in a model of the generation of inequality of educational opportunity has become the mark of a 'deficit theorist'.[2]

The sociology of education is a conversation of 'competing discourses'. Bernstein, for example, protesting his innocence against the accusation of deficit-theorising, notes that accounts that focus on the home distract attention from school processes and their significant contribution to social disparities in achievement. This response, however, may concede more than is necessary, and is more political than scientific. The construction of an adequate model of the origin of social disparities in educational achievement should be developed in accordance with the nature of the world, rather than shaped by an ideological mould. It is rather as if a complex model of the causes of road causalities were to be inhibited by the fear that to recognise the importance of drunk driving would distract attention from the need to improve the state of the roads. One might even conceive that to be so, but it should have no bearing on the fact that an adequate explanatory framework must be competent to reveal whatever is the case, that twice as many accidents are caused by drunk drivers as by 'black spots', or vice versa, as things may be. The widespread acceptance of the essentially political view that the educational system is responsible, at least by default, for social disparities in achievement makes it unnecessary in certain respects to develop an account of the mechanisms that actually generate the inequities it fails to correct. If the initial disparity is actually rooted in home resources and practices, then, given the doctrine that such differences can be eliminated by pedagogical action, the implications for educational policy are minimal. The utility of causal theories to programmes of equalisation is never, in any event, a straightforward matter.

A dictionary might tell us what the word 'deficit' means, but knowing what the word means does not tell us what is a deficit, and, indeed, there is a well-supported movement to redefine all terms that so attempt to refer to characteristics of individuals as references to 'deficits' in social provision. The questions of what is to count as 'deficit theory', and what actions are blameworthy, are worth a brief examination. There is always a normative consideration when a 'deficiency' is identified, and the basis of that judgement should be explicit. A family with an income below the poverty line is in that respect 'deficient' because it does not have enough to provide a decent life by the standards of the community, but a family with 20 books is not therefore deficient in books merely because the average is about 100. It is one thing not to have enough money to make ends meet, and another to choose to spend one's time collecting and reading books. A similar degree of attention can be paid to the concept of blame. There is good evidence that pre-school children whose parents read to them everyday are likely to read better

---

2   The reluctance to consider family resource accounts is now so deeply embedded in educational thought that the 2003 PISA questionnaire to schools asks the question: 'In your school, to what extent is the learning of students hindered by:' and includes among the 13 permitted responses not one about home resources and practices, the cognitive dispositions of students, or the nature of the local community.

than those who are read to less frequently. Are parents who do not read to their children every day to blame both for that conduct and for whatever consequential effect it has on their reading performance? The answer, in this case, is a little subtle. It is arguable that parents' failure to make bedtime stories part of the daily routine is not actually blameworthy, but there may well be some responsibility to be accepted should the relative level of their children's future achievements fall below what it might have been. Parents are not culpable if they do not read to their children in the way they are if they allow their children to stay awake all night playing video games, but, in as much as listening to stories structures the cognitive habitus, parental actions are to that extent responsible for whatever effects that has on their school achievements. Such judgements, being moral and quasi-judicial, cannot be made automatically, but only after a proper consideration of the relevant social facts in their full context.

There are well-grounded objections to those normative accounts of social disparities in achievement that may justly be criticised as deficit theories. It is not the intention of this chapter to turn back the hands of the clock. It may be pertinent to recall, however, that Flude's critical review of theories of differential achievement concluded with respect to deficit theory that, 'there is an urgent need to rethink the problem and relocate it – *initially at least* – in the manner in which teachers' and administrators; categories of social class, ability and knowledge constitute part of the institutional context with which pupils' careers are formed' (Flude, 1974: 45; original italic), and did not deny that pupils' material conditions of life had a significant effect on their response to school. The advice to rethink, 'initially at least', was not an injunction to reject out-of-hand and once-and-for-all the significance of causal processes dependent on family resources and practices. Flude suggested, in fact, that the issue for sociology might be a matter of 'avoiding the ethnocentric and normative characterization of low-status groups' (Flude, 1974: 45); in other words, of minding our cultural p's and q's. The language of description and analysis should not be conflated with the language of responsibility and blame, and what is 'deficient' should be distinguished from what is just different. This essay in conceptual analysis is a long way from the rhetorical stigmatisation of all accounts that refer to family resources and practices as 'deficit theories' that 'blame the victim', but it may encourage a more sophisticated debate.

A Note on Ethnic Disparities

In the case of ethnic differences a somewhat different question is asked and can be answered by a number of techniques. In order to show that the educational system is characterised by racial discrimination, it has conventionally been argued that the achievements of students from communities held to be disadvantaged are lower than those when all relevant conditions are satisfied when these conditions are satisfied. These conditions might include parental education and income, student properties, such as cognitive ability scores (in as much as these are not generated by the educational system), and so on. In as much as it is acceptable to test for the presence of racial discrimination in a system by making like-with-like comparisons between different groups, then regression analysis is an adequate tool for the purpose (Jencks and Phillips, 1998). It is a straightforward matter to compare the observed scores of an ethnic sub-population with those predicted on the basis of properties other than those of ethnic origin. If the observed and predicted scores were not significantly different, it is plausible to argue that that the effect on educational disparities of processes unique to the social relations between ethnic groups is minimal. This methodology cannot, of course, be applied to the investigation of disparities between social classes. It also runs the risk of being criticised as reductionist and of failing to recognise the autonomy of ethnic identity as a social reality. The question asked, nevertheless, is motivated by concerns that should be acknowledged as legitimate within a democratic polity.

If the achievements of students from certain ethnic communities cannot be distinguished from those of others given their class location, then the causes of the observed disparity seem to lie outside the educational system. The educational system can be held responsible only on the ground that it has failed to meet a policy directive to provide opportunities to students of all class and ethnic groups. As these withheld 'opportunities' are identified only by the fact that the achievements of disadvantaged groups are low by comparison with those of advantaged groups, the entire argument rests on the standard assumption that the educational system actually has the power to generate levels of group equality that it fails to exercise. Whether these powers do exist is an open question: no system has ever demonstrated such powers, and, as demonstration is the test of existence, those not required by their position, as policymakers often are, to insist on their reality may be allowed the privilege of science to entertain an alternative hypothesis.

Many theoretical difficulties in the race versus class – ethnicity versus SES – contest arise from the attempt to categories resources and practices as those generated by relations of a specific kind. It is not always a straightforward matter to make the judgements involved. And it is always possible, of course, that class and ethnic relations in a given society are interlinked in such a way that no sensible basis exists for making a determination in the matter of certain resources. A complex structure–disposition–practice narrative recognises the possession of material and symbolic resources by institutions and individuals as a precondition for social practice. The principles regulating the social distribution of effective resources are open to theoretical and empirical investigation. It is a matter of theoretical definition that the relation of class determines whether income from that that source accrues from the possession of capital or the exchange of labour power. The dispositions generated as a result of class relations are, of course, a proper object of sociological investigation. A great deal of celebrated sociological research has exactly that character (for example Charlesworth, 2000; Willis, 1976). The same approach may be taken with respect to ethnic relations. Where resources are distributed according to ethnic classification then that social fact will be included in any accurate explanation of group disparities.

Conclusion

Marked social differences in educational attainment are a legitimate matter of public concern. Whatever can be done within the realms of practicality to eradicate them should be done. It matters to parents, teachers, politicians, educational administrators and advocacy groups that, in the UK, GCSE A* – C passes are achieved by about 70 per cent of children from families classed as professional and by about 15 per cent from those classed as unskilled manual (Gillborn and Youdell, 2001). The business of constructing a satisfactory explanation of this state of affairs is, if not the definitive undertaking of the sociology of education, certainly part of its core business (Erikson and Jonsson, 1996; Shavit and Blossfield, 1993). One of the fundamental tasks of the sociology of education is thus to discover what actions, by what people, in what social organisations, contribute to what extent in bringing about social differences in educational achievement. The difficulties involved in developing and testing theories capable of providing robust explanations prove, however, to be unexpectedly severe. The sociology of education has, for example, never conceded that it possesses no adequate technique that will allow fractions of the disparity between social classes, such as that between the upper and lower fifths of the household income distribution, to processes localised to the home rather than the school. Statistical models used in this field are almost invariably designed to account for the variance in the total population rather than to isolate the causes of the lesser disparity between population subgroups and provide no more than one strand of evidence in the construction of integrated sociological explanations with a structure–disposition–practice scheme.

Policymakers might find this discussion of some value in helping to clarify the theoretical and methodological limitations sociology of education necessarily faces in its attempt to construct realist explanations of the origins of social disparities in educational achievement. These limitations cannot be overcome, but they can be accepted without great loss, and may even provide a context in which the relationship between the concerns of policymakers and those of sociologists can be placed on a more secure basis.

References

Baragwanath, S. (1998). Making the system work for the at-risk student, *Social Policy Journal of New Zealand*, 11: 95–110.

Bernstein, B. (1970). A critique of the concept of 'compensatory education'. In D. Rubinstein and C. Stoneman (eds), *Education for Democracy* (Penguin, Harmondsworth): 65–76.

Bernstein, B. (1975). *Class, Codes and Control 3: Towards a Theory of Educational Transmission*, 2nd edn (London: Routledge & Kegan Paul).

Bernstein, B. (1995). A response. In A.R. Sadovnik (ed.), *Knowledge and Pedagogy: The Sociology of Basil Bernstein* (Norwood, NJ: Ablex): 165–218.

Bernstein, B. (1996). *Pedagogy, Symbolic Control and Identity: Theory, Research, Critique* (London: Taylor and Francis).

Boudon, R. (1974a). *Education, Opportunity and Social Inequality: Changing Prospects in Western Society* (New York: Wiley).

Boudon, R. (1974b). *The Logic of Sociological Explanation* (Harmondsworth: Penguin).

Bourdieu, P. et al. (1993). *The Weight of the World: Social Suffering in Contemporary Society* (Stanford, Calif.: Stanford University Press).

Charlesworth, S.J. (2000). *A Phenomenology of Working Class Experience* (Cambridge: Cambridge University Press).

Coleman, J.S. (1966). *Equality of Educational Opportunity* (Washington, DC: US Department of Health, Education and Welfare/US Government Printing Office).

Erikson, R. and Jonsson, J.O. (1996). *Can Education Be Equalized?: The Swedish Case in Comparative Perspective* (Oxford: Westview Press).

Feinstein, L. (2003). Inequality in the early cognitive development of British children in the 1970 cohort, *Economica*, 70(277): 73–97.

Flude, M. (1974). Sociological accounts of differential ability. In M. Flude and J. Ahier (eds), *Educability, Schools and Ideology* (London: Croom Helm): 15–52.

Gillborn, D. and Youdell, D. (2000). *Rationing Education: Policy, Reform and Equity* (Buckingham: Open University Press).

Goldthorpe, J.H. (1996). Class analysis and the representation of class theory: The case of persisting differentials in educational attainment, *British Journal of Sociology*, 47(3): 481–512.

Halsey, A.H. (1975). Sociology and the equality debate, *Oxford Review of Education*, 1(1): 9–28.

Jencks, C., Smith, M., Acland, H., Bane, M.J., Cohen, D., Gintis, H., Heyns, B. and Michelson, S. (1972). *Inequality: A Reassessment of the Effect of Family and Schooling in America* (Harmondsworth: Penguin).

Jencks, C. and Phillips, M. (eds) (1998). *The Black–White Test Score Gap* (Washington, DC: Brookings Institution Press).

López, J. and Scott, J. (2000). *Social Structure* (Buckingham: Open University Press).

Moore, R. (2004). *Education and Society: Issues and Explanations in the Sociology of Education* (Cambridge: Polity Press).

Organization for Economic Co-operation and Development (2003). *Programme for International Student Assessment*, data-set.

Shavit, Y. and Blossfield, H.P. (1993). *Persisting Inequality: Changing Educational Attainment in Thirteen Countries* (Boulder, Col.: Westview Press).

Willis, P. (1978). *Learning to Labour: How Working-class Kids Get Working-class Jobs* (Farnborough, Saxon House).

Index

Page numbers in italics refer to tables and figures; numbers preceded by n refer to footnotes.